Mason Gallagher

Was the Apostle Peter ever at Rome?

A Critical Examination of the Evidence and Arguments Presented...

Mason Gallagher

Was the Apostle Peter ever at Rome?
A Critical Examination of the Evidence and Arguments Presented...

ISBN/EAN: 9783744780636

Printed in Europe, USA, Canada, Australia, Japan

Cover: Foto ©Lupo / pixelio.de

More available books at **www.hansebooks.com**

WAS THE APOSTLE PETER EVER AT ROME?

A CRITICAL EXAMINATION OF THE EVIDENCE AND ARGUMENTS PRESENTED ON BOTH SIDES OF THE QUESTION.

BY

REV. MASON GALLAGHER, D. D.,

AUTHOR OF "TRUE CHURCHMANSHIP VINDICATED," "THE DUTY AND NECESSITY OF REVISION," "A CHAPTER OF UNWRITTEN HISTORY," "THE TRUE HISTORIC EPISCOPATE."

INTRODUCTION BY

REV. JOHN HALL, D. D.,

Pastor Fifth Avenue Presbyterian Church, New York.

NEW YORK
PRINTED BY HUNT & EATON
150 FIFTH AVENUE
1894

"The origin and prevalence of the tradition respecting Peter's supposed Episcopacy at Rome are among the curiosities of history, and well worthy of the attention of the critical scholar."—SAWYER'S *Organic Christianity.*

"The validity of the Petrine claims directly affects every matter, and every act within the spiritual domain of the Papacy, whether belonging to the sphere of Faith or that of Discipline."—LITTLEDALE, *Petrine Claims.*

"The question of the supremacy of Rome is far enough from being out of date. It is one of the chief living, burning questions of our time."—S. H. KELLOGG, *Christian Treasury.*

"There is no evidence from Scripture that Peter ever was in Rome, and it is far from being probable that he could have visited heathen Rome and have said nothing about it and have given no account of his labors there; and as the evidence of Scripture is negatively against his being there the burden of proof is upon the shoulders of those who assert the fact."—*Princeton Review,* iii. 252.

COPYRIGHT, 1894,

By REV. MASON GALLAGHER, D. D.

THE MERSHON COMPANY PRESS,
RAHWAY, N. J.

TO THE

TRUSTEES AND FACULTY OF U. S. GRANT UNIVERSITY,

Athens and Chattanooga, Tennessee.

THIS VOLUME IS INSCRIBED

IN TOKEN OF THEIR COURTESY IN CONFERRING THE DEGREE,

DOCTORIS DIVINITATIS, UPON THE AUTHOR,

CHAPLAIN U. S. GRANT POST, 327, G. A. R.,

BROOKLYN, N Y.

"For though you believe all the Scripture, yet if you believe not that Peter was at Rome, you know who will tell you, you had as good believe nothing."—Dr. JOHN LIGHTFOOT.

"The great fact of the Roman Church is founded solely on the coming of St. Peter to Rome. This fact would be absurd, it would be inexplicable, it would be madness, if it be not admitted that St. Peter came to Rome to preach. It is by the coming of St. Peter, that the Roman Church exists."
—Father GUIDI, Diss. at Rome, 1872.

"We cannot find fault with a Protestant, when relying on the proofs which the oldest Fathers, Clement of Rome and Justin, present, he holds the abode of Peter at Rome, and all connected with it, for a tale derived from the Apocrypha."
—ELLENDORF, Roman Catholic Professor, Berlin.

"St. Peter the good, honest, married Apostle of Babylon, and the East, who left as the last legacy to his followers, not to make themselves 'lords over God's heritage.'"—*Edinburgh Review*, July, 1893.

INTRODUCTION.

THERE has not been given much attention by the good people of the United States to the arguments by which the doctrines and practices of the Church of Rome have been assailed from the one side and defended from the other. The reasons for this are not discreditable to a young Nation busily engaged in shaping its own life, and satisfied that religious convictions are a man's own affair and need not be discussed by his neighbors. There is, however, an increasing attention being given to History, and the element of Religion cannot be ruled out of historical investigation.

It is, moreover, being shown to thoughtful students of the questions of the day, that there are such religious convictions as do affect others than those who hold them, and that they become a factor in social and political life. We rejoice in freedom, but we must scrutinize forces, even though "religious," that appear to be opposed to accepted ideas of human freedom.

Is there an infallible, visible, divinely appointed Head of the Church—the whole and only Church of Christ in the world? How much submission is due to such a Head, if the title to the position be accepted? Can the title be sustained? Did the Chief Shepherd and Bishop of souls make Peter his representative, and arrange for an unbroken line of successors to the Apostle? More than one field of investigation must be traversed in seeking for replies. We must go into the exegesis of our Lord's words to his disciple. They who read in these words a Primacy conferred have to face another question. Where is the evidence of Divine selection of Rome as the seat of this Primacy of the universal Church?

It is easy to see how, in the absence of any authoritative reply to this question, the pleaders for such an appointment would welcome tradition and take references to the Apostle's stay in Rome as a providential indication of the Divine will. Even the language of 1 Peter v. 13, "The Church that is at Babylon . . . saluteth you," has been grasped as an argument for the apostle's sojourn and labors in the Roman capital, which, they say, for reasons of his own, he describes as "Babylon." One wonders that they do not fear to identify it with the "Babylon" of John, the character and doom of which are so vividly presented in the Revelation.

Is there real historical evidence of Peter's being in Rome, in any such sense as would make him the Founder and Head of the local Church? To this question Dr. Gallagher has given thought and careful investigation. He has not ignored the arguments of the adherents of the Papal view, whether in traditions or Patristic literature. He has tried to set their true value upon points of supposed evidence, and he has presented calmly and dispassionately the arguments upon the other side. He has shown, by the admission of scholarly Roman Catholics, how necessary it is to have settled beliefs on this matter, if one is to be a sincere and loyal subject of the Vatican.

I can cordially commend the book to careful study. It would moderate the views of candid Roman Catholics regarding Protestants, to have shown to them the uncertainty to our minds of a matter which they have accepted as proved.

They would not blame us for rejecting their theory when the Scripture reference to it will not stand the test of exegesis, and when the historical evidence at so many points suggests the verdict "not proven."

And it would be profitable to many Protestants to have their attention called to the alleged basis of a spiritual claim of authority in the gravest human affairs—a claim which is becoming a real thing to American citizens. We reject the claim, for cause. We should be able to give a reason for this objection. Dr. Gallagher's book, it is to be hoped, will strengthen intelligent Protestant conviction, and give encouragement to us all to speak to our Roman Catholic fellow-citizens, "the truth in love."

J. HALL.

PREFACE.

ROME rests her claim on Peter. That our Lord conferred an especial distinction on this Apostle must be conceded.

When he said : " Thou art Peter, and on this Rock I will build my Church, and the gates of hell shall not prevail against it. And I will give unto thee the keys of the kingdom of heaven ; and whatsoever thou shalt bind on earth shall be bound in heaven ; and whatsoever thou shalt loose on earth, shall be loosed in heaven," Matt. xvi. 17, 18 ; whatever was meant by these words, the honor conferred was great.

We read of no authority given him to exercise over his fellow Apostles. He never claimed it. His fellows never admitted it. Instead of regarding it, they strove among themselves who should be greatest. The wife of Zebedee desired the pre-eminence for her sons.

Peter disowned the claim when he styled himself " a fellow elder." He discouraged such aspirations when he wrote : " Be clothed with humility," under divine guidance ; he gave us no charge to build on a dead Peter but to " come to a Living Stone and be built up a spiritual house," to offer praise to God through Jesus Christ.

Paul does not direct the Corinthians to build on Peter, who had followers among them, but declares : " Other foundation can no man lay than that is laid, which is

Jesus Christ." This he says, Divinely inspired, and with all who give due honor to the word of God, it will be enough to condemn a Petrine Foundation.

But Rome interprets the charge to Peter as a gift of authority over the universal church : that Peter has been made the foundation, and that, apart from him, no soul can be built up in the faith of Christ ; can obtain forgiveness of sin ; can be sanctified by the Spirit, and be prepared for eternal judgment and heavenly glory.

When Rome sends her heralds to this land who come to me in the name of Peter and demand my adherence, and complete subjection, I reply : Granted that Peter had such power, proved by Holy Writ, did he convey that power to any other mortal, and was it to be handed down from generation to generation, and to the end of time ?

If this is proven, I ask again, what connection has the city of Rome with Peter, the Apostle of the Circumcision, and how can the Bishop of Rome derive power from the dead Peter in the nineteenth century, over any immortal soul in this distant land ? By what right can an Italian minister of Christ interfere with the spiritual liberty of an intelligent American, who has the Bible in his hand, and who there finds that some of the doctrines and usages of Rome are clearly and emphatically condemned, and woes denounced against those who present " Another Gospel " ?

Examining carefully the history of the Church of Rome, and all the evidence she presents for the validity of her authority, I find none that will bear an impartial and thorough scrutiny. I find no ancient writer whose testimony to a Roman visit would be received in any court of justice, or even in a matter which concerned worldly property. Shall I risk my immortal soul on such an uncertainty?

I find that the vast body of enlightened scholarship, outside the Roman communion, decisively reject the claim that Peter lived and labored in Rome, and consider the statement too improbable to be believed.

I find that learned lawyers have thoroughly investigated the subject, and discover no evidence that is reliable, and likewise numerous Roman Catholic authors assert that Peter lived and labored in the East.

I am justified therefore in rejecting the proposals of Rome, and in regarding her claim to authority, through Peter, as baseless and vain, and that all who have bowed to her dictation have been deceived; and considering the influence that Church has exercised on nations to their spiritual and temporal harm, I am bound to make known the truth, that others may be benefited by its reception.

All evidence that Rome has presented for her Petrine claim is here considered, and the views of the leading scholars of different nations, with respect to the life and labors of the Chief of the Apostles, together with other matters cognate to the subject.

It will be seen that in this inquiry the title of Saint has been omitted. This course has been pursued, inasmuch as there is no precedent or authority in Scripture, nor in the Primitive Church for the practice.

The Apostles were not thus styled in the best days of Christianity, nor for many generations after their decease.

As for later and uninspired men, the practice originated in a degenerate age, and cannot be defended on reasonable grounds.

There was no especial merit to warrant this invidious

appellation, neither have those who received the distinction excelled the Christians of our own time in divine knowledge, or in the possession and manifestation of the graces of the Christian character.

By the Apostles all the members of the one body were equally styled " saints."

By departing from the Scriptural statement some of the brethren have been unduly magnified. Distance has lent enchantment to the view, and clothed imperfect humanity with a false luster. Evil has naturally followed. Those styled saints have been honored with a species of *worship*. *Adoration*, instead of being confined to one Supreme Being, has been offered in some measure to his creatures, and the displeasure of the Almighty has been manifested, in the withdrawal of his presence and favor from an Institution which has favored such a practice.

Superstition has widely extended, the truth of the Divine Word has been corrupted into falsehood, and spiritual darkness has enveloped both priests and people.

Such being the undeniable results, we regard the use of the title to be honored more in the breach, than in the observance.

That the Divine Head of the Church may bless this investigation to the extension of the truth, and to the removal of error, and thus to the enlightenment of souls, is the author's earnest prayer.

BROOKLYN, N. Y., March 9, 1894.

CONTENTS.

CHAPTER		PAGE
I.	Statement of the Case,	1
II.	Ignatius,	23
III.	Clement of Rome,	32
IV.	Fathers of the Second Century,	51
V.	Testimony of the Scripture,	58
VI.	Was the Babylon of Peter, Rome?	68
VII.	Origin of the Story: Babylon Meant Rome,	74
VIII.	Canon Farrar on the Question of Babylon,	81
IX.	The View of the Orientalist Lightfoot,	87
X.	Dr. G. W. Samson's Argument,	92
XI.	Rome not Babylon—Arguments of English Authors,	100
XII.	Views of Continental Writers,	107
XIII.	Gavazzi's Argument,	117
XIV.	The Apostles Peter and John,	123
XV.	The Second Epistle of John, To Whom Addressed?	131
XVI.	Results of Inquiry Thus Far,	141
XVII.	Rome's Appeal to Antiquity,	150
XVIII.	Irenæus,	160

CHAPTER		PAGE
XIX.	"The Trophies" of Caius,	174
XX.	Tertullian and Hippolytus,	184
XXI.	Origen, Clemens, Cyprian,	194
XXII.	Eusebius,	206
XXIII.	Professor Ramsey's Theory,	218
XXIV.	Recapitulation,	234
XXV.	Index,	247

WAS THE APOSTLE PETER EVER AT ROME?

CHAPTER I.

Statement of the Case.

"THE conclusion which follows from the fact of St. Peter being Bishop of Rome is important, and one which every Catholic looks upon as the foundation of his faith."—Rev. S. B. Smith's, D. D., TEACHINGS OF THE HOLY CATHOLIC CHURCH. Imprimatur: Cardinals McCloskey and Gibbons; Bishops Gilmour, Lynch, and Elder. 1884.

"The simplest way of proving that the Bishop of Rome is not the successor of St. Peter, is by establishing as a stubborn fact that St. Peter himself, the presumed source of the Roman claims, never was Bishop of Rome; in fact that he never was in the Eternal City."—Rev. Reuben Parsons, D. D., STUDIES IN CHURCH HISTORY. Imprimatur: Archbishop Corrigan, New York. 1886.

Considering the generally accepted opinion on this question, it is remarkable that the weight of modern argument is so largely with those who deny that there is satisfactory or respectable evidence that the Apostle Peter ever resided in, or visited the Imperial City; evidence based on testimony *judicially scrutinized*, which alone is worthy to be accepted in an investigation so important with respect to the spiritual, eternal interests involved.

For if Peter went to Rome, and the results followed which over half the visible Christian Church are taught to believe as an essential article of faith, then the writer, and all who with him reject and oppose the Roman Catholic Church, because not a sound and pure part of the kingdom of Christ, are thereby doomed to eternal and irretrievable damnation with the devil and his angels.

WHAT ROME TEACHES.

"If anyone should deny that it is by the institution of Christ, the Lord, or by Divine Right, that blessed Peter should have a perpetual line of successors in the primacy over the Universal Church, or that the Roman Pontiff is the successor of blessed Peter in the Primacy, let him be anathema!"—DECREE OF VATICAN COUNCIL, 1870.

"He that acknowledgeth not himself to be under the Bishop of Rome, and that the Bishop of Rome is ordained of God to have Primacy over all the world, is a heretic and cannot be saved, nor is of the flock of Christ."—CANON LAW CH. OF ROME.

CREED OF POPE PIUS IV., 1564: "I acknowledge the Holy Catholic, Apostolic, Roman Church, for the mother and mistress of all Churches; and I promise true obedience to the Bishop of Rome—successor to St. Peter, Prince of the Apostles, and Vicar of Jesus Christ. I do at this present freely profess, and sincerely hold, this true Catholic faith, without which no one can be saved."

Catechismus Romanus, ii. vii. xvii. : "The Roman Bishop . . . occupying as he does the chair of St. Peter, the Prince of the Apostles, who most assuredly himself occupied it till the time of his death, is, in it, entitled to the highest honors, and the most unbounded jurisdiction, as having been conferred on him, not by the decrees of any council or other human authority, but by God himself."

Decree of Boniface VIII., ed. Gregory XII., 1648: "There are one Body, one Head of the one and sole Church, viz., Christ and Christ's Vicar, Peter, and the successors of Peter. . . Moreover we say, determine, and pronounce, that every human creature is subject to the Roman Pontiff, as of absolute necessity to salvation."

"After the death of St. Peter, the Pope, the Bishop of Rome, has always been taken as the visible head of Christ's Church, because St. Peter established his See at Rome and consecrated it with his blood."—Fam. Ex. Cath. Doctrine, p. iii, 1888. Imprimatur: Cardinal Gibbons.

"Whoever would seek for salvation must adhere to this unity ; to this authority of St. Peter and his successors."—Barras., Gen. Hist. Catholic Church, i. 24. Imprimatur: Archbishops McCloskey, Spalding, and Purcell.

WHERE THE BURDEN OF PROOF LIES.

I am aware that the Roman claim of the Primacy of Peter would not be established by such a visit, nor by an asserted residence of twenty-five years in that city. I insist, also, that the burden of proof in this matter rests with those who make the eternal salvation of mankind depend upon their belief in Peter, as living and ruling in Rome, supreme Bishop of the Christian Church.

For it is absolutely essential for the confirmation of

Roman Catholic claims that Peter should have lived in Rome; should have been Bishop of Rome; should have handed down plenary apostolic power to his supposed successors. The whole fabric of the Roman edifice needs for its support, the production of well authenticated and indisputable testimony to establish Peter's visit to and residence in Rome.

Cardinal PERRONE, one of the most learned of recent Roman controversialists, in a work published in 1864, says: "None but an apostate Catholic could assert that Peter was not at Rome; for the reason of that fact is that the coming of St. Peter at Rome, and the seat there established by him, is connected with an article of our faith—that is, the Primacy of Order and Jurisdiction belonging of Divine Right to the Roman Pontiff. Hence it follows that he cannot be a Catholic who does not believe the coming, the episcopate, and the death of St. Peter in Rome." Cardinal BELLARMINE acknowledges that "the right of succession of the Popes is founded on this, that Peter established his seat in Rome by Divine command, and occupied it till his death."

It overthrows the foundations of the Church of Rome to show, that there is no clear or reliable proof that Peter visited Rome, because the whole fabric of Popery falls without the establishment of this assumption. It is as essential to this argument as the brain or the heart is to the human body.

RECENT CRITICAL INVESTIGATIONS.

This whole subject has received of late years a more thorough investigation on the part of legal minds accustomed to sift evidence; and it has been clearly shown *that there is not a tradition of the first century after Peter's death, that he was in Rome; and that there is no assertion of the fact till the beginning of the third century, in any authentic document.*

That Holy Scripture makes no such statement is conceded by all, except those who unwarrantably assume that the Apostle, when he writes Babylon, means Rome, a position denied by many eminent Romanists, and by the great bulk of scholars outside that Church, of which the proof will be presented.

ROMAN CATHOLIC ADMISSIONS.

A marked feature of this controversy is the character of the admissions made by Roman Catholic writers. Simon, in his "Mission and Martyrdom of St. Peter," refers to some of these admissions. Introd., p. 10:

"Charles Du Moulin, the great ecclesiastical lawyer (A. D. 1566), whom Father Calmet speaks of as a steadfast Roman Catholic, and than whom no writer ever enjoyed a higher reputation for learning and intelligence, has unequivocally stated it as his opinion, that there never was even a vague tradition among the ancients about Peter's having left the East, and that one might very well be a Roman Catholic without thinking there was."

In one passage he writes thus: "Even when, after the breaking up of the empire, the Bishops of Rome began to extend their authority over other Churches, they never alleged or put forward this story of Peter's being at Rome, and of his Primacy devolving in succession upon them, which they would not have omitted to do if there had been any such thing to put forward; a clear proof that there was not; the story, I suppose, not having yet been invented." (Vol. iv. p. 460.)

Father Leland, the celebrated English Antiquarian (A. D. 1552), and Marsilius, a distinguished Italian jurist (A. D. 1324), both of whom Calmet also mentions as members of his Church, were equally positive on this point. Father Caron, an Irish Franciscan of the highest eminence (A. D. 1666), took the same view of the matter; as also did Father Hardouin, a French Jesuit (A. D. 1729), likewise in very high repute in Rome. "We Roman Catholics hold," says Father Hardouin, "that at least Peter's head was brought to Rome after his crucifixion, and that it ought to be duly worshiped there; but that the Pope is Christ's substitute and Peter's successor is clear enough without our being bound to suppose that Peter himself ever came to Rome."

De Cormenin, a Roman Catholic, Hist. Popes, pp. 17, 18, remarks: "We are compelled to admit the force of reasoning of the Protestants, who steadily deny the existence of the journey of St. Peter to Rome. There is no proof that his blood was shed at Rome, despite the opinions of Baronius, Fleury, and others."

Ellendorf, Roman Catholic professor at Berlin, Bib. Sac., January, 1859, 105: "Peter's abode at Rome can never be proved."

Francis Turretin, Op., p. 144, presents, as openly denying the visit of Peter to Rome, John Bapt. Mantuan, M. Cæsenas, Marsilius Patavinus, J. Aventinus, Car. Molinæus, and others, all Roman Catholics.

THE VERDICT OF PROTESTANT SCHOLARSHIP.

CONTINENTAL AUTHORS.

George Stanley Faber, among England's ablest writers, refers to one who was regarded as the greatest scholar of his age : "Many persons will incline to rest, either partially or wholly, in the strongly expressed judgment of the learned SCALIGER : 'As for the coming of Peter to Rome, his Roman episcopate of twenty years, and his final martyrdom at Rome, no man, whose head can boast a grain of common sense, will believe a single syllable.'"—Facts and Assertions, etc., p. 58.

In a treatise on the Feigned Departure of Peter, etc., SPANHEIM maintains that "Peter never was in Rome."

SALMASIUS asserts that "there is no better evidence for Peter having gone thither, than for the preaching of James in Spain, or of Joseph of Arimathea in Britain; and by calculation of dates it is proved, with the utmost certainty, "that the Apostle was never at Rome." (See ROBINS' "Evidence of Scripture Against the Claims of the Roman Church," p. 106.)

F. TURRETIN, Op. iii. 148, Am. Ed.: "That Peter was at Rome is doubtful and extremely uncertain; it is far more certain that he never saw Rome."

RANKE affirms: "Historical criticism has shown that it is a matter of doubt whether the Apostle ever was at Rome at all." (Ref. C., ii. ch. 3, p. 472.)

VAN OOSTERZEE, Christ. Dogm., p. 702: "Even if we allow that Peter was actually at Rome (though the Scriptures do not actually decide it, and hardly leave room to suppose it), nothing is thereby determined in favor of his episcopate over that church."

LIPSIUS, a great German critic, asserts: "The Roman Peter Legend proves itself to be from beginning to end a fiction, and thus our critical judgment is confirmed. *The feet of Peter Never Trod the Streets of Rome.*"—Pres. Quar., April, 1876.

Kurtz says : "It is by no means clear that Peter ever went to Rome."—Ch. Hist. i. 64.

Quoting one of the most eminent of Church Historians, Professor BLEDSOE, himself among the most profound philosophers of the century, asks : "Was St. Peter ever at Rome at all ? This question is carefully discussed by NEANDER in his Planting and Training of the Christian Church ; and after candidly weighing the evidence on both sides, he evidently inclines to disbelieve the tradition respecting St. Peter's visit to Rome, and still more his residence there as bishop. But unless we are greatly mistaken, there are several forcible, if not irresistible considerations, which are overlooked by Neander, and which negative the idea that St. Peter ever was Bishop of Rome."—South. Rev., July, '72.

VIEWS OF BRITISH SCHOLARS.

Of the Reformation writers we have CRANMER and COVERDALE asserting, "It is not certain that Peter was ever in Rome."—Cranmer, Wks., ii. 76.

Bishop HOOPER says : "Whether Peter was in Rome at all is still a disputed question. I never knew a man yet able to prove it."

BRADFORD argues strongly against it. WILLET, in his "Synopsis Papismi," does the same.

In the seventeenth century we have the Orientalist, LIGHTFOOT, asserting : "In all the Scripture you cannot find Peter nearer Rome than Joppa ; and our Protestant writers have made it plain as the sun at noonday, that he never was there."—Wks., vii. 2.

JOHN OWEN writes : "As to what is recorded in story, the order and series of things, with the discovery afforded us of Peter's course and place of abode in

Scripture, do prevail with me to think steadfastly he was never there."—Vol. xix. 202.

Bishop Bull, Wks., ii. 193 : "All this while the city of Rome lay in darkness ; till at length, in the reign of Claudius, as Eusebius relates it, St. Peter came to Rome, (and certainly *then* he came if *ever*,) and brought the light of the heavenly doctrine from the East, into the parts of the western world. . . St. Clement, Bishop of Rome in the Apostolic age, speaking of the labors of St. Peter and St. Paul, briefly touches on the former, but dwells on the praises of the latter (*not so much as mentioning St. Peter coming to Rome*)."

"Some very learned men have observed that the above tradition of St. Peter's voyage to Rome was first derived from Papias, an author indeed very ancient, but also very credulous, and of a mean judgment."—Vind. Ch. of England, p. 42.

J. H. Browne, "Peter the Apostle never at Rome," p. 45 : "Since the ancient tradition of the journey of the Apostle Peter to Rome in the reign of Claudius is untrustworthy, as I have shown, and very generally rejected ; and since the same Apostle's going to Rome at any subsequent time rests on no foundation in sacred or ecclesiastical history, as I have also pointed out in the foregoing pages ; the conclusion of Bishop Bull, as it seems to me, must be assented to, and the *testimony* accepted which he considers must be drawn from the silence of Clement of Rome, *that the Apostle Peter was never in that city.*"

John Howe writes : "All their learning, wit, and sophistry will never answer what hath been written to make it highly probable that St. Peter was never at Rome, much less that he sat twenty-five years there.

It must therefore be a strong delusion which makes them build so mighty a fabric on so infirm and weak a foundation."—Wks., v. 524.

Bower, in Hist. Popes, i. 5, says: "From what has hitherto been said, every impartial judge must conclude that it is at best very much to be doubted whether Peter was ever at Rome."

Of modern writers of great learning we have Adam Clarke, who asserts: "I am of opinion that St. Peter did not write from Rome—that he was neither Bishop of Rome, nor martyred at Rome—in a word, that he never was at Rome."

Dr. Kitto says in his Encyclopædia: "There is no sufficient reason for believing that Peter was ever even so much as within the walls of Rome."

In Dick's Theology, ii. 468, we read: "The sum of all that has been said is, that we have no evidence that Peter went to Rome now, or at any other time."

Hill, Divinity, p. 70, remarks: "When you examine the evidence that Peter died Bishop of Rome, you will find it extremely doubtful whether he ever was in that city."

Robert Hall writes: "That Peter was ever at Rome we have no evidence but vague and uncertain traditions. That he exercised the episcopal function there is still more uncertain, or rather extremely improbable."—Wks., iv. 254, Eng. Ed.

Bishop Copleston, in Errors of Romanism, says: "It is even a matter of serious doubt whether Peter was ever at Rome. There is no historical evidence of the fact, and there is much probability against it."

Greenwood, in Cathedra Petri, writes: "It may be stated generally with perfect certainty that no visit of the Apostle Peter to the West is asserted, in direct and positive terms, by any extant Christian writer for the first three centuries."

EDGAR, Var. Popery, p. 68 : "History has preserved a profound silence on the subject of the first Roman bishop . . . the evidence of Peter's visit to that city is not historical but traditional. History for a century after the alleged event presents on this topic an universal blank, which is supplied from the very suspicious testimony of tradition. A single hint on this subject is not afforded by Peter himself, nor by his inspired companions."

TIMPSON, Ch. Hist. 35, remarks : "We have no satisfactory evidence from history that Peter ever was at Rome, much less bishop of that city."

POWELL on Succession, 119 : "It is a question never yet settled whether Peter was at Rome."

ALEX. BISHOP, Two Babylons : "That Peter the Apostle was ever Bishop of Rome has been proved again and again an arrant fable. That he ever set foot in Rome is at best highly doubtful."

McGAVIN's Protestant : "That Peter was Bishop of Rome, or that he ever saw Rome, remains yet to be proved."

ARROWSMITH, Geog. Dict. Script. : "It is by no means certain that Peter was ever at Rome at all (being the Apostle of the circumcision, Gal. ii. 9).

SEELEY, Essays on Rom., 182 : "So far from such being the case (St. Peter, Bishop of Rome), long arguments have been constructed to show that St. Peter never was at Rome at all."

J. A. WYLIE, "The Papacy," p. 233 : "If ever Peter did visit Rome, of which there exists not the slightest evidence, his stay must have been short indeed."

LITTLEDALE, in Plain Reasons, says: "That St. Peter was ever at Rome at all, there is no first-hand or contemporaneous testimony to the opinion, whether in Scripture or elsewhere; whence it is clear that God has not considered it important enough to be certified for us as being a matter of faith."

DAVIDSON, Intro. N. Test., i. 142: "The connection of Peter with Rome, though it appears in early ecclesiastical literature, rests on an insecure basis. Distinguished critics reject it, not without reason."

KENNARD affirms, Cont. with McLachlan, 49: "I boldly and advisedly assert that there is no *evidence* to show that St. Peter ever was at Rome."

BAGBY'S Trav. in East. p. 702: "I do not believe that Peter was ever at Rome at all; at any rate for any length of time. There are no authentic records to prove it, though the Romanists profess to show the spot on which he was put to death, and assert that he was crucified, head downward, in the reign of Nero. Peter is never once named as having been at Rome, in the New Testament."

MASSEY, Secret. Hist. Rom., 2: "The Roman Church, like the Roman Empire, rose to its palmy greatness from the poorest and most obscure origin. The researches of the historians Milman, Merivale, Mosheim, Giesler, and Bunsen, as I have fully shown in my history of Rome, have detected as 'transparent fabrications,' all the legend, by which Romish writers glorify their early Church. They expose the monstrous absurdity of the Romish claim to St. Peter as its founder and bishop. They point to the undeniable fact that there is not the slightest allusion in the Holy Scriptures, to any connection between that Apostle and Rome. . . Milman also shows from that curious first religious romance, the Clementina, that this story of St. Peter's sojourn at Rome is of fabulous origin."

NORTH BRITISH REVIEW, November, 1848, p. . "It is *possible* that Peter may have gone to Rome, ἐπι τέλει as Origen has it, *but there is not the very remotest reason for such a supposition.*"

BLAIKIE in Bible History, p. 418, writes: "The tradition that Peter went to Rome in the reign of Nero, and was condemned at the same time as Paul, is now generally abandoned as destitute of trustworthy authority."

ENCYC. BRITAN., Article, Popedom: "It is maintained, by the great majority of Protestant scholars, that there is no proof that Peter was ever in Rome at all."

AMERICAN WRITERS.

SMYTH, Apostolical Succes., p. 233: "We have sought for Peter at Rome, and could not ascertain that he ever was at Rome at all."

C. HODGE, Syst. Theol., i. 132: "It is very doubtful whether Peter was ever at Rome. The sphere of his labors was in Parthia and the East."

ELLIOTT on Romanism, ii. 223: "There is no evidence that Peter ever was at Rome, no proof that he ever wrote from Rome, or was bishop there."

BETHUNE, Lect. Cat., ii. 350: "It is doubted by many learned investigators that Peter ever was at Rome at all."

JACOBUS, Com. Acts, xii. 17: "There is no proof that Peter went to Rome now, or at any other time."

Hurst, Short. Hist. Early Ch., p. 6: "There is no historic proof that Peter founded the Church in Rome, or was bishop there."

Strong, Syst. Theol., p. 507: "There is no conclusive evidence that Peter ever was at Rome."

Dr. N. Murray (Kirwan), Let. to Bp. Hughes, 57. "As to Peter being Bishop of Rome, or being even at Rome, the Scriptures are silent. The amount of your testimony resolves itself into the truth or falsehood of a prattling Papias, who told Irenæus that somebody told him, that Peter was Pope of Rome."

H. C. Vedder, Bapt. Quar. Rev., xi. 509: "It cannot be proved that Peter ever was at Rome, much less that he was a bishop of the Church of Rome."

R. E. Thompson, Mag. Christ. Liter., August, 1892: "Peter was probably never at Rome."

W. M. Taylor, Life of Peter, 343: "It is not by any means certain that Peter ever was at Rome, and facts may yet be brought to light to make it certain that he never was."

Lansing, Rome and the Rep., 205: "From the best evidence that I can get on both sides, Peter was never in Rome, and that has been the opinion of many of the most learned theologians and historians."

Emerton, Intro. Mid. Ages., 102: "In later times the Roman Church claimed that it had been founded by the Apostle Peter, but that cannot be proved."

Shimeall, End of Prelacy, p. 289: "We deny that Peter was ever at Rome. The New Testament Scriptures are, of course, entirely silent on the subject. . . From A. D. 49 or 50, for all further information respecting him, we are wholly dependent on the bewildering uncertainty of early tradition."

New Englander, October, 1872: "Rome was the only city in the West where an Apostle, Paul, had labored; though it was claimed that Peter had been there, against all the intimations and teachings of Scripture."

Princeton Rev., iii. 252 : "There is no good evidence that Peter was ever in Rome. It certainly does not appear from Scripture; indeed there is nothing in Scripture which would lead to such a supposition."

T. V. Moore, South. Meth. Rev., January, 1856: "The fact that we press is that there is not a particle of evidence for a hundred years after the death of Peter that it was ever dreamed that he had been in Rome; that it is not until A. D. 176 that a doubtful testimony occurs; and that it is not until the first quarter of the third century that we find clear evidence that this fact was believed, and then only in connection with many admitted falsehoods. There is absolutely no clear satisfactory proof that Peter ever was at Rome : the probability clearly is that he died at Babylon."

Bacon, Lives of Apos., p. 253-257: "In justification of the certainty with which sentence is pronounced against the whole story of Peter's ever having gone to Rome, it is only necessary to refer to the decisive argument on pp. 228-233, in which the whole array of ancient evidence is given by Dr. Murdock. . . All those writers who pretend to particularize the mode of his departure, connect it also with the utterly impossible fiction of his residence at Rome."

Dowling, on Romanism : "There is no mention in the New Testament that Peter ever was at Rome, and hence Scaliger, Salmasius, Spanheim, and Adam Clarke and many others have denied that he ever visited that city."

SNODGRASS, Apos. Succ. 221 : "The challenge has often been given to the Papacy and to all others who claim to be successors of Peter as Bishop of Rome, to produce any proof that he ever was at Rome at all, and they have never done it. The probability is that he never was."

N. L. RICE, Rom. not Christianity, p. 139 : "It is sufficient to state the fact, that the most learned men who are not Papists are unable to find any trace of the doctrine of the Pope's supremacy in the Primitive ages of Christianity, that they even doubt whether Peter was ever at Rome."

NOURSE, Prot. Rev., July, 1846, p. 220: "The truth is this, the Scripture is wholly silent in regard to any visit of Peter to Rome, either for one purpose of another. And this is strong, nay, *conclusive evidence* against such a visit. For so remarkable a fact (had it existed) as the prince of the Apostles going to Rome to exercise his supremacy there, could not have been left unrecorded. There is, therefore, no evidence in Scripture that Peter ever exercised his office in Rome."

SAWYER's Organ. Christianity, p. 49: "The tradition of Peter's death at Rome is a natural accompaniment of the fiction that he lived and labored there ; and has no solid foundation. The manifest error of supposing that he had lived there sufficiently accounts for the tradition that he died there. There is no evidence in favor of either ; but the contrary. . . The origin and prevalence of the tradition respecting Peter's supposed episcopacy at Rome are among the curiosities of history, and well worthy the attention of the critical scholar."

Professor CLEMENT M. BUTLER, formerly a chaplain

in Rome, remarks in his work, St. Paul in Rome, p. 260 : "We find no contemporaneous witness saying that St. Peter was at Rome, nor even *saying that it was said*. We find no witness *near that period* making that assertion. It is not until several generations after his death that it began to be said that St. Peter had lived and been crucified at Rome. After it once began to be said, it matters not how many may have repeated the saying on the authority of those who went before. They do not add any strength to the testimony. The chain of testimony fails for the want of connecting links between the first witnesses and the facts alleged. Nothing is accomplished by adding a thousand links to the other end of the chain. . . We see from an examination of those references which we have considered, of how little weight, in the way of historical testimony, would be the statements of Eusebius and Jerome, and twenty or thirty other fathers who lived from a century and a half to four centuries after Peter, as to the question of his residence, his life and death at Rome. They could but repeat the statements of those who had gone before. They could but assert over and over that such and such were traditions of the Church. How much credit would be due to traditions thus created we have already seen. For it would not be difficult to show that whatever weight may be due to that which may be called traditions, the alleged statements with regard to St. Peter are not in fact entitled to that name."

A HISTORIC PARALLEL.

I would not extend this article, but having all the Greek and Latin passages before me ever alleged in testimony of St. Peter's having left the East, thirty-seven in number, I am prepared to show that all, combined, do not present satisfactory or decisive proof that this Apostle ever visited Rome.

Indeed, the case resembles that of the story of the female Pope Joan, which, although accepted by one Pope and 150 Romish authors, and sustained by monuments prior to A. D. 1600, is yet rejected by numerous Protestant writers. It requires no more credulity to believe the one than the other. There is about as much certainty that the one was Pope, as that the other ever visited Rome. It is equally idle to base any matter of importance, any scheme of doctrine, on the supposition that either event ever transpired. The errors and delusions of the Papal scheme are built, like the story of Peter's Roman visit, on traditions suited to superstitious minds, not on reason or fair argument, which will abide the test of sound criticism and candid and thorough examination.

Bishop JEWEL, than whom there is no higher authority on such questions, in his controversy with Harding, states that "the fable was raised at Rome, and thence only, and from no place else, was published abroad to the world." Then presenting the names of nineteen Roman Catholic authors, who affirm the truth of the story, he writes: "of these some lived four hundred, some five hundred years ago, and have ever been counted worthy of some authority; notwithstanding, for your dame Joan's sake, you, M. Harding, begin now to clip their credit. Howbeit, whatsoever they were, certain it is they were not Lutherans. All these, with one consent agree together, that dame Joan was Pope of Rome."— Defense, p. 352.

Dr. GEORGE PECK, Meth. Quar. Rev., January, 1845,

p. 152, writes: "Here is a strong array of Roman Catholic authorities in favor of. the fact of a female Pope. We do not pretend to say that the evidence is conclusive, indeed we doubt whether it is sufficiently sustained, BLONDEL and BOWER, two great Protestant writers, have investigated the matter more fully than others, and come to the conclusion that the story is fabulous. Their conclusions are based upon the want of contemporaneous history, the first notice taken of it being by an author who lived some two hundred years after the event is said to have transpired.

"BOWER, however, says what no one denies, that 'the female Pope owes her existence and her promotion to the ROMAN CATHOLICS themselves; for by them the fable was invented, was published to the world by the priests and monks before the Reformation, and was credited upon their authority, even by those who were most zealously attached to the Holy See, and among the rest by ST. ANTONINUS, Archbishop of Florence, nor did they begin to confute it till Protestants reproached them for it, as reflecting great dishonor upon the See of St. Peter."

We simply ask Roman Catholics and others to deal as candidly and intelligently with this Peter-Roman question, as Blondel and Bower have with the Joan-Roman story. We have no question as to what will be the result of this investigation.

Bishop COXE pithily remarks: "If you ever find a Jesuit disposed to be impudent, there is one way to silence him which seldom fails of success. Remind him of the great cloud of Romish witnesses who have believed in Pope Joan; and challenge him to produce a tenth part of such evidence as confirms her historic character, in behalf of his fable about St. Peter's residence and Pontificate in Rome."—N. Y. Observer, December 12, 1872.

THE SOCIETY OF JESUS.

With regard to the so-called "Society of Jesus," the writer feels fully justified in using plain language. As an American citizen, and a friend of truth and right, he is irreconcilably opposed to an organized system of double-dealing and deceit. He distinguishes between this irreformable and unchangeable body, morally isolated from mankind, and the great mass of honest Christian men and women in the Church of Rome, in this and other lands. He fully adopts the judicious language of a learned and godly scholar, Professor McDonald of Princeton, who in his Life and Writings of St. John, p. 220, says: "We shall now have occasion to speak of Rome, as it is, or has long been, since the fall of the empire, but we mean Rome, strictly, Papal Rome, Jesuit Rome, and not that great venerable Body called the Catholic Church, as it exists in Europe, on which this Papal power has been sitting like a close and stifling incubus.

"This is a distinction that ought ever to be made, as enabling us, on the one hand to preserve charity, and on the other to maintain the true interpretation of those solemn prophecies which point to the terrible evil that was to be developed in the history of the Christian Church. It is thus only we can preserve a feeling of brotherhood to our fellow Christians, and love them for the saintliness often exhibited in their characters. But with Jesuit Rome, the Rome of Hildebrand and Borgia, there can be no communion. She herself utterly repels it, and her ban is to be preferred to her embrace."

The simple fact that every Roman Catholic government has publicly expelled the Jesuits, will justify us with every reasonable member of that Church.

The order was driven out of Portugal in 1759; from France, Spain, and Naples, 1767. In 1773 Pope Clement XIV., for meddling in politics, quarreling with other religious orders, conforming to heathen usages in the East, raising disturbances which brought persecution on the Church, required the order, for the peace of the Church, to be suppressed, extinguished, abolished, and abrogated forever, with everything pertaining to it; all the property to be confiscated, and the General to be confined in prison till his death.

The Jesuits reappeared in France in 1814, and were again expelled in 1880; again expelled from Spain in 1820 and 1835; from Portugal in 1834; from Russia in 1819 and 1830; from Holland in 1816; Switzerland in 1867; Germany in 1872.

It was re-established in Rome by Pius IX. in 1849. It is swarming extensively in our own land.

Monseigneur DEPRADT, Roman Archbishop of Malines, writes: "So atrocious, extensive, and continual were their crimes, that they were expelled either partially or generally from all the different countries of Europe at various intervals, prior to the abolition of the order in 1773, thirty-nine times—a fact unparalleled in the history of any body in the world."—Christ. Treasy., vii. 510.

The rejoinder to the statements previously presented that Protestants of eminent reputation, like Pearson, Grotius, Drs. Lardner, Macnight, Whitby, and many others, have accepted the tradition of Peter's visit to Rome, is conclusively met by its utter rejection by numerous writers of equal learning and standing, as has been seen, and will be more fully shown.

Mere unauthenticated traditions, and unsustained assertions, are not conclusive in this inquiry.

A claim which involves consequences so momentous as the salvation of the human soul, demands of necessity, proof clear, positive, impregnable—in fact, absolute demonstration. A Divine mandate is imperatively required, else the doctrine has no claim whatever on the conscience of man. All anathemas and excommunications based upon it have been utterly valueless in the court of Heaven, and such maledictions have been visited upon those who have proclaimed them.

CHAPTER II.

Ignatius.

It may be asked, Why discuss a question of this nature at this time? Are not the minds of Roman Catholics inaccessible to all argument against the accepted doctrines of their Church? Is it not an established principle of the Papal Communion, that to doubt one dogma of their creed is damnation? Is it not, therefore, a waste of time, labor, and thought to prove that what is distinctively Roman is neither Catholic, reasonable, nor revealed? To the first inquiry we answer, Yes, in most cases. The adoption of the principle involved in the second question, necessarily produces this result.

It is, however, a cheering fact that in our land of religious liberty, universal education, and political independence, there is an advancing freedom of thought among the laity of the Church of Rome. It is encouraging to witness the formation of such societies as the Columbian Reading Union, the Catholic Summer School, and the recent meeting of the Roman Catholic Congress. Vast results for good may be anticipated in the line of emancipation of the lay Roman Catholic mind.

It is in the hope of reaching this class that the argument which vitally concerns the foundation of the Roman Scheme, as to the fact of the Apostle Peter's visit to Rome, is here presented.

The fact that the minds of a number of PRIESTS have

recently been opened to the full divine light of Holy Scripture, is a strong stimulus and encouragement to efforts in this direction.

The establishment of the fact that there is no satisfactory proof on record that the Apostle Peter ever saw the city of Rome, while at the same time the silence of Scripture renders the supposition highly improbable, may lead some Roman Catholic minds to doubt the truth of the System which is built on the doctrine, that Peter was in Rome; was a Bishop of Rome; and handed down to succeeding Bishops of Rome plenary apostolic authority and supreme spiritual domination.

A general survey of the subject was presented in the previous chapter, where was briefly mentioned the arguments of learned writers against the fact of the journey to Rome by Peter, and the admission of Roman Catholics that proof of the same is wanting. The language of all early writers, whose works have reached us, appealed to to substantiate the claim that Peter visited Rome, will be examined in detail. Alleged testimonies which Roman Catholic writers have confessed to be forgeries will be briefly disposed of.

FORGED TESTIMONY: LINUS AND ANACLETUS.

Of this character are Linus, A. D. 70, and Anacletus, A. D. 91, Bishops of Rome, whom Father Feuardent, in his notes on Irenæus, b. iii. c. 3, states: confirm "with wonderful unanimity" the statement of that writer, that "Peter proclaimed the Gospel at Rome, and laid the foundation of that Church."

This same writer wonders at "the abandoned effrontery with which Velenus, Illyricus (otherwise called Flacius, 1520–75), Funccius, and other French Protestants, have the impudence to jabber about Peter's having never been at Rome."

After such a stout assertion, how surprising to read in Father CEILLIER (vol. i. p. 490) concerning Linus: "The work that we have in two books under the name of St. Linus is full of ridiculous fables, and is not worth reading."

Cardinal BELLARMINE, in his Ecclesiastical Writers, states: "We consider that Linus' writings are not extant, and that those which now pass under his name are forgeries."

With respect to ANACLETUS we have similar statements from Papal authors. TILLEMONT (1637-98) writes: "We have three Decretals under the name of St. Anacletus. All the learned are agreed nowadays that these letters are frauds and forgeries, and that all the Decretal letters attributed to the Popes who lived prior to Pope Siricius (A. D. 385) are equally so."

Father DUPIN (1657-1719), the learned historian, in his chapter on the False Decretals, gives his reasons for regarding these epistles as a "forgery" and an "imposture."

"Works have been published attributed to St. Linus as their author. They are now pronounced apocryphal, because they are infected with errors resembling those of the Manicheans."—ARTAUD., Hist. Popes, i. 19.

IGNATIUS.

IGNATIUS, bishop at Antioch (A. D. 107), is appealed to by Bellarmine, Pearson, Baratier, and by Father McCorry in his tract "Was St. Peter Ever at Rome?" as a witness on the affirmative side of this question.

Baronius, Feuardent and Valesius (Henry De Valois, 1603-76), wisely decline an appeal to him.

This supposed evidence of Ignatius is found in his Epistle to the Romans, ch. iv.—"Not as Peter and Paul do I give you directions. They were Apostles, I am condemned. They were free; I am still a slave. But if I suffer I am a freed man in Jesus, and I shall arise in him a free man."

Bunsen's rendering is: "I am not commanding you like Peter and Paul; they were Apostles, I a condemned convict; they were free, I am hitherto a slave. But if I suffer, I am a freed man in Jesus Christ, and I shall rise from the dead like him, a free man."

Pearson on these words remarks; "For what can be more manifest than it is from those words to the Romans, that Ignatius must have had an idea that Peter proclaimed the Gospel at Rome, was put to death there, as well as Paul."

Baratier exclaims: "Why does this writer mention Peter and Paul together in this way, if it were not that they were both at Rome. . . It is evident that Ignatius believed that Peter had been at Rome."

McCorry argues: "This proves that the Romans had been taught by St. Peter and St. Paul, and had received their commands, and of course shows that both Apostles had been at Rome."

To prove that the Apostle Peter left the field to which our Lord had especially assigned him, the Jewish people; entered upon his brother Paul's work, that of converting the Gentiles of the West; that he forsook Babylon, in whose neighborhood were over a million of his people, and from which city he wrote his first Epistle; and came to the eight thousand Jews at Rome under the care of Paul, Clement, Andronicus, Junia, and other teachers, will demand the most overwhelming testimony; so improbable and inconsistent would be such a proceeding on the part of a wise and faithful Evangelist.

So far from such an assertion, Ignatius simply says, Peter and Paul had directed and instructed the Roman Christians.

This Peter had done with respect to the strangers from Rome on the Day of Pentecost; and these had returned to found the Church, which Paul at a later day instructed.

"The Church of Rome seems to have been founded by laymen. Bunsen, Michaelis, Rambach, Rosenmuller, and others suppose that the Church at Rome was founded by some of the Roman converts under Peter's preaching on the day of the great Pentecostal blessing. Among the hearers were 'strangers of Rome, Jews and Proselytes,'" Acts i. 10.—SAWYER'S Organic Christianity, p. 32.

OWEN, Pref. Calvin on Romans, remarks: "The only thing which Peter appears to have had to do in forming and founding a Church at Rome was to have been the instrument in the conversion, at the Day of Pentecost, of those who in all probability were the first who introduced the Gospel unto Rome; and it is probable that it was this circumstance which occasioned the tradition that he had been the founder of that Church.

"Less occasion has often produced tales of this kind."

It should be borne in mind that the ancient writers, in speaking of the combined common work of the twelve Apostles in founding Churches, use the names of Peter and Paul to include all who engaged in this evangelical mission.

Greenwood, in his Cathedra Petri, vol. i. p. 24, remarks: "It has been alleged with great plausibility that the distinctive ministries of each—that of Peter to the Circumcision, and of Paul to the Uncircumcision—had been acknowledged by themselves, and had become a matter of notoriety to the whole Church. These two functions together comprehended one entire ministry, in such wise that the association of the names was in fact rather an association of ideas than of persons. The names of Peter and Paul could thus come to represent the community or union of the ministry of the Jews and Gentiles, the twofold foundations or pillars of the Gospel dispensation; a sense in which they are frequently spoken of by subsequent Christian workers."

Nor do these writers regard the presence of an Apostle as necessary, when alluding to the founding of a Church by the same mode of expression. We have a marked instance of this in Baronius (1538-1607), a later Roman writer, who says, A. D. 39, paragraph 19: "For what does it mean when Peter is said to have founded the Church at Antioch? They are quite wrong who think that Peter must have gone to Antioch for that purpose."

Though Peter never preached in Rome in person, and remained in Babylon and its neighborhood, still he was connected closely with the Christians of Rome, who had been converted in Jerusalem by his preaching, and had returned to preach the Gospel in the Imperial City.

Thus had Peter preceded even Paul in the work at Rome, and in this way may be truly said to have been the founder of that Church, and of others whither his converts were dispersed.

Thus, naturally, may the language of the Martyr Ignatius be understood, without supposing that he gave countenance to the improbable supposition that Peter had forsaken the millions of Jews of the East to visit the thousands at Rome, so carefully tended and instructed by his brother Apostle, Paul, together with the Heathen, as previously arranged.

WYLIE, on Papacy, p. 233, justly says: "There was a formal arrangement among the Apostles touching that matter. Peter, along with James and John, gave his hand to Paul, and struck a bargain with him that he (Paul) should go to the Heathen, and they (James, Cephas, and John) unto the Circumcision. If then, Peter became Bishop of Rome, he violated the solemn paction." (See Gal. ii. 9.)

We have thus far seen that from the language of Ignatius, the Church of Rome derives no support from her claim to the residence and episcopate of Peter in the Imperial City.

But Ignatius, in one aspect, may be regarded rather as an antagonist to the claims of the Roman Communion. This point is forcibly presented in the *Christian Observer*, November, 1883, p. 742: "The words of Ignatius, as Archbishop Wake gives them, are these: '*I write unto the Churches*, and signify to them all, that I am willing to die for GOD, unless you hinder me . . . I do not, as Peter and Paul, command you. They were Apostles, I a condemned man. They were free, but I am even unto this day a servant.'

"The Apostles had written unto the Churches; so did Ignatius. But the Apostles, so writing, could *command* the Churches, while he, Ignatius, did not pretend to do so. Is not this one plain meaning of the words? But where is there one word implying that Peter had visited Rome?

"On the other hand, see what is implied in the *silence* of Ignatius. The assumption of Father McCorry is that Peter had founded the Church of Rome, was its bishop for five-and-twenty years, and was finally martyred there; and that he left his primacy, the popedom, to the bishops who should follow him in that chair.

"Well, we now have an aged bishop, in the next century, writing seven letters to various Churches just before his martyrdom. *In six of these epistles, he particularly notices their bishops.* But when he comes to the Church of Rome for the first time he is silent. The Romish hypothesis now is that at Rome there was the Chair of St. Peter; that the bishop of that city was St. Peter's successor, the Primate of the whole Church, and in that city they showed the burying place of the Apostles. How can it be accounted for then, that Ignatius —fond to an excess of bishops, and just about to follow St. Peter in his martyrdom—should write to Rome, without once alluding to St. Peter's chair; and should even refer to St. Peter's epistles without remembering the fact (if it *were* a fact)—that the remains of the Apostle rested in that soil?

"Truly, that remarkable *silence*, to use Father McCorry's own phrase, 'speaks volumes.' How *could* that aged bishop, who in no other case forgets to address and compliment the bishop and the Church to which he was writing—how comes he to forget to venerate the successor of St. Peter, the primate of the whole Church? Only in one way can this omission be accounted for. Ignatius knew nothing of any successor of St. Peter; in his days there was no Pope. To believe that there was a Pope at Rome in A. D. 147, and that St. Peter's tomb was known to be there, is exceedingly difficult, in the face of Ignatius' silence on both these topics."

In the following critical investigation, we shall find that the few expressions of the Fathers with respect to Peter's connection with Rome, may be made to correspond with the Scripture, by a rational and consistent interpretation, on principles exacted in all courts of law.

The Scripture is utterly silent with respect to this alleged Roman visit of the Apostle; history presents no reliable testimony that Peter ever deserted Babylon for Rome.

The original words of Ignatius are herewith presented:

οὐχ ὡς Πέτρος καὶ Παῦλος διατάσσομαι ὑμῖν· ἐκεῖνοι ἀπόστολοι, ἐγὼ κατάκριτος· ἐκεῖνοι ἐλεύθεροι, ἐγὼ δὲ μέχρι νῦν δοῦλος, ἀλλ' ἐάν παθω ἀπελεύθερος Ἰησοῦ Ξριστόῦ, καὶ ἀναστήσομαι ἐν αὐτῷ ἐλεύθερος· νῦν μανθάνω δεδεμένος μηδὲν ἐπιθύμειν.

—Ignatius *to the Romans*, § iv.

CHAPTER III.

Clement of Rome.

CLEMENT OF ROME, a contemporary of the Apostle, is appealed to both by Protestant and Roman writers in support of the tradition that Peter visited the Imperial City. If this writer makes this affirmation, it is enough to settle the question. "Clement," says Chevalier in his Introduction to his translation of the Epistle of this writer: "is believed upon the general testimony of ecclesiastical historians, to have been the same whom St. Paul mentions among his fellow-laborers, whose names are written in the book of life."—Philippians iv. 3.

"The epistle of Clement to the Church at Corinth is the only genuine work of any uninspired writer of the first century, now extant."—RIDDLE's Eccles. Chron., p. 13.

"By ecclesisatical writers generally nothing that is not divine is admitted to be of higher authority."—COLEMAN's Apos. and Prim. Ch., p. 164.

Clement, according to BUNSEN's Chronology, Hippolytus, vol. i. p. 44, was bishop between the years 78 and 86.

Of this Epistle Bishop LIGHTFOOT writes: "We cannot hesitate to accept the universal testimony of antiquity that it was written by Clement, the reputed Bishop of Rome." Of his office he remarks: "He was rather the chief of the presbyters, than the chief over the presbyters."—Christ. Ministry, p. 67.

The testimony of this earliest and most esteemed of uninspired writers is of great importance as settling the question, that the order of bishops and presbyters was the same, in both the Churches of Corinth and of Rome; and no argument whatever can be based on it in support of the authority of the Episcopal office as a distinct order.

As to the hypothesis of Peter's visit to Rome, some Roman Catholic and Protestant writers have claimed Clement as a witness for the affirmative.

Baronius, Bellarmine, and Pearson prudently refrain from appealing to his testimony.

Feuardent, Baratier, Lardner, and McCorry claim him as an authority for Peter's residence at Rome.

McCorry writes thus in his Treatise, p. 67: "The first witness that we shall bring is Clement the Roman, a disciple of Peter. After the persecution of Diocletian had subsided, he wrote an epistle to the Corinthians; in which he speaks of those who had suffered martyrdom at Rome, and makes distinct mention of St. Peter as the great bishop who had founded and governed the Roman Church. He says: 'Let us always have before our eyes those good Apostles: Peter, who endured so many labors, and who, dying a martyr, departed to glory; and Paul, who obtained the reward by patience, and suffered martyrdom under the emperors. To these men, who had led so angelic a life, a vast multitude of the elect were added, who rivaling one another in suffering reproaches and torments, have left behind them for our sake the most beautiful example.' Now here is a declaration from a contemporary writer bearing evidence to the fact that the prince of the Apostles died a martyr at Rome."

Dr. LARDNER, in his History of the Apostles, in the

article on Peter, renders Clement's language thus: "Let us set before our eyes the excellent Apostles: Peter, who through unrighteous zeal underwent not one or two, but many labors, till at last being martyred, he went to the place of glory that was due unto him. Through zeal, Paul obtained the reward of patience. Seven times he was in bonds; he was whipped, he was stoned. He preached both in the East and West, and having taught the world righteousness, and coming to the borders of the West, and suffering martyrdom under the governors, so he departed out of the world, and went to the most holy place, being a most eminent pattern of patience." Similar is the translation of this writer, by Wake, Chevalier, Greenwood, and Simon, except the passage, "the borders of the West." Wake renders it, "the utmost bounds"; Chevalier, "the furthest extremity"; Simon, "the remotest limits"; Greenwood, "the extreme verge."

With respect to the false version of this passage of Clement, offered by Father McCorry, SIMON, p. 309, remarks: "The *translations* of this writer are invaluable as showing to what lengths a few of the Roman clergy now among us go, and are obliged to go upon this subject, and these passages."

We have another illustration of this style of version, in Bishop Kenrick on the Primacy, p. 94, ed. 1848, who says: "Clement. . . . declares that Peter and Paul suffered martyrdom in Rome, before his eyes."

The argument of LARDNER founded on these words of Clement, for the supposed Roman residence of Peter, is as follows; "From these passages I think it may be justly concluded that Peter and Paul were martyrs at Rome, in the time of Nero's persecution. For they suffered among the Romans, where Clement was bishop, and in whose name he was writing to the Corinthians. They were martyrs, when many others were an *example*, or *pattern*, of a like patience *among them*. To *these Apostles*, says Clement, *was joined a great multitude of choice ones*, that is, Christians. This is a manifest description of Nero's persecution at Rome, when a multitude of Christians there were put to death, under grievous reproaches and exquisite torments, as we are assured by Tacitus. These were joined to the excellent Apostles, Peter and Paul, before mentioned. Therefore Peter and Paul had suffered at that place, and at that time; and as it seems, according to this account, at the beginning of that persecution, which may be reckoned not at all improbable.

"When Clement says that Paul *suffered martyrdom under the governors*, he may be understood to mean *by order of the magistrate*. It cannot be here inferred that Peter and Paul did not die by Nero's order, or in virtue of his edict against the Christians. It should be considered that Clement is not an historian. He is writing an epistle containing divers exhortations. It is not needful for him to be more particular. He does not name the city in which Peter and Paul died, nor the death they underwent. But he intimates that they suffered a cruel death, together with many choice ones *among them*, which must mean Rome; and he plainly represents these Apostles as martyrs, who had suffered through envy and unrighteous zeal. The place and the manner of their death were well-known to the Christians at Corinth, to whom Clement was writing."

Lardner goes on to say that Clement was obliged to be "circumspect" in his language in that period of "persecution." Lardner argues, against Pearson, that Nero was in Rome in the year 68, and that therefore the term "governors" may refer to that Emperor. "As for the word being in the plural number; it is no uncommon thing to prefer that to the singular when we are obliged to be cautious, etc. . . So that I must take the liberty to say, that Pearson's observation, that Peter and Paul were put to death, not by Nero, but by the Prefect of Rome, or some other great officer, in the absence of the Emperor, appears to be of no value, and it is destitute of all authority."—See Watson's Theological Tracts, vol. ii. pp. 433–435.

Dr. Lardner has made as much of Clement's words for his argument as is possible. (See *N. Brit. Rev.*, November, 1848, p. 32.)

We give on the other side the comments of three barristers who have thoroughly examined the question.

Ecclesiastical events demand as careful investigation as any matters of importance.

The one we are considering has been made by the Church of Rome one of vital import, and it is bound to furnish irresistible, incontestable evidence.

The supposed journey of Peter to Rome does not appear to be sustained by trustworthy testimony, according to the view of the learned lawyers whose opinions are herewith presented.

Greenwood, who has written the political history of the Latin Pontificate, in his Cathedra Petri, i. 20, writes on Clement's language:

"In proof of the facts here stated respecting Peter and Paul as parts of one transaction, it has been observed that, the sufferings and death of both being mentioned, as it were in the same breath, by one who was in a position to be an eye-witness of the things he relates, a presumption arises that both Apostles were together at Rome, at some point of time between the closing incidents of St. Luke's narrative and the death of Paul in the Neronian persecution. Peter's martyrdom, however, is only remotely alluded to, and not in any way as synchronous with that of Paul. Several things are said of Paul that are not said of Peter, more especially the act of preaching the Gospel in the far West. Lastly, neither time nor place of the martyrdom of either is mentioned; consequently, all ground for concluding, from this passage in the writings of Clement of Rome, that Peter and Paul dwelt and suffered together in that city—seems to fall to the ground."

Simon, another competent legal critic, who, for the purpose of investigating the question here discussed, came to London, and almost dwelt in the British Museum for nine months; in his Mission and Martyrdom of Peter, p. 34, writes with respect to Clement's statement: "The first question that here suggests itself is, Why is Paul's journey into Europe and Paul's martyrdom at Rome, so pointedly stated in the very same paragraph in which nothing more is said of Peter's travels or of Peter's martyrdom, than what manifestly presupposes the Scripture account about his going to the Jews of the Dispersion, as he was directed by his Divine Master, and about his being put to death at Babylon as his own epistles intimate? How is it that Clement makes no allusion to a residence in Europe, or even to a martyrdom there for the Apostle of the Circumcision as well as for the Apostle of the Gentiles? Peter's martyrdom took place in Clement's lifetime; how is it that Clement never heard of anything connected with it at variance with the facts that are laid before us in the Scriptures?

But we do not inquire for the evidences of Peter's having lived and died as is indicated in the sacred text. Our inquiry is for the alleged evidence of his not having done so. Father McCorry supposes St. Clement to speak of the martyrs that had fallen in his own city! whereas Clement speaks of those who had fallen within the memory of that present generation. " 'Let us look at the illustrious examples of OUR OWN AGE,' says the Bishop of Rome; 'let us take, for instance, the Apostles!' "

BOUZIQUE, a recent member of the French bar and legislature, in his History of Christianity, in his examination of Clement, remarks, vol. i. p. 360: "This passage, which clearly excludes the idea of a punishment simultaneously undergone at Rome by the two Apostles, seems nevertheless to have been one of the principal sources whence proceeded the legends on the abode of Peter in that city, and on the tragical end which the Apostle to the Gentiles found there at the same time. It is necessary to remember that in the first centuries Clement's epistle was in some sort received as a sacred Scripture, and read publicly in the Churches of Greece, Asia Minor, and all the Hellenic lands. This habitual reading singularly formed the opinions which legend had got possession of. Clement said nothing else but that Peter and Paul were persecuted through envy, which caused the death of one on the confines of the West, and made the other seven times endure, before God called him to himself.

"But in ceaselessly hearing in the epistle the death of the two Apostles mentioned close together, the Greek Churches came to believe that they perished at the same time, and as the letter came from Rome, at Rome the hearers placed their simultaneous punishment in thought.

"It was supposed that Clement had been the disciple of the one, as of the other, and the ocular witness of their death. . . . If you call to mind the evils endured as much by Peter as by Paul, you see that it is the intention of offering in them illustrious examples of the evil that envy may engender, and not to make them perish in the same time and in the same place.

"But the Christian populace made a mistake. Clement associated the two in the example, the popular legend associated them in suffering and death. It is only two or three generations after the first epistle of Clement that we begin to find some traces of the legend on the journey and the death of Peter at Rome; all this time was needful for it to gain a certain consistency.

"The whole drift of Clement's testimony, then, while it breathes not one word of support of St. Peter's visit to Rome, does imply by the distinction drawn between him and St Paul, that *he* did *not* preach both in the East and in the West—*i. e.*, that he did not visit Rome."

Bacon, in his Lives of the Apostles, thus refers to Lardner's criticism. Alluding to manuscript lectures of Professor Murdock on this subject he writes: "Lardner also gives a sort of abstract of the passage in the Fathers which refers to this subject, but not near so full, nor so close to the original passages as that of Dr. Murdock, although he refers to a few authors not alluded to here, whose testimony, however, amounts to little or nothing. Lardner's disposition to believe all these fully established Roman fables is too pronounced, and on these points his accuracy appears to fail in maintaining its general character.

"However, in the single passage from Clemens Romanus referred to above, he is very full, not only translating the whole passage relating to Peter and Paul, but entering into a very elaborate discussion of the views taken of it; but upon all he fails so utterly in rearing an historical argument on this slender basis, that I cannot feel called on, in this place, to do anything more than barely refer the critical reader to the passage in his Life of Peter."

Faussett, in Com. on 1 Peter, remarks: "Clement of Rome 1 Epist. ad Corinthos, Sec. 4, 5, often quoted for, is really against it. He mentions Paul and Peter together, but makes it a *distinguishing* circumstance of Paul, that he preached both in the East and West, implying that Peter was never in the West (2 Pet. i. 14). "'I must shortly put off this my tabernacle' implies his martyrdom was near; yet he makes no allusion to Rome, or of any intention of visiting it."

Giesler's comment is brief: "Clement testifies to his martyrdom, Ignatius alludes to it."—Hist. i. 81.

As we are dealing with a question of vital import, as related to the exclusive claims of the Church of Rome, with its one hundred millions of adherents, too much importance cannot be attached to the testimony of the witness who, alone of all appealed to, had personal cognizance of the facts in the case.

Clement, as we have seen, was a contemporary of the Apostle Peter, and is the only writer of the period who has written a line bearing on the subject, now extant.

Peter's residence in Rome is "the very *neck* which attaches the head to the body—the 'Primacy of Peter' to the Roman Papacy." We must do justice to the arguments of the eminent writers, both Papal and Protestant, who claim for the Apostle a residence in Rome. No one has argued in the affirmative more ably than the "celebrated" Protestant scholar, Lardner. To the argument drawn from one of Clement's expressions to establish clearly the fact that the Apostle was not at Rome, Dr. LARDNER thus replies. He refers to the Preface to St. Peter's 1st Epistle, written by the commentator Dr. BENSON, who says:

"Clemens Romanus (who was personally acquainted with the Apostles and knew very well where they traveled) writes a letter from Rome to Corinth, and mentions St. Paul's traveling very far to spread the Gospel; but in the same section, though he mentions St. Peter's sufferings and martyrdom, yet he says nothing of his traveling much, not one word of his ever having been in Rome." To this Lardner replies: "*First.* It seems to me that Clement says Peter and Paul suffered martyrdom at Rome. For speaking of the *great multitude of the elect, who had been an excellent example of patience among them,* meaning the Romans, he says *they were joined* to or with the *good Apostles,* before mentioned. Therefore the Apostles had suffered in the same place. Certainly Clement, who wrote this, did not think that Peter died at Babylon in Mesopotamia, and Paul at Rome in Italy.

"*Secondly.* The reason why Clement so particularly mentions St. Paul's travels probably was because the extent of his preaching was very remarkable. And it is likely that Clement refers to Rom. xv. 19.

"*Thirdly.* His omitting to speak of Peter's travels is not a denial of his having traveled a great deal. Nor does it imply that he had not been at Rome. St. Paul must have been some time in the West, and at Rome, if he suffered martyrdom there. But Clement does not say so, though he knew it very well. As did the Corinthians likewise. But when we speak or write of things well known (as these things were at that time), there is no need to be very particular. It was sufficient if Clement mentioned such things as would render his exhortations effectual.

"Upon the whole I cannot but think that these passages of Clement bear a testimony to the martyrdoms both of Peter and Paul, and that at Rome, which cannot be evaded."

See Beecher's Pap. Conspiracy, p. 248: Shepherd's Hist. Ch. of Rome, p. 529: Ellendorf, Bib. Sac., January, 1859, p. 117, Butler's St. Paul in Rome, p. 266.

The Christian Observer, November, 1853, p. 741, takes an entirely opposite view of Clement's words. He writes: "We remark two things: *First.* There is no allusion whatever to Rome. That city is not named or referred to in any way whatever. The Apostle does not allude to our own country, or our own Church, but he passes from ancient examples to the examples of *our own age* or time.

"*Secondly.* But, speaking of the two most eminent Apostles, Peter and Paul, he particularizes one characteristic of St. Paul, which does not apply to St. Peter. Peter, he says, underwent many sufferings, till at last, being martyred, he went to the place of glory that was due to him.

"But of Paul he says, seven times he was in bonds, he was whipped, he was stoned, *he preached both in the East and in the West;* and so having taught the whole world righteousness, and for that end *traveled* even unto the utmost bounds of the East, he at last suffered martyrdom. Here is a feature ascribed to St. Paul which is not touched upon in the description of St. Peter.

"Now, when I describe two eminent men, and speak of one of them as deeply learned, I thereby imply that this is a point in which he is distinguished from the other.

"If I say of two brothers that the younger one has traveled much, the hearer quite understands me to imply that the same thing cannot be said of the elder.

"And so in like manner, when, panegyrizing the two apostles, Clement points out the feature in St. Paul, that he preached *both in the East and in the West*, and speaks especially of his travels; we rightly understand now, to-day, by implication, that this was a point in which he exceeded St. Peter—in short, that St. Paul, going to the Gentiles, preached both in the East and in the West; while St. Peter, the Apostle of the Circumcision, stayed in Babylon, where the Jews were chiefly resident.

"The whole drift of Clement's testimony, then, while it breathes not one word in support of St. Peter's visit to Rome, does imply, by the distinction drawn between him and St. Paul, that *he* did *not* preach both in the East and in the West—*i. e.*, that he did *not* visit Rome. His testimony, therefore, is not in Father McCorry's favor, but rather against him. Thus, the very first witness produced, instead of proving the advocate's case, goes far to establish the very *opposite.*"

The NORTH BRITISH REVIEW, November, 1888, on Scheler's translation of Ellendorf's essay on Peter's Roman residence, says of Clement: "The earliest testimony which is generally alleged in support of the tradition is that of Clement, third Bishop of Rome, who, in his first Epistle to the Corinthians (p. 5), exhorts the latter to look for courage and perseverance to the examples set by the Apostles; and then draws a parallel between Peter and Paul both having suffered martyrdom for the sake of Christ. But he does not add one word as to *where* and *when* they suffered, and the inference drawn from his words is therefore wholly gratuitous; the more so, as he nowhere else mentions that St. Peter ever set foot in Rome. A similar interpretation is forced upon an expression of IGNATIUS, in whose Epistle to the Romans the words occur: *I command you not like Peter and Paul;* but surely, if such expressions be proof, what is there that may not be proved?"

DICK, Theology, ii. p. 468, observes: "Clement, who is so favorably mentioned in the New Testament, in an Epistle written from Rome to the church at Corinth, says that Paul suffered martyrdom in the West, but takes no notice of the martyrdom of Peter. His silence is absolutely unaccountable if, as the Papists tell us, Peter had been Bishop of Rome, and had been crucified before the eyes of Clement."

FROSCHAMMER, Romance of Rom., p. 20, remarks: "If Peter had labored and died in Rome as well as Paul, why does not Clement say also of him, that having preached in the East and West, he also died in the West? Manifestly Clement in these words means to say something of Paul which could not be ascribed to Peter."

ELLENDORF, a Roman Catholic Professor in Berlin, has written an exhaustive critical inquiry on the subject here discussed, which was translated in the *Bibliotheca Sacra* for July, 1858, and January, 1859. With respect to Clement's language he remarks: "When we remember that according to Tertullian's account, Clement was consecrated by Peter as Bishop of Rome, the strange way in which Clement here mentions Peter is very remarkable, and renders the account suspicious. When Clement says distinctly of Paul, that he came to Rome and suffered martyrdom under Nero, the same reason he had likewise in the case of Peter, if he really had been at Rome, and was his friend and teacher."

With respect to the alleged testimony of Ignatius, the same writer says: "Are the Epistles of Ignatius genuine? Is that, particularly, to the Romans genuine? And if it be genuine, is not that *Petrus* smuggled in, like so many other things of which criticism must clear these Epistles before they have their former shape? They can hardly serve as testimony in so important a matter: least of all can that passage, which in every respect has nothing of evidence in itself, even if it be genuine" (1859, p. 85).

CLEMENT'S EPISTLE SUPPRESSED.

How this epistle of Clement was practically suppressed and lost in the Western Church, for so many centuries, is an interesting subject of inquiry—we have not time to dwell on it. KENNION in his work, "St. Peter and Rome," p. 25, thus writes on this point:

"As an instance of the attempt to get rid of documents which are found inconvenient, I may mention perhaps that very epistle of Clement you allude to. When we remember the high character and prominent position of Clement, and the great estimation in which this epistle was held, we cannot but wonder how it came to be so completely suppressed that for many centuries no copy was known to exist, and that when found it was not in the Western, but in the Eastern Church—the first MS. coming from Alexandria, the second from Constantinople, and the third from Syria. The wonder ceases when we find that the epistle is altogether inconsistent with the pretensions of the mediæval Romish Church. Clement of Rome writes as a Protestant bishop might do, but certainly not as Pio IX. would have done under the same circumstances."

"Clement was a Roman bishop," writes EDGAR in his "Variations of Popery," p. 44, "and interested in a peculiar manner in the dignity of the Roman See. An apostolic predecessor, besides, would have reflected honor on his successor in the hierarchy. He mentions his pretended predecessor indeed, but omits any allusion to his journey to Rome, or his occupation of the Pontifical throne."

There were good reasons for the panegyrists of the Roman See, who boasted that *two* Apostles founded their church, and that they possessed their bones and their sepulchers, to put out of their way the letters of a Roman bishop, a contemporary, who, writing of these Apostles, says nothing of the execution of one, whose martyrdom he must have witnessed, and whose funeral services he would naturally have conducted, if this Apostle had died at Rome. Especially, moreover, as it is claimed that Clement had been consecrated by Peter. The silence of this letter of Bishop Clement on these points was too convincing a negative argument, and efforts would be made to consign it to oblivion, by those who were so busy in manufacturing evidence from idle Romances, to establish a Roman residence for Peter. TURRETIN, Op., iii. 148, well argues: "Who could believe that Clement would omit to mention Peter's visit to the West, and his stay in Rome, and his martyrdom under the governors there, which he narrates of Paul, if these events had occurred?

"In what obscurity are involved the far more important contests of Peter at Rome, his punishment like that of Christ—nay, more severe—his body inverted, overlooking Rome; and moreover, the previous consecration of his church and appointment of his successor, even as they would have it, of Clement himself?

"Neither are these authors to be mentioned, on the other part, who relate the visit and the martyrdom of Peter at Rome, as Ignatius or Papias, who were either later than Clement, or were certainly of doubtful authority or judgment."

UHLORN in Schaff-Herzog. Encyc. presents the history of the Epistles: "Clement's two *Epistles to the Corinthians*, especially the first, belong among the most important documents still extant.

"In the ancient Church they were held in the greatest esteem, and in many places they were read in Divine Service. Nevertheless, after the fifth century, they disappeared from the Western Church, and remained completely unknown until Junius rediscovered them in the celebrated Cod. Alex., a present from Cyrillus Lucaris to King Charles I., and published them at Oxford (1633).

"Up to 1875 this manuscript remained the only one known. . . In 1875 BRYENNIOS, Metropolitan of Serræ, gave an edition from a newly discovered manuscript in the library of the Holy Sepulcher at Farnari, Constantinople."

WAS PETER MARTYRED?

Another point of great importance in this inquiry is the fact, that Clement does not affirm that the Apostle Peter *suffered martyrdom*. He is the only authority worthy of consideration as to the matter who has been appealed to, and this from a misconception, we think, of his language. Clement's words are thus rendered by an able writer in the *New Brunswick Review*, August, 1854, p. 293:

"It is certainly a remarkable fact that Clement, whom the 'Letters of the Pope' makes the immediate successor of Peter in the Roman Pontificate, should have written this long and important letter and never have spoken directly or indirectly of Peter having been 'in Rome.' The only allusion it contains to Peter is the following sentence: 'Peter having on account of zeal, suffered not one, but many hardships (*ponous*), and thus having given his testimony (*houtos marturesas*), went to the deserved place of glory.'

"The testimony of death is plainly not alluded to here, for the expression 'thus' implies that it was the testimony of '*many hardships.*'"

When we consider that the *primary* meaning of the verb here used, and as always employed in the New Testament, is merely "to witness"; that it had no other meaning for a century after Clement's time; that Clement uses the same word with respect to Abraham (Sec. xvii.), who certainly was not executed; it is clear that he gives no testimony to show that the Apostle Peter died by violence. This point is fully discussed in Bacon's "Lives of the Apostles," pp. 265–67. He writes:

"The only authority which can be esteemed worthy of consideration on this point is that of Clemens Romanus, who in the latter part of the first century (about the year 70, or as others say, 96), in his Epistle to the Corinthians uses these words respecting Peter: 'Peter on account of unrighteous hatred, underwent not one, or two, but many labors, and *having thus borne his testimony*, departed to the place of glory which was his due' (οὕτως μαρτυρησας ἐπορευθη εις τον ὀφειλομενον τοπον δοξης).

"Now it is by no means certain that the prominent word (*marturesas*) necessarily means 'bearing witness by death,' or *martyrdom* in the modern sense. The primary sense of this word is merely '*to witness*,' in which simple meaning alone it is used in the New Testament: nor can any passage in the sacred writings be shown, in which this verb means 'to bear witness to any cause, *by death*.' This was a *technical* sense (if I may so name it), which the word at last acquired among the Fathers, when they were speaking of those who bore witness to the truth by their blood; and it was a meaning which at last nearly excluded all the true original senses of the verb; limiting it mainly to the notion of a death by persecution for the sake of Christ. Thence our English words *martyr* and *martyrdom*.

"But that Clement by the use of the word, in this connection, meant to convey the idea of Peter's having been killed for the sake of Christ, is an opinion utterly incapable of proof, and rendered improbable by the words joined to it in the passage. The sentence is, 'Peter underwent many labors, and having THUS borne witness to the gospel truth, went to the place of glory which he deserved.' Now the adverb '*thus*' (οὕτως) seems to me most distinctly to show what was the nature of this testimony, and the manner also in which he bore it. It points out more plainly than any other words could, the fact that his testimony to the truth of the Gospel was borne in the zealous labors of a devoted life, and *not* by the agonies of a bloody death. There is not in the whole context, nor in all the writings of Clement, any hint whatever that Peter was killed for the sake of the Gospel: and we are therefore required by every sound rule of interpretation to stick to the primary sense of the verb in this passage." Bacon refers to Suicer's Thesaurus, and to several Fathers, to substantiate his position.

We have the more critically investigated the testimony of Clement, as he is the only contemporary of Peter whose writings have come down to us, and because he is claimed as a witness to the fact of Peter's presence in Rome.

We have seen that a careful examination of Clement's words presents a damaging argument against the pretensions of the Roman Church, and goes far to explain the fact why the noble epistle of this eminent Apostolic Christian laborer was apparently suppressed for centuries in the Western Church. The silence of Clement, like the silence of Paul, and the entire New Testament, including the Apostle Peter himself, immeasurably outweighs all subsequent traditions and fables with respect to the latter's residence in Rome.

"When we come to the very *coupling* which is to hold the long train of the Papacy to its motive power, we look for a bolt, and we find instead a *bulrush*."

CHAPTER IV.

Fathers of the Second Century.

We have seen in our previous examination of this question that neither Ignatius nor Clement, of the first century, alludes to any visit of Peter to Rome.

If the fact be true that Peter was in Rome, and all the schemes connected therewith by the Church of Rome be considered; is it not marvelous that Clement, a Bishop of Rome and writing from Rome, and Ignatius a Bishop of Antioch and writing to Rome, present no testimony whatever bearing on the point in question; both writers living in the first century.

If it can also be shown that in the five additional authentic documents of the century after Peter's death, which alone have reached us, there is a similar silence on this matter, regarded by so many as of vital import, will it not require absolute demonstration to establish the Roman claim?

"The authority of the Bishops of Rome is either a divine ordinance to which all Christian people are bound to submit, if they would not incur the guilt of rebellion, or it is a shameless usurpation, and an intolerable tyranny, which it is our duty to resist." The claim rests upon the supposed residence of the Apostle Peter in Rome—we are examining now that question—and after presenting all in Clement and Ignatius, claimed as evidence, and finding it without value; we shall inquire whether Polycarp, or Barnabas, or Hermas, or

Justin Martyr, or the newly found Didache, all of the century following Peter, present any testimony to establish the claim that this Apostle was ever at Rome.

POLYCARP.

Polycarp is supposed to have been born in the city of Smyrna, in Nero's reign, about the year 67. After the death of Buculus, the Bishop of Smyrna, by whom he had been ordained deacon, he was selected to succeed him. Irenæus states that Polycarp "had been instructed by the Apostles and had familiar intercourse with many who had seen Christ." He has left us one letter to the Church at Philippi, written about the year 108. Its authenticity has not been disputed. Le Moyne writes that "there is not, perhaps, any work extant that has more entire evidence of its being genuine than this." Eusebius says of it that "it was publicly read in the churches." We can only remark of this letter of Polycarp exhorting the Philippians to the performance of Christian duties, that there is no mention made of Rome, or of Peter. This omission cannot be reconciled with the existence of a just claim of the Roman Church as the See of the Apostle Peter.

Polycarp visited Rome to confer with Bishop Anicetus as to the time when the festival of Easter should be kept. The Roman Church observed the Feast on the Sunday after the Jewish Passover; the Asiatics kept it on the third day after the fourteenth day of the first month. The two bishops conferred as to the matter; neither could persuade the other to change his views. Each held to his own opinion, and after an amicable discussion and the celebration of the Lord's Supper, at which the Bishop of Rome requested Polycarp to preside, the bishops separated. Bower in his "Lives of the Popes" remarks: "St. Polycarp, though well acquainted with the doctrine of the Apostles, was a stranger, it seems, to that of Bellarmine, Baronius, etc.—viz., that the whole Catholic Church is bound to conform to the rites, ceremonies, and customs of the Church of Rome." Vol. i. p. 13, Am. Ed.

BARNABAS.

Whether the Epistle of BARNABAS was written by the companion of Paul, the associate of the Apostles, or some other Christian, does not affect the bearing of the testimony on the matter we are considering. If written by the former it has been largely interpolated, like the letters of Ignatius, for there are statements in it which could not have been made by an Apostolic writer. The best critics make the time of its composition in the reign of Hadrian—the first quarter of the second century. In the latter part of the Epistle there are directions with respect to the "Way of Light," which are a summary of what a Christian is to do that he may be happy forever; also the "Way of Darkness" is described, and what kind of persons shall be forever cast out of the kingdom of heaven.

No modern Roman Catholic writer could allude to such a topic without directing his readers to the Church of Rome as the "Way of Life," the Church founded by Peter at Rome. As neither Rome nor Peter is ever mentioned by this author, who wrote within fifty years after the Apostle's decease, the silence of the Epistle is an additional argument that the Petrine claims were not known at that period. The Apostles and their associates surely knew better what was essential to the faith than any successor.

HERMAS.

There is a work written about the same time as the letter of Barnabas, entitled " THE SHEPHERD OF HERMAS." It is of a much higher order than that last described, and was regarded by some of the early Christians as inspired, and publicly read in the Eastern Churches. It is an allegorical work, written somewhat in the style of the "Pilgrim's Progress." There is internal evidence that the book was written in Italy, probably in Rome. In the vision the writer is directed to write two books, and send one to Clement and one to Grapte. "But thou shalt read it in this city with the elders who preside over the Church." Archbishop Wake in his edition strangely omitted the word "preside." We read again, "I say unto you who are set over the Church and love the first seats;" elsewhere, "The earthly spirit revealeth itself and will have the first claim;" and again, "They are such as had some envy and strife among themselves for principality and dignity."

The writings of Hermas so far from bearing any witness to a primacy of Peter as Bishop of Rome, make no allusion to him, and testify to the fact that the Church was then ruled by elders, and warns these elders against the sin of aspiring to precedence, as the Lord Jesus Christ warned his Apostles. The testimony of Hermas is, therefore, still more strongly against the claim that Peter was at Rome, and its bishop.

Bishop LIGHTFOOT, a high authority, confirms this opinion, Ignatius and Polycarp, i. 399. "The next document emanating from the Roman Church is 'The Shepherd of Hermas.' Here again we are met with a singular phenomenon. If we had no other information, we should be at a loss to say what was the form of government when 'The Shepherd' was written. . . The episcopate, though doubtless it existed in some form or other in Rome, had not yet (it would seem) assumed the same strong and well defined monarchical character, with which we are confronted in the Eastern Churches."

JUSTIN MARTYR.

Our next witness is a converted heathen philosopher who was born soon after the death of Peter, and died about the year 160. His apology for Christianity is regarded as written about the year 140. JUSTIN names the Apostles a few times, and alludes to Peter, James, and John as having had their names changed, but there is not the slightest trace in anything that he had said of any distinction of power, or of any primacy among them. He never even names any Bishop of Rome. Justin speaks of Simon Magus, his magic, and his deification at Rome, but makes no mention of Peter's going to Rome to combat him, nor does any Father narrate this fable till after the year 300.

Justin describes the worship of the early Christians on the Lord's day, the Lord's Supper, and the presiding Presbyters, with the Deacons; but no mention is made even of a third order of the ministry, much less of a Bishop, or Pope, the Vice Regent of God and successor of Peter. The absence of such witness, in the works of this learned man, written at Rome, bears very strongly against the force of the Petrine claim.

THE DIDACHE, OR TEACHING OF THE APOSTLES.

We speak last of this recently discovered work, edited by Bryennios, Metropolitan of Nicomedia, though it possesses deeper interest and value than those previously mentioned. It is a discovery of inestimable value, as it is the first Church Manual we possess, written, according to the best critics, at the beginning of the second century, and perhaps earlier. "It contains a true and graphic picture of the faith, discipline, and practice of the Christians of the second century."

Here we would expect to find, if anywhere, a statement with respect to the Apostle Peter's claim to the primacy, and his position as Bishop and Pope of Rome, if Peter had been at Rome, and had presided there. But though the work discourses on the ministry, the Apostles and other ministers, on baptism and the Lord's Supper and the duties of Christians—there is no mention of Peter, nor of the Church of Rome. The subject is entirely ignored, as of no importance. The writer appears not even to have heard of such a claim as Peter's residence and precedence in Rome. Outside of the Scriptures, we do not possess another such interesting and authoritative document, on this matter, as the DIDACHE.

Taken in consideration with the utter silence on this point of Justin, Hermas, Barnabas, and Polycarp, the above writings are, with this precious document, the sole authentic testimonies preserved from the century following Peter's death. Its abstinence from all allusion to the subject under consideration, seems to settle conclusively the fact, that the Church of Christ was not aware that the Apostle Peter had been in Rome, had founded the Church there, had given it precedence over other Churches in consequence thereof; and whatever later writers might state could not give force or efficacy to any claim of the Church of Rome, which it is clearly evident the early Christians had no knowledge of for a century after the death of the Apostle. We feel authorized to assert with Lipsius, the great German critic, "The Roman-Peter legend proves itself to be, from beginning to end, a fiction, and thus our critical judgment is confirmed: THE FEET OF PETER NEVER TROD THE STREETS OF ROME." *

* See Examination of Lipsius—*Presb. Quarterly*, April, 1876.

CHAPTER V.

Testimony of Scripture.

If it were a matter of great importance to the Church of Christ to know that the Apostle Peter had resided in Rome, and was its Bishop while there, the Word of God would have contained the narrative, and thus have settled the fact beyond contradiction, for all time.

The Holy Scriptures contain the names of a number of Christian workers in Rome. Peter's name is not among them. In our previous examination we have presented the writings of all the authors who wrote during the century after Peter's death, whose works have reached us, and find that in them, as also in the Didache, a work of the same period, nothing is said of a visit of Peter to the Imperial City. Clement, Ignatius, Barnabas, Polycarp, Hermas, and Justin are silent on this topic.

THE TRADITIONAL TIME OF PETER'S RESIDENCE.

The Roman doctrine of the time of Peter's visit to Rome, and the length of his sojourn there, are based on the statement of Eusebius, A. D. 340, and that of Jerome, transcribed from that of Eusebius. Binius, Labbeus, Petavius, Bede, Baronius, and Valesius agree with the above Fathers, in sending Peter to Rome in the reign of the Emperor Claudius. This is now the universally accepted teaching in the Church of Rome. We need only to present the language of the latest extended Church history, that of the Abbé Darras, which bears the Imprimatur of Pope Pius IX., Archbishops McCloskey, Spalding, and Purcell. In vol. i., page 42, we read "The pontificate of St. Peter lasted thirty-three years, of which twenty-five were passed in Rome." Having the dictum of their infallible Pope, Romanists are bound henceforth to adhere to this declaration.

In view of claimed infallibility, the discrepancy among the Papal writers is remarkable. The Bullarium states Peter was in Rome twenty-four years, three months, and twelve days; Eusebius, in the Armenian version of his Chronicon, twenty years; in the Latin, twenty-five; Jerome, twenty-four; Baronius, twenty-five; Herbst, not beyond a year; Valesius Pagi, Baluze, Hug, Klee, during the later years of Nero's reign. The Dominican Fathers, in their Bibliothèque Sacrée, dismiss the subject very briefly, stating: "What is certain is that Peter did not go to Rome until the reign of Nero."

TURRETIN, Op., iii. p. 144, remarks: "Some think that Peter came to Rome in the second year of Claudius, as Eusebius and Jerome. Others in his fourth year, as Thomas, Beda, and Fasciculus Temporum; others in Anno 43, as the Passionale de Vitis Sanctorum; others that he remained there twenty-three years, and others twenty-five years. The common opinion which Baronius and Bellarmine adopted is, that Peter after the death of our Lord remained in Judea five years, whence, A. D. 39, he came to Antioch, accepted the Episcopate, whence he departed and came to Rome after seven years, when he established the Church, and presided.

"In the meantime it happened that in the year 51, by the edict of Claudius, Peter with the rest of the Jews was expelled from Rome, and took occasion to come to the Council at Jerusalem, held that year. Then on the death of Claudius, he returned to Rome, where he presided till his death by martyrdom."

MEYER, an accurate and judicious writer, Intro. Epis. Rom. p. 20, says: "We may add that our Epistle—since Peter cannot have labored in Rome before it was written—is a *fact destructive of the historical basis of the* Papacy, in so far as the latter is made to rest on the founding of the Roman Church and the exercise of the Episcopate by that Apostle.

"For Paul, the writing of such a didactic Epistle to a Church of which he knew Peter to be the founder and bishop, would have been, according to the principle of his Apostolic independence, impossible in consistency."

Meyer writes elsewhere of "the tradition of the Roman Church having been founded by Peter; a view disputed even by Catholic theologians like Hug, Feilmoser, Klee, Ellendorf, Maier, and Stengel." DUFF, Early Church, p. 64, writes: "The tradition, which cannot be traced back further than the end of the fourth century (Jerome's version of Eusebius), is not only unsupported by satisfactory evidence, as may be said of the legends given above, and even of the position that Peter was ever at Rome at all; but with the Scripture data we have in our hand, it is so incredible that some Roman Catholic writers have abandoned it; and have reduced it twenty-five to one. The truth is we know nothing with certainty of Peter, but what we learn from the New Testament itself."

But what do we learn from Scripture as to Peter's residence in Rome? EDGAR, Var. Popery, p. 44, wittily remarks: "A single hint is not afforded by Peter himself nor by his inspired companions, Luke, James, Jude, Paul, and John. Pope Peter, in his epistolary productions, mentions nothing of his Roman residency, episcopacy, or supremacy. Paul wrote a letter to the Romans, and from the Roman city addressed the Galatians, Ephesians, Philippians, Colossians, Timothy, and Philemon. He sent salutations to various Roman friends, such as Priscilla, Aquila, Epenetus, Mary, Andronicus, Junia, and Amplias; but forgets Simon, the supposed Roman hierarch. Writing from Rome to the Colossians, he mentions Tychicus, Onesimus, Aristarchus, Marcus, Justus, Epaphras, Luke, and Demas, who had afforded him consolation; but strange to tell, neglects the sovereign pontiff! Addressing Timothy from the Roman city, Paul of Tarsus remembers Eubulus, Pudens, Linus, and Claudia, but overlooks the Roman bishop! No man, except Luke, stood with Paul at his first answer, or at the nearer approach of dissolution. Luke also is silent on this theme. John, who published his Gospel after the other Evangelists, and his Revelation at the close of the first century, maintains, on this agitated subject, a provoking silence."

Turretin, Op. iii. p. 147, on the singular neglect of Peter to welcome Paul on his arrival in the Imperial City, if he were present there, says: "When Paul came to Rome, the brethren hastened to meet him at the Appii Forum; if Peter had been there, he surely would have accompanied them, but his name is not mentioned.

"Afterward, on the third day, Paul assembles the Chief Jews. These, who certainly were not Christians, desired to hear the sentiments of Paul. And if Peter was in Rome, and its bishop, would not these have heard concerning the Christians from him, especially if he were their Apostle?

"In vain does Bellarmine assert that Peter was at that

time absent. Who can believe that Peter would have been absent so long from his Church, where he could be in safety? If he was bishop of that Church, where ought he to have been, rather than at Rome? How otherwise could he escape the charge of idleness and neglect of duty?"

J. A. WYLIE, The Papacy, 234, writes: "We have eight instances of Paul communicating with Rome—two letters to, and six from that city—during Peter's alleged Episcopate, and yet not the slightest allusion to Peter occurs in any of these letters. This is wholly inexplicable on the supposition that Peter was in Rome."

CALVIN writes, Tracts, iii. 272: "Paul writes various Epistles from prison; he mentions the names of certain persons of no mean rank; there is no place for Peter among them. If he were there, such silence would be a marked insult.

"Then, when he complains that at his first defense no man stood by him, would he not affix the stigma of extreme perfidy on Peter, if he were then the pastor of the city?"

WHAT THE SCRIPTURE SAYS.

The Scripture informs us that Jerusalem was the residence of Peter. It is said (Acts viii. 1) that, "At that time" (the stoning of Stephen, A. D. 34), there was a great persecution of the Church which was at Jerusalem. And they were all scattered abroad throughout the regions of Judea and Samaria except the Apostles." Chapter viii. 14, we read of Peter and John being sent to Samaria. Here Peter met Simon Magus. In the 9th chapter, Peter's visitation at Lydda and Joppa is narrated. In the 10th chapter, at Cæsarea, he admits Cornelius to the Church by baptism. He returned to Jerusalem, and was present at the Council, A. D. 52. It is obvious that he could not have gone very far from Jerusalem on journeys, or that, if he had gone to the Imperial Capital, no mention could have been made of it.

Peter was, therefore, not at Rome when the Council sat in Jerusalem, A. D. 52. Gal. i. 8, we read that Paul went to Jerusalem to see Peter, three years after his conversion, A. D. 38, and found him there. Fourteen years after (Gal. ii. 1), he goes again to Jerusalem, and there meets Peter. If, according to Pope Pius IX., and the Roman Church, Peter was then at Rome, why did not Paul seek him there? According to their statement, he would have been there six to eight years. This, we have seen, the Scriptures plainly contradict.

On Peter's alleged journey to Rome after his escape from Herod (Acts. xii. 17) J. ADDISON ALEXANDER remarks: "That Peter went to Rome is a 'conjecture' in order to sustain the tradition that Peter was for many years the bishop of the Church there, a tradition inconsistent with the absolute silence of Paul respecting him, in writing to and from Rome."

BAUMGARTEN on the same points, Apos. Hist., i. 325, says: "The opinion of the Romanists, who look upon Rome as the unnamed locality to which Peter betook himself, is the very widest from the truth."

TESTIMONY OF ELLENDORF.

We now present the criticism of a learned Roman Catholic professor in Berlin, who has exhaustively treated of Peter's claimed visit to Rome, and finds it to be a fable. His treatise may be found in the Bibliotheca Sacra, July, 1858, January, 1859. He writes, p. 582:

"In A. D. 45, Peter had not yet come to Antioch, to say nothing of his coming to Rome; he had not even crossed the boundaries of Palestine. The opinion, then, that Peter went to Rome in the second year of Claudius, A. D. 42, is proved to be wholly false." That he was Bishop of Antioch, as the Pope and others claim, Ellendorf emphatically denies. After examining all authorities presented, he writes, p. 590: "We see what is the weight of these testimonies—just nothing at all: they are from the fifth, sixth, and seventh centuries. Peter's bishopric at Antioch is shown to be, in all respects, a fable."

In p. 576 he says: "If Paul's conversion occurred, as we have proved above, in A. D. 38 or 39, then the Council of Jerusalem is to be placed in A. D. 52 or 53. In this year, therefore, Peter had not gone to Rome. All that is maintained of the journey to Rome is not above a mere story or fiction, at the bottom of which there lies nothing solid. . . Peter had not come to Rome in the beginning of the reign of Nero, that is in A. D. 54 and 55; we will now prove that he had not come there up to A. D. 64."

Analyzing Paul's Epistles and the book of Acts minutely, Ellendorf arrives at the conclusion (p. 605): "We must have lost all common sense and regard for truth if we maintain, under these circumstances, that Peter and his disciples were with Paul at Rome in A. D. 61-63, when he wrote these Epistles.

"While Paul developed such a widespread and deeper penetrating activity at Rome; while there he concentrated the action of almost the whole body of the important intellects of the Church, or pointed out to them abroad the circle of operation; and while he formed, organized, founded, and governed the Church at Rome, and from it lending form and aid, he made his attacks on the East and West, *nothing is perceived of Peter, not a word is breathed of his abode at Rome, or of his activity there.* The stale conversion of the name of Babylon into Rome (1 Peter v. 13), is the only argument by which they venture to prove Peter's abode at Rome, his Episcopate, and his Popedom from the Holy Scriptures. It would not pay for the trouble to waste a word on it."

Page 620: "Finally, we have proved from the above-mentioned authorities that *not the slightest share can be shown for Peter in the founding of the Church at Rome,* and much more that this was exclusively owing to Paul and his disciples. The mode and manner of conducting this proof has been twofold, *positive and negative.* In the former we proved that Peter was elsewhere at the time in which he is placed at Rome; in the latter, that the silence of the authorities renders that residence of Peter at Rome wholly inadmissible."

We have preferred to present the argument at the hands of a candid, cultured Roman Catholic scholar, inasmuch as it comes with twofold force from one who was obliged to disregard the doctrine of his powerful Communion with its infallible head, while presenting historical truths.

ELLENDORF'S ADMISSION.

"We cannot find fault with a Protestant," writes Ellendorf, "when, relying on the proofs which the Holy Scriptures and the oldest Fathers, Clemens of Rome and Justin, present, he holds the abode of Peter at Rome, and all connected with it, for a tale drawn from the

Apocrypha. This much is certain, that no one of the arguments which can be opposed to him has so much weight that he is morally bound to acknowledge the story as truth. *Peter's abode at Rome can never be proved;* neither, therefore, can the *Primacy of the Romish Church*, based on it, be so."

Bouzique, a French barrister and statesman, in his History of Christianity, i. 362, briefly sums up a similar examination thus: "The sojourn of Peter in Rome, and his journey through Asia Minor, Greece, and Italy can be reconciled neither with the Acts of the Apostles, nor with the Epistles of Peter and Paul; nor can they be reconciled with the absolute silence of the first century and of the Apostolic times. The journeys and the preaching of Peter in those divers lands would have been facts too considerable in the history of the Church for Paul or Luke, or any other writer of that time, not to have spoken of them directly or indirectly. That silence, and the different facts supplied by the Acts, the Epistles, and the other parts of the New Testament, offer then an insurmountable obstacle for every unprejudiced mind."

Marsilius of Padua, jurist and counselor to the Emperor Lewis of Bavaria, and under him, Papal Vicar at Rome, and at one time rector of the University of Paris; in his Defensor Pacis, written 1322, states that he finds no proof in Scripture that St. Peter was Bishop of Rome, or ever was in Rome.

"If this were so, how surprising it is," he remarks, "that St. Paul, in rebuking the Jews in Rome for their want of faith, makes no allusion to the preaching there of St. Peter; and though he resided in Rome two years does he appear to have met him; nor does the historian of the Church state that Peter was in the city." The original language may be seen in Neander (Church History, vol. ix. p. 45, Bohn's edition).

FARRAR in his "Early Days of Christianity," p. 77, refers to DÖLLINGER, WATERWORTH, and ALLNATT, additional Roman Catholic authorities, as holding that "if Peter was ever at Rome at all, it could only have been very briefly before his martyrdom." Waterworth, Engl. and Rome, ii; Allnatt, Cathedra Petri, p. 114.

The argument of these Roman Catholic investigators, combined with that of this acute French lawyer and the erudite scholars which have been presented, we may safely say, leaves no ground for an opponent to stand upon.

We have the more thoroughly treated this point because, if the visit of Peter to Rome cannot rest upon any testimony of Scripture, but simply on tradition and inference, it is taken out of the domain of faith and conscience; and clearly has no connection with the salvation of the human soul, as is asserted by the Roman Catholic Church. Our Heavenly Father will not require us to believe any doctrine which we cannot find plainly set forth in His revealed Word, the infallible standard and constitution of His Church; of whose existence and authority we have satisfactory proof in that Word alone.

As we have seen, Scripture, thus far, is against the Petrine claim. It remains to consider WHERE WAS BABYLON, WHERE PETER WROTE HIS FIRST EPISTLE?

CHAPTER VI.

Was the Babylon of Peter, Rome?

In the course of our examination of this question, we have seen that in the New Testament, and in the writings of early Christian authors who lived in the first century after Peter's death, whose works have reached us, there is nothing to be found to show that this Apostle was ever in or near Rome.

When the scheme and claims which rest upon the residence and Episcopate of Peter in Rome, are considered, what has already been established would reasonably appear to be enough to decide the question against the Papacy.

In connection with the Scripture argument it remains, however, that we notice the controversy with respect to Babylon, where the Apostle wrote his First Epistle.

In chapter v. verse 13, 1st Epistle, the Apostle writes: "The Church which is at Babylon, elected together with you, saluteth you; and so doth Marcus my son."

Babylon, argue many writers, is Rome; for so the Apostle John designates the Imperial City in his Revelation; hence Peter wrote his Epistle there.

We have seen that Professor Ellendorf, a Roman Catholic, alludes to this view, but deems it not worthy of notice, remarking "The stale conversion of the name of Babylon into Rome (1 Peter v. 13) is the only argument by which they venture to prove Peter's abode at

Rome, his Episcopate and his Popedom, from the Holy Scriptures."

"It would not pay for the trouble to waste a word on it." (p. 608.) Simon, in his work on the Mission and Martyrdom of St. Peter, for the preparation of which work he spent nine months in the British Museum Library in London, remarks on this point : " Father Calmet mentions several members of his Church as having abandoned this interpretation of the carnal-minded Jews. 'Some [Roman] Catholic writers,' says he; 'for instance, Peter de Marca, John Baptist Mantuan, Michael de Ceza, Marsile de Padua, John Aventin, John Leland, Charles du Moulin, and perhaps some others, have expressed their misgivings as to the truth of this interpretation.'" (Calmet's Com., Prelim. Diss., on 1 Peter.) But it is not misgivings that they express, it is unqualified denial, as anyone may see by reference to their works. For instance : "St. Peter went to Antioch," says Peter de Marca, Archbishop of Paris, a writer of extreme celebrity and favor in the Roman Church, "and from there to Babylon, where the hereditary Patriarch of the first dispersion of the Jews resided. When established in that city he wrote his First Epistle, as is clear from the words, 'the Church at Babylon salutes you.' For although the ancients supposed Peter to have here meant Rome, Scaliger can be shown to be right when he says that this letter was written from Babylon itself to those dispersed Jews whose provincial synagogues depended upon the Patriarch of Babylon." (De Marca de Concordia Sacerdotii et Imperii, lib. vi. c. 1.) "It is not misgivings, then, that these writers have expressed."—Simon, p. 189, 190.

Father Dupin writes, i. 343, Lond. ed., 1713 : "The

First Epistle of Peter is dated at Babylon. Many of the ancients have understood that name to signify Rome; but no reason appears that could prevail with St. Peter to change the name of Rome into that of Babylon. How could those to whom he wrote understand that Babylon was Rome?

"We cannot precisely assign the time it was written. but we may consider that it was written at Babylon, A. D. 65."—Prelim. Diss., sec. 4.

The learned Hug, Professor at Freiburg, in his Introduction, and Erasmus, both Roman Catholics, take the same view. "Why," says Erasmus, "is the Apostle here supposed to put Babylon enigmatically for Rome? Because idols were worshiped in Rome? That was done everywhere. That he might not reveal his own whereabout? Whence this so great timidity in him?"

De Cormenin, another Romanist, writes: "The First Epistle of St. Peter is dated from Babylon, which has led some visionary to declare that he gave this name to the capital of the empire."—Hist. of Popes, p. 17.

We might properly regard this question as settled by these Roman Catholic authors, De Marca, Erasmus, Hug, De Cormenin, Ellendorf, and others, in favor of the obvious and natural interpretation; but inasmuch as learned Protestants have held to the mystical interpretation that Babylon means Rome, and also to another view; the opinions of the most learned scholars, generally, on this interesting topic will be presented.

BABYLON IS ROME.

The learned Dr. McKnight, in his Diss. sec. v. Pref. to St. Peter, writes: "Whitby, Grotius, and all the learned of the Romish communion are of opinion that by Babylon Peter figuratively meant *Rome*, called Babylon by John likewise. (Rev. xvii., xviii.) And their opinion is confirmed by the general testimony of antiquity, which, as Lardner states, is of no small weight."

These are strong Protestant names, and to their side may be added those of Bede, Hales, Cave, Hammond, Tomline, Milner, Wells, Buckley, Horne, Cook, Farrar, Ellicott, Seabury, Samson, Schaff, Fry, Doyly and Mant, Coglan, A. I. Mason, Bishops Hinds and W. Alexander, Poole, T. Jones, Townsend, Lundy, Quarry, Cumming, Salmon, Maclaren, Rees' Encyclopedia. Of Continental scholars, Luther, Hoffman, Hengstenberg, Cludius, Schott, Thiersch, Wiesenger, Windishman, Mynster, Renan, Hitzig, Godet, Valckn, Ewald, Est, Hilgenfield, Weisacker, Mangold, Deitlein, Sieffert, Olshausen.

BABYLON WAS IN EGYPT.

Another opinion has been held by some learned men that Babylon was an Egyptian city where Peter resided. Such was the opinion of Fulke, Pearon, Mill, Greswell, Leclerc, Calov, Pott, Burton, Bertram, Wolf, Wall, Vitringa, Fabric, and Trevor.

"This Babylon was a town of considerable importance near Heliopolis, mentioned by Strabo and Ptolemy. Josephus reports that the Jews afterward built a temple there. We may thence conclude that they were already there in considerable numbers. And as Mark, who was generally in attendance on Peter, is supposed to have planted the Church of Alexandria, it is not improbable that Peter visited Egypt and may, therefore, have dated his First Epistle from Babylon near Heliopolis." This view gives increased interest to the Church of Alexandria.

Canon Trevor, in his work on Rome, p. 62, regards this view favorably. He writes : " Peter was at this time probably at Babylon, the place from which his Epistle is dated ; and though Eusebius, with most of the Fathers in reference to the tradition, interpreted this word as a mystic name for Rome, this interpretation is now universally exploded. The visions of the Apocalypse which, however, had not then been revealed, do indeed call Rome by this name. With the date of a letter must, in all reason, be the actual name of the place. This was either the well-known city on the Euphrates or, more probably, Babylon on the Nile. These were the two largest seats of Jewish population out of Palestine, and, therefore, as appropriate to Peter's mission as Rome, the capital of the world, was to St. Paul." He refers to his work on Egypt, p. 115.

"The only existing Babylon as a city was that of Egypt. It is not probable, though some of the ancients so understood it, that Peter wrote from Rome, disguising the place under the name of Babylon. Egypt, according to the testimony of Church History, was the Province of St. Mark's missionary labors."—Chester and Jones, N. Test. Illust., 1, 108.

Murray, in his Handbook of Egypt, relates an interview with the Patriarch of Alexandria, in which the latter says, " there is no tradition in the Coptic Church that Peter ever visited Egypt."

"The view that by Babylon is meant Egypt, has nothing to commend it, the less so that this Babylon was simply a military garrison."—Meyer on 1 Peter.

"A most unnatural interpretation."—Neander, Hist. Plant. Ch. i. 373.

In Hertzog's Encyc. we read : "There was another

Babylon in Egypt, founded by Babylonians, who settled along the Nile after the Persian invasions, but it is nowhere alluded to in the Bible. 1 Peter v. 13 refers to ancient Babylon, a portion of whose ruins was occupied by Jews."—*Art. Babel.*

Dr. T. L. Cuyler, in his "Travels From the Nile to Norway," writes, p. 751: " From the Museum we drove to that wonderful region of antiquity, 'Old Cairo,' which lies three miles from the present city. It was built as an Arab city right after Mahomet's death ; but even then an old Roman town stood there, part of which was called 'Babylon.' It seems quite probable that the Apostle Peter wrote his Epistle in that ancient Roman town, or in a part settled by a colony from the Persian Babylon. We rode through the spot where this Babylon stood, and gazed with awe upon the solid Roman bastions which have withstood both the sieges of the Caliph Omar and of time itself. Inside of these walls, oh, what delicious oddities of antiquity ! "

That by Babylon, Jerusalem was intended by the Apostle, was the opinion of Capellus, Spanheim, Hardouin, and Semler.

CHAPTER VII.

Origin of the Story: Babylon meant Rome.

It is interesting to inquire how the opinion arose that by Babylon the Apostle Peter meant Rome.

PAPIAS, Bishop of Hierapolis, who died A. D. 155, is charged with the origin of the story.

Professor WHITTAKER of Oxford, whom Bellarmine styles "the most learned heretic he had ever read," Disp. p. 664, makes this charge and remarks: "Papias was the father and master of tradition. Eusebius says he wrote many things from unwritten traditions, but they are full of commentititious fables. He wrote, as Eusebius tells us, five books concerning the Lord's discourses, but these, through the goodness of God, are lost."

Bishop BULL, Vindi. Ch. England, p. 42, writes: "Some very learned men have observed that the above tradition of St. Peter's voyage to Rome was first derived from Papias, an author indeed very ancient, but also very credulous and of mean judgment."

CHARLES ELLIOT, on Romanism, ii. 222, writes: "Because Papias had among his traditions *strange and novel* parables and doctrines concerning *our Saviour, and other things more fabulous,* and that he fell into these errors chiefly by his ignorance and misunderstanding of Scripture, yet he is the principal witness that the Church of Rome has to prove that Peter was at Rome. They have no other place in Scripture to favor their interpretation, and only Papias for that. For all the other ecclesiastical historians do nothing more than copy the error of Papias. Such is the *only* and the best ground that Rome has to show that Peter ever was at Rome."

KIRWAN (Dr. N. MURRAY) to Bishop Hughes, p. 57, states: "At about the close of the second century, Irenæus records it as a tradition received from one Papias, and is followed by your other authorities. But who Papias was, whilst there are various conjectures, nobody knows. And Eusebius speaks of the matter as a doubtful tradition. Here, sir, is the amount of your testimony, and it resolves itself into the truth or falsehood of a prattling Papias, who told Irenæus that somebody told him that Peter was Pope at Rome."

S. T. BLOOMFIELD writes, Notes on 1 Peter: "Others suppose that by Babylon is here figuratively denoted Rome. Yet for this no stronger testimony exists than a bare *tradition* derived from *Papias*; and as it rests on no sufficient authority, so neither is it borne out by *probability*, for no probable reason has ever been alleged why the Apostle should here call Rome by the name Babylon, and withhold its true name."

F. TURRETIN, who has written so ably and fully with respect to the Roman residence of Peter, presents the same view with respect to Papias, as the author of the tradition. He says, Op. iii. p. 148: "The unanimity of the ancients, who firmly held that Peter lived and died at Rome, has absolutely no weight, for this story has its origin in Papias, Bishop of Hierapolita, in Phrygia, who, according to the testimony of Eusebius, was not merely of mediocre talents, ignorant and credulous, but deceptive and inclined to fables; who has handed down many incredible and unrecorded stories, more like fables than reliable histories (Eus. Lib. iii. ch. 3). He was also the author of the story of the Chiliasts. He was the first to write that Peter had been at Rome. After him followed Hegesippus, Irenæus, Clemens Alex., and others after, and so their statement is valueless, according to the testimony of this same Eusebius, who stated that the majority of the ecclesiastical writers, especially Irenæus, gave occasion for this same error. Since, therefore, the credibility of this same writer is so doubtful in other matters, how can he have our assent when there are so many arguments from the Scriptures, which have been taken up in order, to the contrary? After Eusebius, Jerome is authority that Papias was not a hearer of John the Apostle, but John the Presbyter, bearing the same name, but another than the Apostle; and Baronius proves that in many ways, and plainly shows Papias' veracity to be doubtful, quoting the words of Eusebius, 'from which you can easily understand,' he says, 'that discrimination should be shown regarding traditions, so that whoever says that he has accepted any of the traditions of the elders, considers them all credible."

Professor McGiffert, who has given a new and accurate translation of Eusebius, and has enriched his work with notes as valuable as they are extensive, thus expresses his view of Papias, vol. i. p. 171: "Eusebius' judgment of Papias may have been unfavorably influenced by his hostility to the strong Chiliasm of the latter; yet a perusal of the extant fragments of Papias' writings will lead anyone to think that Eusebius was not far wrong in his estimate of the man."

CAN THE CHARGE AGAINST PAPIAS BE PROVED?

Notwithstanding that Papias is so generally regarded as the author of this statement, it is not clear that the charge is proven. Eusebius, referring to a statement that Mark's Gospel was written at the request of Peter's hearers, writes (ii. 15): "This story is given by Clement of Alexandria, and corroborated by Papias. There is, however, a report that it is this Mark that Peter mentions in his First Epistle, which it is also pretended was written at Rome, and that Peter intimates this himself by using the term 'Babylon' in a metaphorical sense for Rome." The translation is by Simon.

Cardinal BELLARMINE, attributing this metaphorical use of Babylon to Papias, to whom it does not belong, places it at the head of his proofs for Peter's residence in Rome. This is his sole Scriptural authority for Peter's Roman residence.

Does PAPIAS here state that Peter used *Babylon* in a metaphorical sense? Many able authors deny the charge.

VALESIUS, the Roman Catholic editor of Eusebius, writes: "These words are to be kept perfectly distinct from the preceding, as I find has been carefully done by Jerome and Nicephorus." (Lib. ii. c. 15.) Father DUPIN on this point remarks: "Some have thought that Papias and St. Clement of Alexandria, cited in this chapter by Eusebius, were of this opinion, but it is not on this point that Eusebius cited them."

BOUZIQUE, the French jurist, writes: "According to Papias, John the Presbyter ascribed that Gospel to Mark, a disciple of Peter, but without saying it was put together in Rome (Eus. iii. 39). Eusebius, reading this passage agreeably to the opinion of this time, inferred from it, as Clement of Alexandria, that the interpreter of Peter was then in Rome in company with the Apostle; while Papias says, solely with John the Presbyter, that Mark wrote the Gospel such as it was taught by Peter. Neither the Presbyter nor Papias, his disciple, speaks of sojourn or preaching in the Imperial City." (History of Christianity, pp. 364, 371.)

Dr. JARVIS remarks (Church Review, i. 166): "It is not certain, as Valesius and other critics of the Roman communion admit, that these were the words of Papias; and if so, we have only the testimony of the fourth century."

Thus according to Jerome and Nicephorus; Valesius and Dupin; Bouzique and Jarvis; all scholars of note; two of them Roman Catholics; the advocates of the opinion that Peter wrote Babylon for Rome, are deprived of Patristic authority, founded on a mistaken assertion with respect to Papias.

Not until the fourth century do we find that the Babylon of Peter was interpreted as representing Rome.

If the view is correct, as taught by Auberlin and others, that the Apocalypse is a sequel to Daniel, the name Babylon was naturally used in the Revelation symbolically; but inasmuch as the book was probably written at the close of the century, there is no good reason to believe that Peter ever saw it, or knew of such use; the contrary is most reasonable. Nor would the dispersion have understood such an allusion, for we read in Lange: "According to Schottgen the Jews did not begin to call Rome Babylon till after the destruction of Jerusalem;" and this event occurred, according to Wiesler, more than six years after Peter's death. It is also to be noticed that John employs the term "Babylon the Great."

Kitto writes (Int. to 1 Peter): "The strongest argument against the Babylon of the Apostle being taken for Rome seems to be that urged by Professor Stuart in his note on Hug's Introduction—'That mystical Babylon,' *i. e.*, Rome, is meant, is still less probable. Mystical names of this kind in a prosaic epistle, consisting of plain and hortatory matter, are not to be expected, and cannot be admitted without strong reasons."

Arguing in the same line, Michaelis remarks: "The plain language of epistolary writing does not admit of figures of poetry; and though it would be very allowable in a poem written in honor of Göttingen, to style it another Athens, yet if a Professor of this University should in a letter from Göttingen date it Athens, it would be a greater piece of pedantry than was ever yet charged upon the learned."

"Our own city is sometimes called Athens, from its situation and from its being a seat of learning, but it would not do to argue that a letter came from Edinburgh, because it is dated from Athens."—Brown, 1 Peter i. 548.

We therefore prefer to believe that the Apostle of the Circumcision traveled six hundred miles to Babylon, where Josephus says (Antiqui. xxxi. 5) the Jews in Peter's time were "infinite myriads, whose number it is not possible to calculate;" and with Philo, another contemporary, that they constituted "almost one-half the inhabitants." We see no good reason why he should travel two thousand miles to Rome (a two months' journey at that time) to preach to eight thousand of his countrymen, who were all sometimes banished by a single order."

The great Dr. Barrow wisely says, Wks. i. 509: "Peter was too skillful a fisherman to cast his net there, where there were no fish."

CHAPTER VIII.

Canon Farrar on the Question of Babylon.

AMONG modern writers Canon FARRAR has strongly advocated the opinion that the Apostle Peter wrote his Epistles in the City of Rome. We present and examine his argument.

In the "Early Ages of Christianity," p. 595, he writes: "*Against* the literal acceptance of the word 'Babylon' there are four powerful arguments. (1) There is not the faintest tradition in those regions of any visit from St. Peter. (2) If St. Peter was in Babylon at the time this Epistle was written, there is great difficulty in accounting for his familiarity with the Epistle to the Ephesians, which was not written till A. D. 63. (3) It becomes difficult to imagine circumstances which could have brought him from the far East into the very crisis of the Neronian persecution in the Babylon of the West. (4) If Marcus be the Evangelist, he was with St. Peter between A. D. 61–63, and probably rejoined him just before his martyrdom in A. D. 68. We should not, therefore, expect to find him so far away as Babylon in A. D. 67."

In reply to Dr. Farrar, we remark, (1) That it is clear that we have only manufactured and confused traditions concerning Peter, and these framed for an obvious purpose. We have nothing reliable concerning his later years, except the disputed passage concerning

Babylon, and a faint tradition in Origen, that he labored in Asia Minor.

(2) Many authors regard Peter's Epistle as written after the death of Paul, and there was no reason why the Epistle to the Ephesians should not have been carried to Babylon, an eight days' journey, by the hands of Silvanus, whom he states was with him when the letter was written.

(3) It is difficult to imagine circumstances to have drawn Peter from Babylon, his proper field of labor, to Rome, where he was not needed, *at any time*, and particularly in his old age; to lead him to rush into danger, contrary to his Lord's command; leaving his vastly important work, where he was protected by the Parthian authorities. This whole question is largely a balance of probabilities, and this greatly preponderates in favor of the literal interpretation. This, we trust, will be made clear in the course of investigation.

(4) Mark's connection with Peter is a matter of great interest, and will warrant a thorough examination.

PETER'S CONNECTION WITH MARK.

SAWYER, in "Organic Christianity," p. 47, says: "Mark's supposed residence at Rome depends upon the supposition that Peter resided there, and has no other foundation. Mark was Peter's companion at Babylon. 1 Peter v. 13.

"The most probable supposition in respect to the composition of St. Mark's Gospel is, that it was written at Babylon after the death of the Apostle Paul, and designed for general circulation in the Roman Empire."

FAUSSETT in his Bib. Cyclop., Art. Mark, gives a satisfactory statement of this question. "After Paul's death Mark joined Peter, with whom he had been associated in the writing of the Gospel. Mark was with Paul, intending to go to Asia Minor, A. D. 61–63 (Col. iv. 10). In 2 Tim. iv. 11, A. D. 67, Mark was near Ephesus, whence he was about to be taken by Timothy to Rome.

"It is not likely Peter would have trenched on Paul's field of labor, the Churches of Asia Minor, *during Paul's lifetime.* At his death Mark joined his old father in the faith at Babylon. Silvanus or Silas had been substituted for Mark, as Paul's companion, because of Mark's temporary unfaithfulness; but Mark, now restored, is associated with Silvanus (1 Peter v. 12), Paul's companion, in Peter's esteem, as Mark was already reinstated in Paul's esteem.

"Naturally Mark salutes the Asiatic Churches with whom he had already been, under Paul, spiritually connected. The tradition (Clemens Alex. in Euseb. H. E. vi. 14; Clem. Alex. Hyp. 6) that Mark was Peter's companion *at Rome,* arose from misunderstanding 'Babylon' (1 Peter v. 13) to be *Rome.* A friendly salutation is not the place where an enigmatical prophetical title could be used (Rev. xvii. 5).

"Babylon was the center from which the Asiatic *dispersion* whom Peter (1 Peter i. 2) addresses was derived. Alexandria was the final scene of Mark's labors, bishopric, and martyrdom."—Nicephorus, H. E. ii. 43.

"It is very probable that about the year A. D. 63 or 64 Mark visited Colossæ and the adjacent regions, and then went to Babylon to see Peter, and made known to him the affairs of the Churches in Asia Minor, upon the receipt of which information the Apostle addressed his Epistle to these Churches."—HARMAN's Intro. H. Script. ed. Crooks and Hurst, p. 697.

Bishop ELLICOTT's view is, Intro. Com. Mark, p. 189: "Mark accompanied Barnabas (A. D. 52) in his work among the Jews and Gentiles of Cyprus (Acts xv. 39). About eight years after he was with St. Peter on the banks of the Euphrates, which still bore the name of old Babylon, and there must have met Silvanus or Silas, who had taken his place as the companion and minister of St. Paul (1 Peter v. 12, 13)."

BLEEK, Intro. Mark, vol. ii., writes: "When 1st Peter was written Mark must have been with Peter in Babylon, or its neighborhood. This Epistle, as we shall see, was not certainly written at an early date, though we cannot exactly say when; perhaps between the writing of that to the Colossians and of 2d Timothy; so that, in the interval, Mark must have visited Peter at Babylon."

MARK SECRETARY TO PETER.

The general tradition has been that Mark was the interpreter and amanuensis of the Apostle. On this MEYER, Intro. Com. Mark, remarks: "At 1 Peter v. 13, we find Mark again with his spiritual father Peter at Babylon. His special relation to Peter is specified by the unanimous testimony of the ancient Church, as having been that of interpreter . . . denoting the service of a secretary, who had to write down the oral communications of his Apostle, whether from dictation or in a more free exercise of his own activity, and thus became his interpreter *in writing* to others. This view is plainly confirmed by Jerome, ad. Hedib. ii."

Archbishop Thomson, Speak. Com. Intro. Mark, writes: "Somewhat later Mark is with Peter in Babylon (1 Peter v. 13). Some have considered Babylon to be a name given here to Rome in a mystical sense; surely without reason, since the date of a letter is not the place to look for a figure of speech. Of the journey to Babylon we have no more evidence; of its date, causes, results, we know nothing. It may be conjectured that Mark journeyed to Asia Minor (c. iv. 10), and thence went to join Peter in Babylon. . . Ancient writers with one consent make the Evangelist the interpreter of the Apostle Peter."

With regard to the argument drawn from a few Latinized expressions, that Mark wrote at Rome, the *North Brit. Rev.*, November, 1848, p. 30, replies: "We have every reason to believe, as will appear from the sequel, that St. Mark wrote his Gospel at Babylon after the martyrdom of St. Paul, and consequently designed it for the use of the Latin as well as the Asiatic Churches, whose care had then altogether devolved on St. Peter. This appears to us to explain in a most satisfactory manner the occurrence in it of a few Latin words and Latinized expressions, upon which the supposition of its having been written at Rome after all depends."

Steiger, on 1 Peter, ii. 316, writes: "This tradition, so generally received and well authenticated, of Mark's relation to Peter, constrains us, since there is nothing to invalidate it, to regard him as the companion of Peter named here, although we need not on that account suppose with Papias (Eus. 1, ii. 15) and Clemens, what appears to be only their own opinion, that this Epistle was written in Rome, as is also affirmed in the false superscriptions of small copies. We conclude, then, that Mark is *one* and the same person with the John Mark mentioned in the Acts of the Apostles. See Hug's Intro. ii. § 13."

Brown, on 1 Peter, quotes Da Costa, a brilliant converted Hebrew layman of Holland, as presenting a probable and interesting suggestion that Mark was the devout soldier sent by Cornelius to Peter; consequently he was among the first-fruits of the Apostle's work among the Gentiles, and naturally was endeared to him as Timothy was to Paul. He notes the military expressions in Mark's Gospel as a ground for this not improbable opinion.

The Roman name of Mark and the Latin words used by him are, by this view, satisfactorily explained.

It adds greatly to the force of the argument that three pre-eminent Roman Catholic authors, Valesius, Dupin, and De Marca, maintain that "St. Mark's Gospel was written from the Mesopotamian capital, and not from Rome." See Greenwood's Cathedra Petri, i. 245.

Valesius was the editor of Eusebius; Dupin, the eminent Church historian; De Marca, Archbishop of Paris.

The natural view of the Apostle's language is clearly that Mark was with him in Mesopotamia, acting as his secretary, and together with Silvanus assisting in the vast work among the myriads of the Circumcision in that region. The tradition which places him at Rome with Peter is altogether improbable, and has no facts to give it credibility.

CHAPTER IX.

The View of the Orientalist Lightfoot.

There is probably no author who has written on our subject whose authority is of more value than that of John Lightfoot.

"Lightfoot, one of the greatest Hebrew scholars in history, to-day enjoys a universal fame."—Schaff-Herzog Encyc.

"In Biblical criticism I consider Lightfoot the first of all English writers."—Dr. Adam Clarke.

"By his deep researches into the Rabbinical writings he has done more to illustrate the phraseology of the Holy Scriptures . . . than any other writer before or since."—T. H. Horne, Bibl. Intro.

Lightfoot, who flourished in the seventeenth century, preached a sermon on 1 Peter v. 13, before the University of Cambridge, from which we quote, p. 3:

"The falsities and fictions in ecclesiastical story, which are not few nor small, have proceeded, especially, from four originals, one, or more, or all: *First*, from ignorance or misconstruction; *Second*, from over officiousness in the relator; *Third*, from favor to a party; *Fourth*, from a mind or purpose to deceive."

These causes Lightfoot elaborates, and says he ascribes more influence to the two things, "viz., Officiousness to Peter and a study to advance Rome . . . when writers in their relations were minded to honor singular places, persons, and actions, it is hard to find them keeping within bounds." P. 6 : " Every place almost had Paul for their founder, it was fit sure the Church of Rome should outvie others, as being the nobler place ; therefore historical officiousness brings Peter thither also. For that Church strove for dignity of place before it did for dignity of episcopacy. And upon this account it was like it was invented that the minister of Circumcision, Peter, as well as the minister of Uncircumcision, Paul, was brought thither." P. 7 : " Babylon is here to be properly taken for Babylon in Chaldea. *First.* Peter was the minister of Circumcision ; what had he to do with Rome, the chief city of the Gentiles? Paul was there justly, but if Peter had been there he would have been in Paul's line. Herein he held agreement with Paul, Gal. ii. 9. He, with James and John, gave the right hand of fellowship to Paul and Barnabas, that these should go to the Heathen and they to the Circumcision."

Lightfoot continues : " Take Peter, chief minister of the Circumcision, and he is in the midst of the Uncircumcision. Need I show how there were multitudes of Jews in Babylon, who returned not with Ezra ; need I tell you that there were in that country three Jewish universities ; or need I speak how there were scattered ten tribes in Assyria? Then how proper it was for Peter to have been there ?

" *Second.* The word 'Bosor' in St. Peter ii. 15, speaks Peter in Babylon. What would they think of it to whom he wrote, if he wrote from Rome ? But if he wrote from Chaldea it was the idiom of that country ! Bosor was the name of the place where Balaam was, 'Balaam of Bosor.' But in Numbers xxii. 5, it is called 'Pethor,' Pethor being turned into Bosor by a change of two letters, ordinarily done by the Jews of those times; their language being now degenerated into Syriac. . . And Peter speaking in the dialect of Babylon, it is a fair conjecture that he was at Babylon when he spoke.

"I shall add more. Every argument that is used to prove that Peter was not at Rome, is sound argument for this that we are upon, viz., that he was at Babylon. And the consideration that Peter ended his days at Babylon is very useful, if my judgment fail not, at the setting out of ecclesiastical story."

Lightfoot commenting on 1 Cor. xiv., says : "Beginning from the East there was the vast settlement in Babylonia of those Jews who had remained after the return from the captivity. Of the twenty-four courses of priests only four had followed Ezra into Palestine.

"No less than three universities of Jews existed in Mesopotamia alone. It was a well known saying, 'Whoever dwells in Babylon is as though he dwelt in the land of Israel.'"

Doddridge tells us that it was Lightfoot's argument which convinced Bishop Cumberland that Babylon was not Rome.

Ecclesiastical history becomes more luminous and intelligible, with respect to Apostolic experiences, if we keep Peter in his proper place, and do not allow vague traditions, and selfish motives in authors, to transfer him two thousand miles, where he was not needed, and where no rational motive could have taken him.

THE ORDER OF PROVINCES.

A strong *geographical* argument in favor of the Chaldean Babylon is found in the order of the provinces to which the Epistle is addressed. They read from East to West, not from West to East. This interpretation is natural.

Dean Howson, in his valuable "Horæ Petrinæ," p. 132, puts the case strongly : " In approaching the question on which so much has been written, whether it was really the Eastern Babylon or the great city of the West, described under an allegorical name, from which St. Peter sent this letter, we have a strong *prima facie* argument in the geographical order in which at the outset he ranges the Churches addressed by him.

"He begins with the North and sweeps around to the West. This would be quite unnatural in the case of one who was writing from a city of the West, but it would be an easy and obvious order to follow when writing from a city of the East, to residents in Provinces distributed according to that succession. This may seem at first sight a somewhat trivial argument, but it is really a strong one, because it has more obvious naturalness in the style of writing."

Dean Alford in Proleg. 1 Peter, 130, contending for the literal interpretation of the word, adds : " It is some corroboration of the view that our Epistle was written from the Assyrian Babylon, to find that the countries mentioned in his address are enumerated, not as a person in Rome or in Egypt would enumerate them, but in an order proceeding, as has already been noticed, from East to West and South, and also to find that Cosmas-Indico-Pleustes, in the sixth century, quotes the conclusion of our Epistle 'as a proof of the early progress of the Christian religion without the bounds of the Roman empire,' by which, therefore, we perceive that by Babylon he did not understand Rome."

THE ORDER OF PROVINCES.

Dr. LITTLEDALE, in his "Plain Reasons Against Rome," argues in the same line. "There is nothing whatever in Scripture to connect St. Peter with Rome directly, except the ancient guess that 'Babylon,' in 1 Peter v. 13, may mean Rome, while even if it does, nothing is said about any authority there. . .

"St. Peter's own opening words contain a very cogent argument the other way. 'Pontus, Galatia, Cappadocia, Asia, and Bithynia' (1 Peter i. 1), are named in order from *East to West;* natural enough in a writer at Babylon in Mesopotamia addressing people in Asia Minor, but the exact reverse of the order which a writer at Rome would be likely to adopt if sending a letter to the East."

NIEBUHR, the eminent historian, confirms this view: "In St. Peter i. 1, the countries are addressed not from West to East (as would be natural to one writing from Rome), but from East to West (as would be natural in writing from Babylon)." Quoted in Expositor iii. 4. 4.

"In Holy Scripture, whenever a number of different nations, countries, or provinces is mentioned, *the order* is to begin with that which is geographically nearest to the writer at the time of writing, and to end with the more remote. This order is the natural order and it is *never* reversed, which has always seemed to us a conclusive argument against the Roman hypothesis." "Romanism," 156.—J. H. HOPKINS.

JOHN WESLEY writes, Notes, etc.: "He names those five provinces in the order wherein they occurred to those writing from the East."

"The fact that the countries to which the Epistle is addressed are named in the order in which a writer in Babylon would naturally view them, confirms that conclusion."—WHEDON's Com.

CHAPTER X.

Dr. G. W. Samson's Argument.

In *Bapt. Quar. Rev.*, July, 1873, Dr. Samson has an elaborate and instructive article on "Peter and his relations to the Roman Church," which fully summarizes the line of argument in favor of Rome as the Babylon of Peter.

On p. 333 we read: "The place called Babylon is without any reasonable doubt Rome, where Peter was then held for trial, and where he was soon after crucified. The evidence as to this is clear and connected. Two suppositions as to the reference are possible: first, that it is literal; second, that it is symbolic in its meaning; while if it is literal, either Babylon on the Euphrates or Babylon on the Nile must be referred to. It is sufficient here to remark that the universal historical testimony makes Rome the city referred to."

Dr. Samson accepts the tradition as to the early visit to Rome as true: "During seven or eight subsequent years, up to A. D. 50, Peter disappears. . . It is worthy of note that it is during this interesting period of several years' duration, as the early Christian writers all agree, that Peter followed up his influence gained among Romans by a visit to Rome." He alludes here to the conversion of Cornelius.

The allusions of Paul to Peter in 1 Cor. are regarded as proof of Peter's visit to Corinth, and naturally an extension of his visit to Rome. The same writer notes likenesses between the two Apostles' epistles, indicating personal association and intercourse in Rome. He says: "Moreover, the common companionship of Silvanus, or Silas, and Mark with both Peter and Paul is inexplicable, unless we suppose them to have been associated at Rome."

He directs attention to the words of Clement, Ignatius, Papias, Irenæus, the Clementines, the Apostolic Constitutions, Origen, Dionysius, Tertullian, Hippolytus, Clemens Alex., Cyprian, Ambrose, Epiphanius, Eusebius, and Jerome. He says: "Peter was at Rome from A. D. 43 to 49. On a second visit to Rome he was eminently useful to Jewish disciples scattered abroad. . . Finally, Peter met with special firmness the martyr's trial, according to the prophecy of Jesus (John xxi. 18, 19), in the eleventh year of Nero, A. D. 67."

A similar elaborate defense of the same position, will be found in Intro. 1 Peter, Speaker's Commentary, by Canon F. C. Cook. All that can be said on that side of the question is forcibly presented by these two able scholars.

We propose, in reply to the preceding arguments, to present extensively the reasonings of standard authors, who have taught that Peter resided in Babylon in Parthia, and there wrote his Epistles.

At this stage of the investigation we introduce a consideration which has a bearing on the inquiry, and is worthy of notice: What has led Rome to assume the name of the city specially marked with the Divine Curse?

ROME'S FIGURATIVE INTERPRETATION A CONFESSION OF WEAKNESS.

It is acknowledged by the Roman Church that the Babylon of St. Peter is Rome, and that the Babylon of St. John in the Apocalypse is likewise Rome.

Her writers claim that the Divine woes are predicted concerning Rome *Pagan*, some affirming that the destruction foretold was inflicted by the Goths in the fifth century, others that an Apostate Rome of the future is indicated.

Singular is it, that many of her own writers in the past, in view of her history and condition, have pronounced that the predictions of Rev. xvii. and xviii. concern Rome *Papal*.

When we consider that the vast multitude of her children who left her at the period of the Reformation, with remarkable unanimity held to the same view and were influenced in action by this belief; it is certainly a proof that no other passage in Scripture can be claimed in support of Peter's visit to Rome; else this Church, under the circumstances, would not thus have acknowledged the possibility of her being the object of the Divine Curse, as a vast multitude of the most godly and enlightened Christian scholars have believed and affirmed.

Before proceeding to consider Dr. Samson's argument we will further illustrate the point here noticed.

Roman scholars confess that there is no evidence for Peter's Roman visit, outside his first Epistle.

ALBERT BARNES clearly states this question, Intro. 1 Peter: "On the supposition that the word Babylon refers to Rome, rests nearly all the evidence which the

Roman Catholics can adduce that the Apostle Peter was ever at Rome at all."

"There is nothing else in the New Testament that furnishes the slightest proof that he ever was there. The only passage on which Bellarmine relies to show that Peter was at Rome is the passage now under consideration. "That Peter was at one time at Rome," he says, "we show first from the testimony of Peter himself, who thus speaks at the end of his first epistle: 'The Church which is at Babylon, elected together with you, saluteth you.' He does not pretend to cite any other evidence from Scripture, nor does any other writer."

That the Babylon of Revelation is Rome hardly requires argument. Bishop WORDSWORTH, on Rev. xvii. (ii. 250), says: "The voice of the Christian Church, in the age of St. John himself, and for many centuries after it, has given an almost unanimous verdict on that subject: "That the Seven-hilled City, the great city, the Queen of the Earth, Babylon the Great of the Apocalypse, is the city of Rome."

Bishop NEWTON, on the Prophecies, 553, asserts: "By Babylon was meant Rome, as all authors of all ages and countries agree."

All Roman authors here agree. BARONIUS will answer for them, Baronius' Annals, A. D. 45: "All persons confess that Rome is denoted by the name of Babylon in the Apocalypse of St. John."

He also affirms that "the fall of Rome, effected by Alaric, was the fulfillment of the prophecy of St. John." Such also is the statement of Bellarmine, Bossuet, and others.

But as Rome revived, and the Bishops of Rome have lived and reigned for centuries since, a new interpretation was required; which is, that in the *future* a heathen apostate Rome will arise, and in this power will the predictions be accomplished.

Bishop WORDSWORTH writes, Com. ii. 251 : "This is the hypothesis of some learned Romish theologians. It is maintained by Juarez, Viegas, Ribera, Lessius, Menochius, Cornelius a Lapide, and others, particularly Dr. Manning, in our own day.

"This hypothesis is important to be noticed, as an avowal on their part that the other theory, above stated, of their co-religionists, Bellarmine, Baronius, Bossuet, and many more—who say that these prophecies were fulfilled in ancient heathen Rome—is untenable.

"Here, then, is a remarkable phenomenon. Here are two discordant schools of Romish theologians. The one school says that these Apocalyptic prophecies concern the Rome that was destroyed more than *a thousand years ago*. The other school affirms that they relate to the Rome of some *future* time. They *differ* widely from each other in the interpretation of these prophecies, which they *all agree* concern their own *city*. And yet they say they have an infallible interpreter of Scripture resident at Rome. And they boast much of their own unity.

"There is something ominous in this *discord*. It makes their *agreement* more striking. It confirms the proof that these Apocalyptic prophecies concern Rome. Both these schools of Roman Catholic expositors allow that *Babylon* is *Rome*. A remarkable avowal, which is carefully to be borne in mind."

This is not the place to discuss the question of the reference of John xvii. and xviii. to the Papal Church, as held by most Protestant expositors. We simply note the fact, and that with them agreed many preceding Roman Catholic writers.

"This interpretation is not a new one," says Wordsworth. "It may be traced in the writings of *Peter of Blois*, and in the expositions of *Joachim*, abbot of Calabria at the end of the twelfth century, of *Lubertinus di Casali*, *Peter Olivi*, and others in the thirteenth century, Marsilius of Padua, and those of the illustrious Dante and Petrarch."

Dr. C. Hodge, Syst. Theo., iii. 882, writes: "Not only the poets Dante and Petrarch denounced the corruptions of the Church of Rome, but down to the time of the Reformation that Church was held up by a succession of theologians or ecclesiastics, as the Babylon of the Apocalypse which was to be overthrown and rendered desolate."

A CONCEDED WEAKNESS OF PROOF.

In view of the above considerations, that Rome consents to the view that the Babylon of Peter is Rome, it seems clear that this Church sees the necessity for some Scriptural evidence for her Peter-Roman story, and that she can find no other than 1 Peter v. 13.

Some writers have put this matter in forcible terms:

"It is singular that the Romish Church contends earnestly for that figurative meaning. See the *Rhemish New Testament*, where they call the Protestants 'dishonest and partial handlers of God's Word' for opposing this view from which they endeavor to build a proof that Peter was at Rome. Fulke fairly remarks: 'You are content that Rome be the See of Antichrist, so you may have Peter at Rome; seeing you will needs have Rome to be Babylon in this place, as in Rev. xvi. and xvii. you cannot avoid the See of Antichrist from the city of Rome; for the Holy Ghost in the Revelation speaks not only of the persecution of the heathen emperors, but also of the incitements to false doctrine, etc."—Com. Rel. Tr. Soc., 1 Pet. v. 13.

The English version of Poole's Commentary is of like force.

"The Papists would have Babylon here to be Rome as Rev. xvii. and that Peter gives it that name rather than its own, because being escaped out of prison at Jerusalem, Act xii. 17, he would not have it known where he was.

"But how comes it that he who had been so bold before should be so timorous now? Did this become the Head of the Church, the Vicar of Christ, and the Prince of the Apostles? And is it probable that he should live twenty-five years at Rome (as they pretend he did) and yet not be known to be there? Wherever he was, he had Mark with him now, who is said to have died in Alexandria, the eighth year of Nero, and Peter not till six years after.

"If Mark then did first constitute the Church of Alexandria and govern it (as they say he did) for so many years, it will be hard to find him and Peter at Rome together. But if they will needs have Rome meant Babylon, let them enjoy their zeal, who rather than not find Peter's chair, would go to hell to seek it, and are more concerned to have Rome the seat of Peter, than the Church of Christ." Poole himself, in his Synopsis, adopts the figurative view.

W. M. Taylor, Life of Peter, 333, remarks: "When Peter wrote his first epistle he was at Babylon on the Euphrates. An attempt indeed has been made to prove that this means Rome, but such a view is ludicrous in itself, and for the Church in whose interests it is advanced, destructive. . . If it be insisted on that by Babylon Peter actually meant Rome, then to Rome must belong the character and doom of the Apocalyptic Babylon."

"A very old opinion," says Lillie on 1 Peter, "held likewise by nearly all Roman Catholic writers, who would thus succeed, though under a bad name, in getting New Testament evidence of Peter's connection with the Imperial City."

"It is singular," writes Hovey, Am. Com., "Roman Catholics should incline to apply to Rome the name of such a city as Babylon, but it is intended to help a theory which needs all possible support."

"If Peter was at Rome, the text that is quoted to show it, shows that Rome is delineated in Rev. xviii." J. Cumming, Hammersmith Disc., p. 507.

The strait in which the Church of Rome is placed to secure some proof from Scripture of Peter's Roman residence is evident from her appeal to the thirteenth verse of the fifth chapter of his first Epistle.

If we mistake not, the argument works somewhat on the principle of the boomerang, which is apt to return to the injury of the one who uses it.

The figurative interpretation, we hold, therefore, to be a concession on the part of Rome, that the Word of God furnishes no rational or convincing evidence in support of her supreme spiritual claim upon the consciences of men ; her affirmation, with anathema, that there is no salvation beyond her jurisdiction, founded, as it is, on the supposition that the Apostle Peter ruled in Rome, and transmitted the Primacy of Christendom to his successors.

CHAPTER XI.

Rome not Babylon—Arguments of English Authors.

The opinion of the commentator S. T. Bloomfield is of more interest and value from the fact that he had been led, by more thorough investigation, to change his views.

In his "Recensio Synoptica," published in 1827, 8 vols., he accepts the traditional view that Peter by Babylon meant Rome. We quote from the latest edition of Notes, N. Test., 1855:

"Of the city here intended, no little diversity of opinion exists. Some suppose Babylon is *Egypt*, an opinion, however, highly improbable in itself, and which has been completely overturned by Lardner." He then states that the figurative interpretation rests solely on a tradition of Papias. See p. 75, quoted above.

"We may, indeed, justly regard it as mere notion, first originating in error, and afterward caught up by Romanists for the purpose of supporting their assertion that Peter was the first Bishop of Rome. In fact Calvin has almost proved to a demonstration that it cannot mean the Church of Rome, arguing from Eusebius and others, who affirm it, saying what is contradictory and does not hang together, as involving a gross anachronism: whence Calvin is warranted in arguing that since Peter had, when he wrote the Epistle, Mark then with him, as a companion, it is, *a priori*, highly probable that he wrote the Epistle from Babylon, and hence well designates that Church as your 'Sister Church of Babylon.'

"The best founded opinion is, I apprehend, that of Erasmus, Calvin, Beza, Lightfoot, Cave, Scaliger, Salmasius, Le Clerc, Wettstein, Bengel, Benson, Rosenmüller, A. Clarke, Steiger, Dr. Peile, Wiesler, and Dr. Davidson, that it means Babylon in Assyria, though they are not agreed whether we are to understand *Seleucia*, i. e., new Babylon or old Babylon. . . There is every reason to think that Babylon was a sort of metropolis of the Eastern Dispersion of the Jews, where a great number of them had gone to settle, in addition to those who were the posterity of those who remained in Babylon, and did not return."

Of our next authority, Dean MILMAN, Jackson's Concise Dictionary declares, "He was the first (and is still the chief) English ecclesiastical historian, who wrote simply in a fair, scientific spirit, not holding a brief for any party or set of opinions."

Milman writes, Hist. Jews, i. 160: "This Babylonian settlement is of great importance in Jewish history, and not less, perhaps, in Christian. I have long held, and more than once expressed, a strong opinion that the Babylon from which St. Peter's Epistle was dated, is this Babylonian settlement.

"What more likely than that the Apostle of the Circumsion should place himself in the midst of his brethren in that quarter, and address, as it were, a pastoral letter to the conterminous settlement in Asia.

"It must have been to these Jews dwelling among the *Ano-Barbarous*, that Josephus wrote the first version of his Jewish War in their native tongue (Aramaic).

It shows their importance at the period immediately after the Jewish war, even to a man so highly Romanized as Josephus."

W. A. WRIGHT, in Smith's Bib. Dict., Hackett's Ed., of the figurative view, says: "Although this opinion is held by Grotius, Lardner, Cave, Whitby, Macknight, Hales, and others, it may be rejected as improbable. There is nothing to indicate that the name is used figuratively, and the subscription to an Epistle is the last place we should expect to find a mythical interpretation. . .

"The most natural supposition of all is that by Babylon is intended the old Babylon of Assyria, which was largely inhabited by Jews at the time in question (Joseph. Ant. xv. 3, § 1. Philo de Viri, p. 1023, Ed. Franc. 1691). The only argument against this view is the negative evidence from the silence of historians as to Peter's having visited the Assyrian Babylon; but this remark cannot be allowed to have much weight. Lightfoot's remarks are very suggestive. In a sermon preached at St. Mary's, Cambridge (Wks. ii. 1144), he maintained that Babylon of Assyria is intended, 'because it was one of the greatest knots of Jews in the world,' and St. Peter was the minister of the Circumcision. . . Bentley gave his suffrage in favor of the ancient Babylon, quoting Josephus, etc."

Dean MERIVALE, Hist. Rome, substantiates Lightfoot's statement as to the overwhelming number of Jews in that region. "After the fall of Babylon and the distribution of its people, the Jews, if we may believe their own writers, took the place of the native races throughout the surrounding districts."

ROBERTSON, Hist. Christ. Ch., i. p. 2, writes: "St.

Peter is said to have founded the Church at Antioch, and after having presided over it for seven years, to have left Euodias as his successor, while he himself penetrated into Parthia and other countries of the East, and it would seem more reasonable to understand the date of *Babylon* in his first Epistle (v. 13) as meaning the Eastern city of that name than as a mystical designation of Pagan Rome."

In PATRICK FAIRBAIRN'S Imp. Bib. Dict. we read: "There is no reason why Peter should have disguised under such a figurative appellation the place from which he wrote his Epistle; and in an Epistle remarkable for its simplicity and directness of speech, it would have been a sort of anomaly to fall at its close, upon a symbolical designation of his place of residence for which the Epistle itself could furnish no key, and which is also without parallel in any other of the Epistles of the New Testament."

Of LAWRENCE ECHARD, Dean Prideaux says: "The Ecclesiastical History of Mr. Lawrence Echard is the best of its kind in the English tongue." In Cent. 1, B. II., Ch. V., p. 200, this author writes: "While this great Apostle of the Uncircumcision was thus diligently pursuing his ministry, the other of the Circumcision, *St. Peter*, after his departure from *Antioch*, preached the gospel to the *Jews* in several provinces of lesser Asia, and traveling eastward arrived at the ancient city *Babylon* in *Chaldea*, above seven hundred miles east of Jerusalem, where great numbers of *Jews* resided, having a famous Academy and several schools. In this city it is probable Silas or Silvanus came to him, leaving *Paul* at *Ephesus*, and having the evangelist *Mark* with him. From this place and in the year 54, as Mr. Dodwell fairly conjectures, he wrote his first Epistle, which is called a catholic or general Epistle."

RENNEL, Geog. Herod. § 15, testifies to the abounding numbers of the Babylonian Jews: "So great a number of Jews was found in Babylon as is astonishing. They are spoken of by Josephus as possessing towns and districts in that country about forty years after Christ. They were in great numbers in Babylon itself."

SALMOND writes: "The allegorical interpretation becomes less likely when it is observed that other geographical designations in this Epistle (ch. i. 1) have undoubtedly the literal meaning. The tradition itself, too, is uncertain."

WELLS, in Sacred Geography, p. 261, alludes to an interesting point, the connection between the labors of the Apostles Peter and Jude.

"It is of some importance to know that the Apostle Jude labored pretty far eastward in this pious work, because it contributes to account for the similarity of the Epistle with some parts of the second of Peter, which seems strongly to confirm the idea that they were both in the habit of addressing the same kind of people.

"In fact the Oriental style of imagery, elevation, and metaphor which they adopt is altogether conformable to Eastern usage, and marks a phraseology to which the Western world reconciles itself with difficulty, and which it rarely adopts in regular and correct composition."

Bishop WORDSWORTH, on the Canon, puts the argument strongly and concisely: "Hence we see why Peter the Apostle of the Circumcision went to Babylon, in Parthian Babylonia. It was the headquarters of those whom he had addressed with such wonderful success on the day of Pentecost, and who are named first in order by the inspired historian of the Acts.

"Hence we see why, being at Babylon, St. Peter addressed an epistle to the strangers *scattered* throughout Pontus, Galatia, Cappadocia, Asia, and Bithynia. They were derived from Babylon. They were co-elect with the Church there."

We close the present list of eminent English scholars with the venerated name of Dean STANLEY, who thus eloquently writes: "Whether the Babylon from the neighborhood of which the Epistle is dated be the city of Mesopotamia, or, as in Rev. xix., a metaphorical name for Rome, cannot perhaps be settled for certainty. . . On the whole there does not seem sufficient reason for abandoning the literal meaning of the passage; see Com. Steiger, Mayerhoff, etc.

"We catch a glimpse of St. Peter with the partner of his labors and his son Mark, far away in the distant East, by the waters of Babylon, among the descendants of those who long ago had hung their harps upon the willows that are there.

"It was—if we take the most probable conjecture as to the time and place of its composition—it was now that from the Euphrates there came that great Epistle, addressed to all the Asiatic Churches, from the eastern hills of Pontus down to the cities on the Ægean Sea."
—Serm. Apost. Age, p. 91.

A few brief American opinions are here presented:

EDWARD ROBINSON, Bib. Dict., Article Peter: "The Epistle was written from Babylon, but whether the Egyptian or Chaldean Babylon cannot be determined." Art. Babylon: "Some critics have supposed that Peter wrote his Epistle from this Babylon, but we have no evidence that he ever was in Egypt, and probability tends to the opposite conclusion."

Professor Stowe, Bks. Bibl. 399 : "It is only the anxiety of some to give Peter a long residence at Rome, that ever imagined here a spiritual Babylon, that is Rome."

McClintock and Strong Encyl..: "The natural meaning of the designation Babylon is held by Erasmus, Calvin, Beza, Lightfoot, Wiesler, Mayerhoff, Bengel, DeWette, Bleek, and perhaps the majority of modern critics."

Professor Shedd, Com. Rom. : "According to 1 Peter v. 13, Peter is connected with the Church in Babylon as late as A. D. 60.

"That this is the literal Babylon is favored by the fact, that the first Epistle of Peter was addressed to the Jewish Church in Asia Minor (1 Pet. i. 1), whose condition and needs could have much more naturally come under the eye of an Apostle on the banks of the Euphrates, than on the banks of the Tiber."

G. H. Whitney, Hand-Book, Bible Geography: "The Babylon of 1 Pet. v, 13 doubtless refers to ancient Babylon, a portion of whose ruins was long occupied by Jews."

CHAPTER XII.

Views of Continental Writers.

AMONG the most able of Biblical commentators, is the well known JOHN DAVID MICHAELIS. In his Introduction to the New Testament he has answered the arguments of Dr. Lardner, one of the most strenuous defenders of the figurative interpretation. Michaelis' opinion is of special weight, inasmuch as he was of those who, like Bloomfield already quoted, changed their view after more thorough investigation.

He writes: "St. Peter, in the close of his Epistle, sends a salutation from the Church at Babylon, which consequently is the place where he wrote his Epistle. But commentators do not agree in regard to the word Babylon, some taking it in its literal and proper sense, others giving it a figurative and mystical interpretation.

"Among the latter have been men of such learning and abilities that I was misled by their authority in the younger part of my life, to subscribe to it; but at present, as I have more impartially examined the question, it appears to me very extraordinary that, when an Apostle dates his Epistle from Babylon, it should ever occur to any commentator to ascribe to this word a mystical meaning, instead of taking it in its literal and proper sense."

Describing Babylon and Seleucia, he continues: "In

the last two editions of this Introduction I preferred the former sense : but after a more mature consideration, I think it much more probable at present that St. Peter meant the ancient Babylon. . . Before I conclude this section I must take notice of a passage in Josephus, which not only confutes all notions of a spiritual or mystical Babylon, but throws a great light on our present inquiry ; and this passage is of so much the more importance, because Josephus was a historian who lived in the same age with St. Peter."

After quoting this passage, he presents Dr. Lardner's reasons for the opposite view : " *First*, There were no Jews in Babylon in the time of Peter ; *second*, That the ancient fathers mostly explain the word figuratively ; *third*, No mention is made of Peter's journey to Babylon ; *fourth*, Peter's charge to ' honor the king,' which must have meant the Roman Emperor." These arguments Michaelis thoroughly examines.

He thus concludes : " It appears then that the arguments which have been alleged to show that St. Peter did not write his first Epistle in the country of Babylonia are without foundation, and consequently the notion of a mystical Babylon, as denoting either Jerusalem or Rome, loses its whole support.

" For in itself the notion is highly improbable ; and, therefore, the bare possibility that St. Peter took a journey to Babylon, properly so called, renders it inadmissible. The plain language of epistolary writing does not admit of the figures of poetry : and though it would be very allowable in a poem written in honor of Göttingen, to style it another Athens, it would be a greater piece of pedantry than was ever laid to the charge of the learned. In like manner, though a figurative use of the word Babylon is not unsuitable to the animated and poetical language of the Apocalypse, yet St. Peter, in a plain and unadorned Epistle, would hardly have called the place where he wrote by any other appellation than that which literally and properly belonged to it."

Dr. ADAM CLARKE, who quotes in his Com. on 1 Peter the entire argument of Michaelis, thus remarks upon it: "That many persons, both of learning and eminence, have been of a different opinion from Professor Michaelis, the intelligent reader is well aware; but Dr. Lardner, of all others, has written most argumentatively in vindication of the mystic Babylon, *i. e.*, as being the place from which the Apostle wrote this Epistle. His weightiest arguments, however, are answered by Michaelis; and to me it appears that there is a great balance in favor of the opinion that Babylon on the Euphrates is the place intended. The decision of this question, though not an article of faith, is nevertheless of some importance."

He elsewhere writes: "After considering all that has been said by learned men and critics on this place, I am quite of the opinion that the Apostle does not mean Babylon in *Egypt*, nor *Jerusalem*, nor *Rome*, as figurative Babylon, but the ancient celebrated Babylon in Assyria."

With respect to Dr. Lardner, KITTO says: "Lardner's principal argument that the terms of the injunction to loyal obedience (ii. 13, 14,) imply that Peter was within the bounds of the Roman Empire, proves nothing; for as DAVIDSON remarks, 'the phrase "the king" in a letter written by a person in one country to a person in another, may mean the king either of the person writing, or of him to whom the letter is written.'"

J. Owen, vicar of Thrussington, writes concerning Lardner's tendency to credit patristic legends : " Even such a man as Lardner seemed unwilling to reject this tale, for fear of lessening the credit of history, evidently mistaking the ground on which history has a title to credit."

Francis Turretin, whose works Principal Cunningham describes as being "of inestimable" value, has also fully argued this question. This author was of a remarkable family. His father and his son, like himself, were pastors of the Italian Congregation at Geneva, and were, moreover, professors at the Theological Seminary of that city. Turretin argues that Peter was never at Rome : (1) from the silence of Luke ; (2) from that of Paul ; (3) from that of Peter ; (4) from a computation of the times ; (5) from the distribution of work between Paul and Peter ; (6) from the chronology ; (7) from the origin of the tradition. We give a portion of his argument :

"XI. Possibly Babylon, concerning which John speaks in the Apocalypse, is none other than Rome, since it is described as possessing those characteristics which could belong to no other city ; especially because it was Seven-hilled, and at that time held, vested in the kings, the government of the world ; it does not follow that this same is to be understood for Babylon (1 Peter v. 13) 'the Church which is at Babylon saluteth you.' Because John wrote a prophecy, and therefore spoke ambiguously and enigmatically, but Peter wrote as a writer of history, and with simplicity, because he wrote a letter in which everything was narrated in a manner clear and easily comprehended.

"Nor had he other reasons for concealing the name

of the city than Paul, who lets it be openly known when he writes at Rome. And it is a singular thing that the Papists wish to understand the literal Babylon in the Apocalypse, which was written in an ambiguous and prophetic manner, and to take figuratively that name which was mentioned, merely as historical, to show the place where the letter was written. Moreover, there is no reason why he should have designated Rome as Babylon. Was it because idols were worshiped there? But that is done everywhere. From fear lest it be known where he was working? But whence such extraordinary timidity? Had not Paul written to the Romans, and written many Epistles at Rome, without either suppressing or changing its name, but freely mentioning it? Rome is principally spoken of as Babylon in the Apocalypse, on account of the spiritual servitude which the Church was to suffer through her. It cannot be said that Rome was commonly so called. John mentions this name as a type of a figure.

"Nor should the testimony of Papias and those who followed him convince us of this, for it is of trifling weight, as will be shown afterward. For no other can be designated more consistently and plainly as Babylon than the capital of the Assyrians and Chaldeans, which was the head and center of government, the chief city of that dispersion to which Peter wrote, Pontus, Galatia, etc., which had $αἰχμαλωτάρμεν$, and many of the Circumcision, the care of which belonged to Peter and John.

"How great a confluence of Jews was there may be evident from the following: because so many Jewish schools were removed from Palestine to Babylon, whence is the Babylonian name Talmud.

"Finally, when nothing renders it necessary to depart from the proper signification of the text, there's no need of seeking a figurative meaning, for the literal one remains. Bellarmine recognizes this, 'De Eucharistica, Lib. 1, Cap. xii.'"

Turretin's further argument will be found in the previous chapter on Papias, p. 75.

NEANDER, Hist. Plant. Christ., i. 573, writes: "This Epistle of Peter leads us rather to suppose that the scene of his labors was in the Parthian Empire, for as he sends salutations from his wife in Babylon, this naturally suggests the conclusion that he himself was in that neighborhood. . . It appears, then, that after Peter had found a suitable field of exertion in the Parthian Empire, he wrote to the Churches founded by Paul and his assistants in Asia, an Epistle, which is the only memorial preserved to us of his later labors. . . The opinion of the Ancients is perfectly arbitrary, that under this name (Babylon) Rome was meant, and there is nothing against our supposing that an inhabited portion of the immense Babylon was still left."

We give Neander's language inasmuch as he has been claimed as holding the opposite view.

STEIGER, Intro. Epis. Pet. i. 29: "In proof that Peter did not confine his activity to Palestine, speaks also the *Place* from which this Epistle is written. That this is not to be understood symbolically for a designation of Rome as the ancients took it (Clem. Alex. in Euseb. H. E. ii. 15), is now admitted, to say nothing of similar interpretations (see Bertholdt, Hug, etc.). . . By Babylon we understand Babylon $\kappa\alpha\tau'\ \dot{\varepsilon}\xi o\chi\dot{\eta}\nu$ (which is also regarded as probable by Neander, etc.), for, had it been any other, a mark of distinction would have been the more necessary, the more remote and unknown it was." Steiger enters fully into the discussion of the questions involved.

GUERIKE, Ch. Hist. translated by Professor Shedd, p. 52: "From the passage 1 Peter v. 13, if the name of Babylon be taken literally, as the character of the Epistle warrants, the conclusion is justified that Peter, attended by Mark, his frequent companion, and the writer of the second Gospel, which obtained its canonical authority from Peter, had extended his labors into Persia, where many Jews had taken up their residence ; and had chosen this part of Asia, generally, as the seat of his missionary efforts ; from here, or at least soon after his return from here, about the year 60, he wrote his first Epistle."

PRESENSÉ, a French author, in his "Apostolic Age," p. 311, writes: "The Epistle of Peter was written before the Apocalypse, and the persecution under Nero, that is to say before the time when Pagan Rome was to the Church what Babylon had been to the Jews of old. Up to this time the Christians had had much more to suffer from the Jews than from the Gentiles. It is worthy of remark, also, that the style of Peter in his Epistle is not raised to the lyric tone of ancient prophecy, and its conclusion is as simple as possible. There can, then, be no reason for attaching a far-fetched symbolic meaning to a designation perfectly clear in itself.

" Peter had succeeded in founding a Church in Babylon ; this Church had become a center of light to all the Jewish colony. Silas, one of the companions of Paul, joined Peter at Babylon, and the description given by him of the critical condition of the Churches in

Asia Minor doubtless led the Apostle to address to them a letter of consolation.

"Persecution was, in truth, imminent; like a violent tempest it was giving precursive tokens of its approach, and it was well that words of earnest exhortation should be multiplied on the eve of so terrible a conflict. Peter pleaded with holy eloquence, magnifying, like Paul. the greatness and glory of Christian endurance, and himself preparing to seal with his blood his witness to the truth."

REUSS, of the same nation as the last author, Hist. N. Test., is of much the same mind: "The idea that Babylon is a mythical name for Rome accords neither with the spirit of the Epistle, nor with any ecclesiastical combination reaching back into the immediate neighborhood of the Apocalyptic period. A doctrinal Epistle is not an Apocalypse, neither is it demonstrated nor probable that in later times the Apocalyptic use of language, without intimation, was generally accepted among Christians.

"The persecutions, as they are described, do not give the impression of something fierce and bloody like that of Nero. They lend, therefore, no support to a composition at Rome in the last years of Nero. . . That Peter met his death at Rome is a bare possibility."

We close this chapter of authorities with the convincing evidence of three pre-eminent modern authorities, in support of the view of the vast extent of the field of the Apostolic labors among the Circumcision, in the neighborhood of the Parthian Babylon.

Professor SCHÜRER, Hist. Jew. People, etc., vol. i. pt. ii. p. 223, remarks: "In Mesopotamia, Media, and Babylon, lived the descendants of the members of the kingdom of the ten tribes, and of the kingdom of Judah, who had been carried away thither by the Chaldeans and Assyrians. . . The Jews in these provinces were numbered not by thousands but by millions.

"Their attitude was always of political importance to the Empire. Josephus names the strong cities of Nebardea and Nisibis, the former on the Euphrates, the latter in the valley, as the chief dwelling places of the Babylonian and Mesopotamian Jews. Around Nisibis were grouped the descendants of the ten tribes, and around Nebardea the descendants of the tribes of Benjamin and Judah."

Dr. EMANUEL DEUTSCH, a brilliant Hebrew scholar, who died greatly lamented in 1873, assistant librarian to the British Museum, in Kitto's Encycl. Alexander's Ed., Art. Dispersion, writes: "Foremost in the two or three chief groups into which the Jewish Dispersion had been divided stands the Babylonian, embracing the Jews of the Persian Empire, into every part of which, Babylonia, Media, Susiana, Mesopotamia, Assyria, etc., they penetrated. The Jews of Babylonia prided themselves on the exceptional purity of their language, a boast uniformly recognized throughout the nation. What Judea, it was said, was with respect to the dispersion of other countries—as pure flour to dough—that Babylonia was to Judea.

"Herod pretended to have sprung from Babylonian ancestors, and also bestowed the high priesthood upon a man from Babylon. In the messages sent by the Sanhedrim to the whole dispersion, Babylonia received the precedence, although it remained a standing reproach against the Babylonians that they held aloof from the national cause when their brethren returned to

Palestine, and thus had caused the weakness of the Jewish state; as, indeed, living in Palestine, under any circumstances, is enumerated among the Jewish ordinances. The very territory of Babylonia was, for certain ritual purposes, considered to be as pure as Palestine itself."

Edersheim, a converted Hebrew, and among the most valued of modern writers, in his "Life and Times of Jesus the Messiah," has largely dwelt upon this topic. He says:

"Far other was the estimate in which the Babylonians were held by the leaders of Judaism. Indeed, according to one view of it, Babylonia, as well as Syria as far north as Antioch, was regarded as forming part of the Land of Israel. Every other country was considered outside 'the Land,' as Palestine was called, with the exception of Babylonia, which was reckoned a part of it. . .

"It was just between the Euphrates and the Tigris that the largest and wealthiest settlements of the Jews were, to such an extent that a later writer designated them as 'the land of Israel.' . . According to Josephus, with whom Philo substantially agrees, vast numbers, estimated as millions, inhabited the Trans-Euphratic provinces. . .

"Such was their influence that as late as the year 40 A. D., the Roman Legate shrank from provoking their hostility. . . After the destruction of Jerusalem the spiritual supremacy of Palestine passed to Babylonia. . . Only eight days' journey separated them from Palestine. And every pulsation there vibrated in Babylonia. It was among the same community that Peter wrote and labored." Vol. i. 7–14.

CHAPTER XIII.

Gavazzi's Argument.

In February, 1872, a public discussion was held in Rome on the question—"Whether the Apostle Peter had visited that city." Three learned priests maintained the affirmative. Three Protestant divines contended for the negative. At the head of the latter was GAVAZZI, a converted priest, who had held a high official position, had been chaplain to Garibaldi's army, and had acquired much fame by his eloquence, on his visits to England and the United States.

We present a portion of Gavazzi's argument: "The silence of the Bible upon the coming of Peter to Rome is not any means a negative proof, but a positive and most explicit one. Cardinal Bellarmine says that silence is a positive proof. . . Let us look at some parallel. Thiers, for instance, does not say a word in his 'History of the Consulate and Empire,' of Napoleon having gone to Washington in America. This is perhaps proof that he went there? No, quite the contrary. By the same logic it might be said that Peter never went to Rome.

"The Acts of the Apostles, which say not a word of the coming of St. Peter to Rome, are the true, official, authentic history, giving a particular account of the development, of the progress, of the persecutions, of the triumphs of the Church. Their aim is to show the labors of the Apostles. These Acts are a legitimate impartial account, because St. Luke was inspired. How could he be silent about St. Peter going to Rome, when he speaks of so many other cities of minor importance?

"He says he went to Lydda, to Joppa, to Samaria, to Cæsarea, to Jerusalem; why should he not also have said he went to Rome, if he really went there. The Acts of the Apostles are, in short, for the Apostles, what Thiers' account of the Consulate and Empire is for Napoleon. Would it have been possible for Thiers to be silent about Napoleon's going to Moscow? No. Well then, St. Peter's going to Rome would have been a thousand times more important for the Apostolate, and the Church, than Napoleon's going to Moscow for the Empire.

"Our adversaries say that perhaps the going of St. Peter to Rome is not mentioned for fear of compromising him. Fear? No, it was not the case; because when the Acts of the Apostles were written, the danger was past. I respect Peter too much to believe that he was afraid. Peter was not a coward to fear martyrdom. Nor did Paul reckon him as such. The silence of Paul then is a positive proof that, during the time he was in Rome, St. Peter was not there."

One who has written exhaustively on this subject says: "There is no more properly historical evidence that Peter visited Rome than there is that General Washington visited London, or Napoleon, New York. No report, rumor, or legend, to the latter effect, has yet been heard of. It is too soon. There is time enough fifty years hence. . . If history is to be made of tropes, bon-mots, half legends, and the like pliable and expansible materials, there is nothing to forbid the expectation that, fifteen centuries hence, a colossal statue and magnificent monument may mark the identical spot where George Washington stood on Tower Hill, and a perpetual anniversary celebrate the arrival of Napoleon, attended by all his marshals, in New York."

Gavazzi presents an original argument in response to his antagonists: "They defy us to find a prophecy which would allude to the death of Peter anywhere else than at Rome. Well? the prophecy is this. Christ said to the Pharisees these words: 'Some of them ye shall crucify.' Now they were Jews, who, according to the words of Christ, were to crucify some of his disciples —not the Romans. Well, of those crucified, there were only, according to the Church, Andrew and Peter; the others were stoned or beheaded. He alluded then to these two: these two were the 'some' meant of Christ.

"The crucifixion of Peter, that it might fulfill the prophecy of Christ, should have happened by the hand of the Jews, not of the Romans, at least in a country where the Jews exercised the utmost power. Now the Jews in Rome had no power of this kind. In Babylon? Yes, it was possible that crucifixion might take place there; there the Jews were so powerful that it is known that some Babylonish King allowed them to have a high priest. At Babylon the prophecy of Christ could be fulfilled, at Rome it could not. Besides, the mode of Peter's death—crucified with the head downward—is not Roman: it is a punishment in use among the Parthians. The Romans crucified with the head upward, and then broke the legs. The very death of Peter, then, is a proof that it did not happen at Rome."

This conjecture of Gavazzi is well worthy of consideration. It is the strongest confirmation of the tradition that Peter died by crucifixion. The interpretation of our Lord's prediction with respect to this Apostle, in the last chapter of John's Gospel, "when thou art old another shall gird thee and carry thee whither thou wouldst not," etc., that it signified crucifixion, is simply a conjecture. Bacon states, Lives of Apos., p. 254, that Tertullian originated this idea. He says; "The rejection of the forced interpretation is by no means a new notion. The critical Tremellius long ago maintained that the verse had no reference whatever to a prophecy of Peter's crucifixion, though he probably had no idea of denying that Peter did actually die by crucifixion. Among more modern commentators too, the prince of critics, Kninoel, with whom are quoted Semler, Gurlitt, Schott, utterly deny that a fair construction of the original will allow any prophetical idea to be based upon it.

"The critical testimony of these great commentators on the true and just force of the words is of the very highest value: because all received the tale of Peter's crucifixion as true, having never examined the authority of the tradition, and not one of them pretended to deny that he was really crucified . . . they therefore pronounce it as merely expressing the helplessness and imbecility of extreme old age, with which they make every word coincide."

Elsewhere Bacon forcibly remarks: "Take a common reader, who has never heard that Peter was crucified, and it would be hard for him to make out such a circumstance from the bare prophecy given by John. Indeed such unbiased impressions of the sense of the passage will go far to justify the conclusion that the words imply nothing but that Peter was destined to pass a long life in the service of his Master—that he should, after having worn out his bodily and mental energies in his devoted exertions, attain such an extreme decrepit old age, as to lose the power of voluntary motion and die thus, at least, without *necessarily* implying any bloody martyrdom.

"Will it be said that by such a quiet death he could not be considered as *glorifying* God? . . Was not God truly glorified, in the deaths of the aged Xavier, and Elliot, and Schwartz, or the bright, early exits of Brainerd, Mills, Martyn, Parsons, Fisk, and hundreds whom the apostolic spirit of modern missions has sent forth to labors as devoted, and to deaths as glorious to God, as those of any who swell the deified lists of the ancient martyrologies? The whole notion of a bloody martyrdom, as an essential termination to the life of a saint, grew out of a Papistical superstition. . .

"All those writers who pretend to particularize the mode of his departure connect it also with the utterly impossible fiction of his residence at Rome, on which enough has been already said. . . Peter was then in Babylon, far beyond the vengeance of the Cæsar: nor was he so foolish as ever after to have trusted himself in the reach of a perfectly unnecessary danger. The command of Christ was, 'when you are persecuted in one city, flee unto another.' The necessary and unquestionable inference from which, was, that when out of reach of persecution they should not willfully go into it. This is a simple principle of Christian *action* with which papist fable-mongers were totally unacquainted, and they thereby afford the most satisfactory proof of the actions and motives they ascribe to the Apostles."

We may justly affirm that the fables about Peter, which were mostly concocted to aggrandize a particular Church, in an age of ignorance and consequent credulity, are based on a principle in direct antagonism to the commands of our Lord, and forbid us reasonably to believe that the Apostle Peter would journey from his abundant and legitimate field of labor, where he was protected by the authorities, and at great personal risk and expense, on a romantic expedition, to terminate at Rome, by a violent death, needlessly, his life and abounding usefulness in preaching the Gospel of his Lord.

There is no testimony, as has been amply shown, either from Scripture, or from any writer within a century after the death of Peter, that he ever left the East; nor is there a solitary statement on record since, which, on critical examination, as will be made evident, is worthy of credit, that the Apostle's feet ever entered Rome.

This fabulous transfer of Peter from Babylon to Rome, made for an evident purpose, has had the effect in some respects of *dislocating* ecclesiastical history. The correction of the error, in the words of the learned Lightfoot, "The consideration that Peter ended his days at Babylon, is very useful, if my judgment fail not, at the setting out of ecclesiastical story."

CHAPTER XIV.

The Apostles Peter and John.

Professor McDonald, in his commentary on St. John, presents a reasonable and interesting suggestion concerning the joint work of these two Apostles. On p. 138, he writes : "It appears to be as well established a fact, not recorded in the Scriptures, that Peter, following the emigrants and colonists of his own nation, journeyed Eastward, and made the Provinces of the Parthian Empire, and the regions east of the Euphrates, the scene of his labors.

"The number of Jews in the city of Babylon, and the Provinces around it had, it is said, been increased at this time to such a degree that they constituted a very large portion of the population. (Joseph. Antiq., xviii.) St. Peter would be led to follow them as he prosecuted his Apostolic work. His first Epistle seems to have been written from Babylon, and is addressed to the Christians scattered abroad, beginning with Pontus, the place nearest to him on the northeast of Asia Minor. That St. Peter uses Babylon in a metaphorical sense for Rome, is a conjecture which has few supporters among scholars.

"Michaelis (I. D.) very ably exposes the absurdity of the opinion that Peter dates from Babylon in a mystical sense. And as Babylon in Egypt was a mere military station, there can be no doubt the place named by

Peter was the ancient Assyrian or Chaldean Babylon, or the city that in his day stood on its site. It was a city of great importance and interest in a religious point of view, offering a most ample and desirable field for the labors of the chief Apostle, now advancing in years, and whose whole genius, feeling, and religious education and natural peculiarities, qualified him as eminently for this Oriental scene of labor, as those of Paul fitted him for the triumphant advancement of the Christian Faith among the polished and energetic races of the mighty West. With Peter went also others of the Apostolic band." Bacon's Lives of the Apostles, p. 260.

"As there are no traces of John in any other direction, it is not improbable, as he had thus far been so intimately associated with Peter in Apostolic labors in Judea and Samaria, they were not separated now; at least for a portion of the time Peter was in the Parthian dominions. As far back as the time of Augustine, A. D. 398, the First Epistle of John was known as the Epistle to the Parthians. He quotes 1 John iii. 2, which he introduces, 'which is said by John in the Epistle to the Parthians.'

"It seems indeed pleasant to contemplate these eminent Apostles, 'in this glorious clime of the East,' amid the scenes of that Ancient Captivity, in which the mourning sons of Zion had drawn consolation and support from the word of Prophecy, which the march of time 'in its solemn fulfillment,' had now made the faithful history of God's children; amid the ruins of Empires, and natural wrecks of ages, attesting, in the dreary desolation, the surety of the word of God."

This view of McDonald and others, that Parthia was the scene of the Apostolic labors of these foremost ministers to the circumcision, is rendered the more probable from the security then enjoyed both by Jew and Christian in that kingdom.

W. C. Taylor, in his Man'l. Anc. Hist., p. 167, says: "After Christianity began to spread, its progress was tolerated, if not directly encouraged, by the Parthian monarchs, who liberally offered shelter to Christians flying from the persecutions of the Pagans, and we must add, from those of their brethren who belonged to a different sect."

Greenwood, Cath. Petri. II. viii, confirms this statement of the tolerant spirit of this people, when he refers to "that degree of repose and social dignity which, we are authentically informed, the Jews of Babylonia for ages afterward enjoyed, under the patronage of the Parthian and Persian sovereigns."

Again, he writes, vol. i. 244: "When we take into account that Peter's mission was to those of the Circumcision, as Paul's was to those of the Uncircumcision; it is most natural to suppose that they bore their testimony, where it was most likely to continue prudential—the conversion, to wit, of Gentiles by Paul, and of Jews by Peter. . . We cannot therefore help thinking it far more probable that Peter suffered in the Mesopotamian capital, than that he traveled in the latest period of his life to Rome, to partake the honor of martyrdom with his colleague Paul."

The tolerance of the Parthian authorities is confirmed by Dr. Wm. Smith in his New Testament History, p. 636, Am. ed., where he says: "If we suppose that Peter was visiting his Jewish brethren of the Eastern Dispersion, there is no place which he would be more likely to make the goal and headquarter of such a tour. Babylon was at that time, and for some hundreds of years afterward, a chief seat of Jewish culture. Under the tolerant rule of the Parthians the Jewish families formed a separate and wealthy community; and thence they had spread to many of the districts of Asia Minor, to which the Epistle was addressed. Their intercourse with Judea was uninterrupted; and their language, probably a mixture of Hebrew and Nabatean, must have borne a near affinity to the Galilean dialect."

JOHN'S EPISTLE TO THE PARTHIANS.

With respect to the visit of John to Parthia, where it is so reasonable, and highly probable, that he labored for so many years with Peter as his colleague, we find BEDE quoting Athanasius as giving to John's first Epistle the title, "To the Parthians." Many writers have adopted the same view; among them the learned MILL (in Prolegom. in Joan. N. T. § 150). He expresses himself fully in favor of the view that John passed the greater part of his life among the Parthians and the believers near them. LAMPE (Prolegom. in Joan. Lib. 1. cap. iii. § 12, note) favors that supposition.

GROTIUS, Annot. Prolegom., suggests "that the Epistle was written to trans-Euphratic converted Jews, who were Parthian subjects, and forwarded to them by Ephesian merchants: but that the cautious Apostle, foreseeing that such a correspondence of Ephesian Christians with a hostile country, if discovered, would be hurtful to Christians in the Roman Empire in general, omitted the usual beginning and conclusion."

Jesuit missionaries in 1555 found a tradition in India, among the Bassoras, that this same Apostle presented the Gospel in that region. Baronius (Ann.–44. § 30).

As this is a matter of profound interest, throwing light on the careers of the two foremost Apostles Peter and John, we give the satisfactory language of D. F. Bacon, in his Lives of the Apostles, the most complete work in English on the subject. He says, p. 308 : "It has been considered extremely probable, by some, that John passed many years, or even a great part of his life, in the regions east of the Euphrates, within the bounds of the great Parthian empire, where a vast number of his refugee countrymen had settled after the destruction of Jerusalem ; enjoying peace and prosperity, partly forgetting their national calamities, in building themselves up into a new people, beyond the bounds of the Roman Empire. These would afford to him an extensive and congenial field of labor : they were his countrymen, speaking his own language, and to them he was allied by the sympathies of a common misfortune and a common refuge.

"Abundant proof has already been offered to show that in this region was the home of Peter, during the same period ; and probabilities are strongly in favor of the supposition that the other Apostles followed him thither, making Babylon the new Apostolic capital of the Eastern churches, as Jerusalem had been of the old one. From that city as a center, the Apostles could naturally extend their occasional labors into the countries eastward, as far as their Jewish brethren had spread their refugee settlements ; for beyond the Roman limits, Christianity seems to have made no progress whatever among the Gentiles in the time of the Apostles.

"If there had been no other difficulties, the great difference of language and manners, and the savage condition of most of the races around them, would have led them to confine their labors wholly to those of their own nation, who inhabited the country watered by the Euphrates and its branches: or still farther east, to lands where the Jews seem to have spread themselves on the banks of the Indus, and perhaps within the modern boundaries of India."

A most interesting confirmation of the spread of the Gospel in the East comes from the Egyptian author of the sixth century, COSMAS INDICO-PLEUSTES of Alexandria, A. D. 535. Dr. Lardner, vol. v. 57, writes of him: "Cosmas quotes the conclusion of the First Epistle of Peter, 'the Church which is at Babylon saluteth you,' as a proof of the early progress of the Christian religion without the bounds of the Roman Empire, by which, therefore, we perceive, he had not understood Rome, p. 101. He mentions a great many countries remote from each other, where the Gospel had been planted; and particularly, several places in the Indies, where he had been, in which were many churches. He expressly says that 'in Persia were many churches and bishops, and people, and many martyrs; as also in Ethiopia and Arabia.'"

JOHN IN BABYLON.

With reference to the Apostle John, who, as the loved of the Lord, the appointed guardian of his mother, as well as from his writings and character, is especially dear to all Christians; we have seen how little is known of his history and labors after the meeting of the Council at Jerusalem, A. D. 50. By far the most probable supposition is, as already stated, that he labored with Peter in the center of the Jewish population in Babylon.

In charge of her, most "blessed of women," he would naturally seek the most favored spot, where life was safest, and the surroundings most desirable. With Peter and his household, too, would be congenial society.

There is nothing against this supposition, while there is much in its favor. We are justified, therefore, in regard to John, in contemplating him in Babylon, till he went to Ephesus. We again quote from Bacon, p. 313, his sensible and eloquent words. "Where there is such a want of all data, any fixed decision is out of the question; but it is very reasonable to suppose that John's final departure from the East did not take place till some years after this date; probably not till the time of Domitian (A. D. 81 or 82). He had lived in Babylon, therefore, till he had seen most of his brethren and friends pass away from before his eyes. The venerable Peter had sunk into the grave, and had been followed by the rest of the Apostolic band; until the youngest Apostle, now grown old, found himself standing alone in the midst of a new generation, like one of the solitary columns of desolate Babylon, among the low dwelling places of its refugee inhabitants. But among the hourly crumbling heaps of that ruined city, the fast darkening regions of that half-savage dominion, there was each year less and less around him on which his precious labor could be advantageously expended.

"Among the subjects of the Parthian Empire, this downward movement was already fully decided; they were fast losing those refinements of feeling and thought on which the new faith could best fasten its spiritual and refining influences; they there soon became but hopeless objects to missionary exertion, when compared with the active and enterprising inhabitants of the still improving regions of the west. 'Westward,' then, 'the star' of Christianity as 'of empire took its way'; and the last of the Apostles was but following, not leading, the march of his Lord's advancing dominion, when he shook the dust of the darkening lands from his feet forever, turning his aged face toward the setting sun, to find, in his latter days, a new home and a foreign grave among the children of his brethren ; and to rejoice his old eyes with the glorious light of what God had done for the churches among the flourishing cities of the west, that were still advancing under Grecian art and Roman sway."

S. R. GREEN, in his Life of St. Peter, p. 125, also alludes forcibly to the decline of this region : "This interpretation also accounts for the fact that the records of the Apostles' latter days have perished. The memorials of those Eastern lands have passed away with the races which inhabited them. No literature survives from those once favored regions. Modern history has almost nothing to tell of them, but that they were made desolate by war ; and the cradle of the human race, once fondly chosen as the rallying point for mankind, has for ages been a solitary waste. But one memorial of that melancholy land shall survive to all time. For there it was that the Apostle Peter, before he passed away from earth, wrote his first great EPISTLE TO THE SCATTERED CHURCHES."

CHAPTER XV.

The Second Epistle of John. To whom Addressed?

An examination of the Second Epistle of the Apostle John may serve to throw further light on this deeply interesting question, with respect to the field of labor of the beloved disciple. We have noticed the tradition with respect to the most reasonable supposition, that John labored with Peter among the vast myriads of the Circumcision of Babylon and its neighborhood, under the protection of the Parthian rulers.

The language of the Second Epistle suggests that it was written by the Apostle to another *Church*, probably one in the further East, in which he had previously labored. We present the views of highly learned men on this question.

Davidson, Intro. N. Test., p. 319, says: "The words refer to a particular Christian Church, to the *Elect Church*. Even Jerome referred κυρία to the Church generally; and though the word occurs nowhere else in this sense, it is natural for the Christian Church to be called so, because of its relation to the Lord (κύριος). The *children* are the individual members of the Church. The contents of the letter agree best with the figurative sense. There is no individual reference to one person; on the contrary the children 'walk in truth'; mutual love is enjoined them as an admonition, 'Look to yourselves,' and the bringing in of 'doctrine' is mentioned. Besides it is improbable that the children of an elect sister would send a greeting by the writer to an 'elect Kyria' and her children. A sister church might naturally salute another."

Bishop Lightfoot, Epist. Col. and Phil., p. 305, remarks: "The 'salutation' to the 'elect lady' (verse ii) from her 'elect sister' (verse 13) will then be a greeting sent to one church from another; just as in 1 Pet. the letter is addressed at the outset ἐκλεκτοῖς Πόντου, κ. τ. λ. (i. 1), and contains at the close a salutation from ἐν Βαβυλῶνι συνεκλεκτή (v. 13) . . . I take the view that the κυρία addressed in the Second Epistle of John is some *church personified*. The whole tenor of the Epistle seems to imply this, especially verses 4–7, seq."

Döllinger, second to none in learning in this century, also gives his assent to the view that a *church* is here addressed. He says: "First Age of the Church," i.198: "The Second Epistle gives us the impression of being addressed to a Community, for if a private family were signified by 'the elect lady and children,' the writer could not have said that not only he, but all who knew the truth, loved the children of this elect one.

"It is then a Community or part of one that is spoken of: the Apostle rejoices that they walk in the truth, and warns them against false teachers who deny Christ's appearance in the flesh."

This interpretation is adopted also by Cassiodorus, Calov, Hammond, Hoffman, Mayer, Huther, Augusti, Baur, and Ewald.

BISHOP WORDSWORTH'S ARGUMENT.

No one has, probably, discussed this question more fully, more ingeniously, and intelligently than Bishop Wordsworth, on the Canon, 226-232:

"Let me here desire your attention to a remarkable connection between the First Epistle of St. Peter, and the *Second* of St. John.

"The First Epistle of St. Peter, as appears from its commencement, is addressed to the '*Elect*,' scattered throughout Pontus, Galatia, Cappadocia, Asia, and Bithynia: that is, to the Jews dispersed in *Asia* Minor: and at its close we read ' The Church that is at *Babylon, elected* together with you, salute you and so doth *Marcus* my son.'

"The Second Epistle of St. John begins thus: ' The Elder to the *Elect Lady* and her children whom I love in the truth :' and it ends with the words, ' The children of thine Elect Sister greet thee.'

"You are aware that it has been doubted *what* place the *Babylon* was from which St. Peter wrote: and also whether the *Elect Lady* to whom St. John wrote was a person or a church.

"If I may venture to offer an opinion on these controverted points, it seems to me that both these questions may be determined at once ; and that, by the solution of them, we gain an important result with respect to the Canon of the New Testament.

"In some ancient manuscripts, St. John's *First* Epistle is inscribed *ad Parthos*—to the Parthians—and as is probable from earlier authorities, as well as from internal evidence, this inscription belongs to St. John's *Second* Epistle, *as well as* the First. For the *Latin Translator* of a work of Clement of Alexandria (the Greek original of which is not now extant) says, ' *Secunda* Johannis Epistola, quæ ad *Virgines* inscripta est, simplicissima est.' It has been well conjectured that St. Clement wrote πρoς Παρϑoυς (ad Parthos) which was corrupted into προς Παρθενους, whence the *Latin Translator* wrote ' *ad Virgines* '; and this is almost certain from the fact that none of St. John's Epistle is addressed to Virgins; and St. Clement himself says that the Second Epistle was written to a certain *Babylonian*, and that the word Electa, the Elect Lady, intimates the *election* of a *Church*. St. Jerome gives the same meaning of the word Electa; he applies it to a church; and this is still further confirmed by the word Κυρία, or *Lady*, which is very appropriate to a church (Κυριακη) as connected with Κύριος, the Lord.

"But what is to be said of the word *Babylonia*, to whom St. Clement affirms St. John wrote an Epistle; and how is it to be connected with the inscription " Ad Parthos '—to the Parthians ?

"I would suggest the following reply :

"St. Peter was the Apostle of the Jews, and he was the beloved fellow Apostle of St. John; he addresses his First Epistle to the Jews of the Asiatic dispersion; that is, to those of St. John's peculiar province : and he closes his Epistle with the salutation. ' Your *co-elect* Sister Church at *Babylon* salutes you and so doth *Marcus* my son.' And St. John, the brother Apostle of St. Peter, *Elect* together with him—St. John, specially loved by Christ, as Christ was specially by St. Peter—St. John the Metropolitan of the *Elect* of Asia, whom St. Peter had addressed, writes to the *Elect* Lady and her children, *whom he loves in the truth*, and he closes his Epistle with the salutation, ' The children of thine Elect Sister greet thee.'

"' *The Elect Lady*,' I believe was the Church of *Babylon*, and the ' *Elect Sister* ' the Asiatic Church.

"Hence St. Clement says that St. John writes to a

Babylonian Electa, signifying an *Elect Church;* and also according to the conjecture already mentioned to the Parthians, of whose empire, as it *then* existed, *Babylon*, it must be remembered, was the most celebrated city—as far as the Jews and their history are concerned. Hence, Milton thus speaks:

> There Babylon the wonder of all tongues.
>   .   .   .   .   .
> All these the Parthian holds!

"Babylon was the city *to* which the *two* tribes were carried away captive, and *from* which those of the *Asiatic* dispersion, to whom St. Peter writes, were derived; and we know, from Philo and Josephus, that Babylon contained a great many Jews in the Apostolic age.

"In fact, the Second (and perhaps, also the First) Epistle of St. John, who is said to have preached the Gospel in Parthia, appears to have been written to the *Elect* Church of the *Parthian* Assyrian, of which Babylon was the head; and to be of the nature of a *reply* to St. Peter's First Epistle to the '*Elect* of *Asia*'; written from the same Babylon, and bearing the salutation of the *co-elect* Church of that city.

"But what, it may now be asked, had *St. Peter* to do with the *Assyrian* Babylon?

"In reply to this inquiry let me remind you that it has been well observed that there is something very significant in the *arrangement* of the names of the countries specified by the inspired writer of the *Acts* of the *Apostles*, in his enumeration of the Jews of the dispersion who had flocked to Jerusalem on the Day of Pentecost, and were witnesses of the effects of the descent of the Holy Ghost on the Apostles, and listened to *St.*

Peter's sermon on that day, by which three thousand souls were added to the Church. 'How hear we every man in our tongue wherein we were born?'

"Let us remark the sacred historian's order. First 'Parthians, Medes, and Elamites, and the dwellers in Mesopotamia and Judea.' These were the Jews of the dispersion of the two tribes and of the ten tribes, and these Jews of the dispersion of the two tribes and the ten tribes were now subject to the *Parthians*, whence the *Parthians* are named *first;* and of these the metropolis was *Babylon*.

"Next come those of the Asiatic dispersion, who were *derived* from Babylon, and are called in the Acts, 'the dwellers in Cappadocia, Pontus and Asia, Phrygia and Pamphylia.'

"Hence we see why St. Peter the Apostle of the circumcision went to *Baylon*—the Parthian Babylon. It was the headquarters of those whom he himself had addressed with such wonderful success at Jerusalem on the day of Pentecost, and who are named *first* by the inspired historian of the Acts.

"Hence, also, we see why, being at Babylon, St. Peter addressed an Epistle to the 'strangers *scattered* throughout Pontus, Galatia, Cappadocia, Asia, and Bithynia: they were derived *from* Babylon; they were *co-elect* with the church there. He had preached to them also at Jerusalem; and they are placed *second* by the inspired writer of the Acts.

"Hence, also, the Apostle St. John, who was stationed in Asia, among these strangers of the dispersion there, and who had been St. Peter's inseparable companion at Jerusalem, and is particularly noticed as such in the Acts of the Apostles, takes up St. Peter's language, and responds from Asia to Parthia, from Ephesus to Babylon, from the *Elect Sister* of the one, to the Elect Lady of the other.

"Hence, also, we shall see the appropriateness of the mention of *St. Mark* in St. Peter's salutation, 'Thy co-elect sister greeteth thee, and so doth *Marcus my Son.*'

"For, if we turn back to the enumeration in the Acts, we find first, as I have said, the *Parthian* or Assyrian dispersion; secondly, the Asiatic derived from the Parthian; thirdly and *lastly*, the *Egyptian*, who were carried from Judea into Egypt by Ptolemy Lagus, or, as they are called by the sacred historian of the Acts, 'those of *Egypt and in the parts of Libya about Cyrene*, Jews and Proselytes, Cretes and Arabians; we do hear them speak in our own tongues the wonderful works of God.'

"These three dispersions were, if we may so speak, St. Peter's audience at Jerusalem on the day of Pentecost, and they were the spiritual *Province* of that Apostle —the Apostle of the Circumcision.

"Now observe, how did St. Peter provide for all these three dispersions which made up his Province? He provided for the *first*, that of Babylon, by visiting them in person. He provided for the *second*, the *Asiatic*, by writing to it from Babylon.

"He provided for the *third*, the *Egyptian*, by sending to them *Marcus his son*, who was the first Bishop of Alexandria.

"Thus St. Peter, writing from Babylon to Asia and sending the salutation of Mark, connects all the three dispersions together. Thus he took care of them all.

"Time and the occasion do not allow that I should say anything here on the reply derived from these results, to the Romish identification of the Babylon of St. Peter's Epistle with *Rome*, and on the claim to universal spiritual supremacy set up for St. Peter, and through him for the Bishop of *Rome*: neither of which allegations is compatible with what has now been submitted for your consideration."

In a note Bishop Wordsworth adds: "After the above had been written, I read with pleasure the following words of Estius (in Epis. 1. Joh. Praef. p. 1201, ed. Rothermag 1709): 'The tradition of the ancients is that John's Epistle was written to the *Parthians:* Hence the title which Pope Hyginus gives it, Epist. I, Possidius in Indic. op. Augustini, and Augustine himself, Quæst. Evang. ii. c. 39; moreover, Pope John the Second in Epist. ad Valerium Episcopum. He writes to the Parthians, who were a neighboring nation to the Medes, for in that region were many Jews of the ancient dispersion of the ten tribes, whence in Acts, chapter second, the Parthians are first named. Wherefore, just as Peter sent his Epistle to the Jews of the Dispersion in Pontus, etc., whom Luke enumerated later, so also John wrote to the Jews in the East, that is in Parthia and the neighboring localities, not but that each Apostle desired that his Epistle should be communicated also to the Gentiles of those regions who believed in Christ and were members of his church.'"

Bishop Wordsworth also remarks: "If anyone is disposed to doubt whether the Babylon of St. Peter is the Babylon of Assyria, let me refer him to Lightfoot's sermon on 1 Peter v. 13. vol. ii. p. 1144." See p. 87.

Prebendary TOWNSEND, Notes N. Test., 1 Epist. St. John, has presented valuable and suggestive thoughts, which serve to throw light on a subject concerning which we have no authenicated facts, but simply conjectures, and a balance of probabilities, by which to determine our judgment.

He says: "A more important question is, whether St. John lived exclusively among the Greek cities of Asia, in the interval between the overthrow of Jerusalem and the banishment to Patmos in the last year of Domitian. This cannot be satisfactorily decided. The learned Mill places some dependence upon the tradition that the Apostle traveled into Parthia and Asia.

"His first Epistle was called, by Augustine, the Epistle to the Parthians; and the Jesuits' Letters cited by Baronius, affirm that the people of a town in India believed the Gospel to have been preached there by St. John; and the same is asserted, as I find by Lampe, by the people of a town in Arabia.

"It is not probable that he would immediately establish himself in Ephesus, as Timothy, who is generally declared by the ecclesiastical historians to have been bishop of that place, was probably still alive.

"Others, whose opinion is strongly condemned by Lampe, have been of the opinion that St. John did not take up his residence in Ephesus till near the end of the reign of Domitian. This opinion seems to be supported by the little remaining evidence which can enable us to come to any decision on a point so obscure. The Apostles were commanded to preach throughout the world, and they would probably have adopted that plan which they are said to have done, that each should take his peculiar district, and to that direct his attention.

"As part, at least, of Asia Minor had been placed under the care of Timothy, it is not unlikely that St. John would have traveled to other parts of the East before he came to Ephesus, to reside there. The course of his travels might have been from the east of Judea to Parthia and round from thence to India, and returning by Arabia to Asia, he there preached and founded the churches of Smyrna, Pergamus, Thyatira, Sardis, Philadelphia, Laodicea, and others. These he might have established at the conclusion of his route.

"In Parthia, India, and Arabia, he would not have required the Greek language, and during the short period which elapsed between his arrival in Asia and his banishment at the latter end of the reign of Domitian, he would have been more likely to have acquired that kind of language which we find in the Apocalypse, than the more polished style of the Epistles and the Gospel. The former shows less acquaintance with the language than the latter; and the fact is fully accounted for, if we suppose that the Apostle, when he wrote the Apocalypse, had not so frequent intercourse with the people as at a subsequent period; and the course of his travels explains the causes of this fact.

"If we may thus decide respecting the travels of St. John after the destruction of Jerusalem, we reconcile many of the various traditions of antiquity, and account for the difference between the language of the Apocalypse, and the other writings of the Apostle."

Note.—W. M. Thomson, Land and Book, 431, says that John was in Jerusalem, A. D. 50 or 52. Acts xv. "Mary must have been between sixty-five and seventy years of age. If St. John subsequently went to Babylon, before removing to Ephesus, as many suppose, it is highly probable that he had fulfilled the honorable mission of our Lord, in respect to the care of his mother, and that shortly after her decease he left Jerusalem."

CHAPTER XVI.

Results of Inquiry Thus Far.

In our examination of Scripture and ancient authors for a century after the death of Peter, we have not been able to find a trace of him in Rome, or west of Cæsarea. The historian of the Apostles gives no account of his later labors, nor of any visit to the West. Clement, his contemporary, speaks of his abundant labors, and of Paul's, and his language fairly intimates that he did not, like Paul, travel to the West. Ignatius mentions Peter's name, but, writing to Rome, does not refer to him as present there. Justin, Barnabas, Polycarp, and Hermas of the second century do not notice him, an omission which cannot be reconciled with his presence in Rome. The Prince of the Apostles could not thus be ignored.

Dr. LARDNER, the most noted advocate of the Peter-Roman legend, was found to have presented no conclusive evidence in the affirmative, nor to have advanced any reason why Peter should not have labored in Babylon.

Canon FARRAR, who adopts the story of Peter's Roman visit, it was seen, presents no sufficient argument for its reception: enough to answer its exceeding improbability.

Dr. SAMSON, who strongly asserts the Apostle's early visit and death at Rome, was answered, in general, by an extended Catena of the views of English and Continental writers, who deny his position. What these three critics have not presented to establish the residence of Peter in Rome, it is not necessary to notice.

It has been stated, that the great volume of modern opinion of Protestant scholars is against Rome as the field of Peter's labors. Before establishing the fact, a more specific reply will be made to the points of evidence in the affirmative, as enumerated by Dr. Samson.

DR. SAMSON'S ARGUMENT NOTED.

Dr. Samson says, "universal historical testimony makes Rome the city referred to" (as Babylon), and that "the early Christian writers all agree," with respect to the "visit to Rome."

The reply to this is, that it has been shown that no writer for a hundred years after Peter's death speaks of the Roman visit. With respect to the later writers whom he enumerates, the rest of the Examination in this volume will be devoted to their opinions.

That Paul mentions Peter in his first letter to Corinth is regarded as an evidence of Peter's visit there, and subsequently to Rome.

To this it may be said that because it is stated that there was a Petrine party in Corinth, this did not demand a visit from Peter, for the Jews who held to the law of Moses, everywhere appealed to Peter; and moreover it is noticeable that while Paul asserts that he "planted and Apollos watered," he omits to state that Peter likewise labored, which he could not have failed to do if Peter had been present in Corinth.

As to "likenesses between the two Apostles' epistles, indicating personal association and intercourse in

Rome"; Peter was attended by Silvanus and Mark, two of Paul's intimates, who had probably carried to Babylon the letters of Paul, about which they naturally frequently conversed.

In our examination of the relation of Mark to Peter, it has been seen that there is no evidence that Mark wrote his Gospel in Rome under the supervision of Peter, but that the probabilities are far stronger that the work was done in Babylon. Eminent Roman Catholic authorities were given, who confirm this view.

With respect to Dr. Samson's opinion that Peter was in Rome in the time of Claudius and subsequently, this is ably controverted by Ellendorf, a Roman Catholic, pp. 64, 65. Farrar quotes several Roman Catholic authors in proof that Peter could not have been in Rome till the days of Nero, p. 67. See also p. 59, for the further discussion of this point.

The argument that Peter visited Rome because of "influence among Romans," in consequence of the conversion of Cornelius, does not hold good, inasmuch as the Apostle, though providentially selected as the first to preach the Gospel to the Gentiles, was not fitted, by education or training, to evangelize the West. This was the province of the accomplished and eloquent Paul, while Peter was the appointed minister to the Circumcision, for which he was eminently fitted; which office he successfully filled at Babylon, the center and headquarters of the Jewish dispersions. No sufficient or controlling motive has ever been advanced to draw Peter from Babylon to Rome; nor would the statement ever have been made, but for a desire to aggrandize a particular Church. This aggrandizement, produced by a perversion of history, has been the source of evil to the Church, and to the world, such as cannot be described nor estimated.

It has been seen that the most probable and convincing supposition is that Peter and John labored conjointly among the Circumcision in Babylon, and the East. There was a natural and earnest desire on the part of both, and of the other Apostles, to see those converted and baptized on the day of Pentecost, who sojourned in Parthia, and the neighboring countries; and also the multitudes who had annually come up in the years succeeding Pentecost, and to whom the Gospel by them had been preached. These converts needed visitation, instruction, and encouragement, and it would have been almost inconceivable that the Apostles, after leaving Jerusalem, could have neglected such an obvious duty. The more this subject is contemplated, the more light and interest it throws upon the work of the Apostles, whose death and burial Providence appears to have concealed from the knowledge of men, as in the case of Moses, to prevent that worship which superstition would have offered to their remains, if found. We know the result with regard to the fictitious bones and imaginary grave of Peter, and it was a kind and merciful arrangement that history cannot throw a ray of light with respect to the grave of one of the Apostles. "No man knoweth of their sepulchers unto this day." We have a tradition with respect to Paul, but no facts on which to base a correct judgment with regard to his burial place. It is a matter of no importance—it is a sad reflection on human weakness and depravity that there are those who appear to be more desirous to pay reverence to the bones of a departed Apostle, than to obey that doctrine which was given to them by inspiration, and through which they have inherited eternal glory.

CATENA OF AUTHORITIES.

In proof of our position, that modern scholarship has rendered a verdict in favor of Parthian Babylon as the residence and field of labor of Peter's later years, we present the names of writers who maintain this view.

CONTINENTAL AUTHORS.

Calvin, Beza, Bengel, Beausobre, Basnage, Drusius, Gerhardus, Gomarus, Vorstius, Scaliger, Salmasius, Turretin, Suicer, Schleusner, Michaelis, Valesius, Junius, Vedelius, Pareus, Estius, Lipsius, Wiesler, Wettstein, Pott, Weiss, L'Enfant, Grimm, Von Ammon, Niebuhr, Keil, Berthold, Steiger, Neander, Rosenmuller, Mayerhoff, Bleek, Ruetschl, Herzog, DeWette, Reiche, Barth, Credner, Nendecker, Huther, Kuhl, Bruckner, Winer, Meyer, Guerike, Fronmuller, Kurtz, Reuss, Presensé, Bouzique, Gavazzi.

ENGLISH WRITERS.

Among English scholars who agree with the above in regarding Peter as writing from Babylon in the East, are: Whittaker, Willet, Rainolds, Bishops Bale and Andrews, Lightfoot, Mede, Echard, Bowen, Cradock, Bps. Cumberland and Conybeare, Prideaux, Trapp, M. Henry, Doddridge, Benson, Campbell, Adam Clarke, Gill, Scott, Stillingfleet, Stackhouse, Dodwell, Allix, Peile, Hawker, Milman, Robins, Dick, Hill, Edgar, Kitto, Wm. Smith, D. Brown, J. H. Brown, McGavin, Bloomfield, Simon, Greenwood, Angus, Alford, Littledale, Salmoud, Kennion, Young, J. C. Gray, Johnstone,

Blaikie, Cobbin, J. Brown of Edinburgh, J. Brown of Haddington, Lillie, Maclean, McGuire, John Wesley, Bishops Ellicott, Cotterill, Wordsworth, Thorold, and Jones ; Archbishop Thomson, Davidson, Darby, Bentley, Wright, J. Martin, J. Owen, Kennard, W. Palmer, Howson, Conybeare, Ayton, Stanley, J. H. Blunt, Nichols, Exell, Houseman, A. Bishop, Witherow, Adolphus, Edersheim, D. Fraser, Littlewood, Dalton, Boutelle, Robertson, Plumptre, Arrowsmith, Shepherd, Geikie, J. Farrar, McDuff, Eadie, Dodds, Powell, Lewin, S. R. Green, J. Spence, B. W. Newton, Fairbairn, Hatch in Encyc. Brit., Young's Concise Dictionary, Oxford Teacher's Bible, Cambridge Bib. Com., Pulpit Com., Christian Kn. Soc. Com., Annot Par. Bib., Faussett's Bib. Cyc., Relig. Tract Soc., London, N. Brit. Rev., November, 1848, Edinburgh Rev., July, 1893.

AMERICAN SCHOLARS.

Of American writers who hold to Peter's Babylonian residence we have : M. Stuart, Barnes, Barrows, Murdock, Bacon, Elliott, Crosby, Shimeall, Blackwood, Demarest, Fisher, Chambers, Nourse, Harwood, Richardson, E. J. Smith, S. M. Jackson, T. V. Moore, C. P. Jones, C. M. Butler, Pond, J. G. Butler, Abbot and Conant, McClintock and Strong, C. Hodge, Justin Edwards, M. R. Vincent, Bomberger, Harman, B. B. Edwards, Covel, Blackman, Taylor, Binney and Steele, Hague, Whedon, Nast, Jacobus, McDonald, E. M. Hunt, Mombert, Coleman, Dowling, L. A. Sawyer, J. H. Thayer, Broadus, E. C. Mitchell, J. T. Wheeler, Goodrich, Magoun, Shedd, Stowe, A. Bond, J. M. Pendleton, J. H. Hopkins, Kittredge, J. N. Hallock, N. Lawrance, A. E. Dunning, A. R. Wells, M. B. Grier,

E. T. Tomlinson, J. R. Miller, Etter, J. M. Frost, J. M. McDonald, Kephart, J. H. Potts, J. F. Berry, E. H. Dewart, A. H. Vail, J. R. Young, Un. Bib. Dict., M. B. Riddle, Am. Sup. to Encyc. Brit., Benton's Ch. Encyc., Clarke and Williams Am. Com., Inglis Bible Text Encyc., Bible Dict. Am. Tr. Soc., Union Bib. Dict., Princeton Review.

We have seen that Calmet, De Marca, Marsillius, John Baptist Mantuan, Michael de Ceza, John Aventin, Leland, Caron, Hardouin, Dumoulin, Dupin, Erasmus, Hug, De Cormenin, and Ellendorf—distinguished Roman scholars—adopt the generally received view of learned Protestants.

On pages 7–17 we have likewise presented the names of thirty additional eminent writers who have expressed their belief that Peter never visited Rome. These necessarily regarded the East as the scene of his labors.

In addition to these names Dr. Kitto adds those of Baur and Eichorn. Professor Hatch, in Encyc. Britan., gives those of Gundert, Holzman, Hausrath, and Zeller. With these also agree Zanchius, Funccius, Spanheim, Sutcliffe, Hospinian, Sibrandus, Flaccius Illyricus, Schleiermacher, Schwegler, Hase, and Froschammer.

Opposed to the mystical interpretation of Bellarmine and other Papal authors, are likewise the fourteen scholars ennumerated on p. 71, who hold that the Babylon of Peter was in Egypt; moreover, the four who regard Jerusalem as referred to.

THE RESULT REACHED.

We have thus enumerated the names of over 330 prominent theological writers, and among them the most noted authors known; fifteen of whom are eminent Roman authors, who have publicly declared their belief that the Apostle Peter never labored or ruled in Rome; and with few exceptions teach that he never set foot in Rome, or traveled west of Palestine.

A few, relying on the uncertain traditions of ancient authors, regard it as possible that he was brought to Rome to die.

When we reflect that the Roman Fabric has been constructed on Peter as a foundation; that Popes and Councils, and Bulls and Standards, and Roman scholars pronounce that Peter was Prince of the Apostles, Head of the Church, and that Rome was the Center and Seat of his supreme authority; that from him as Bishop of Rome, comes down to his successors in that See universal dominion over all mankind, supreme power over all princes and governments; that they possess the attribute of Infallibility, with respect to the expounding of the truth, and that from them there is no appeal; and then, when, per contra, we consider that the enlightened, unprejudiced, learning and scholarship of the world, (for Roman Catholics are not permitted to question or oppose the determinations of their Church, and are bound to sustain the position of the Pope,) has shown that there is no proof extant in God's Word, or in any historic document within a century of Peter, that he ever saw Rome, or ever left the East; that there is no foundation in truth for the claims of Rome; that the Roman bishop had no righteous jurisdiction outside of Italy; can we fail to perceive that, ere long, this baseless superstructure must crumble, and that the Truth which is mighty must prevail, and men be delivered from this bondage to superstition, and to a hoary, world-wide, and stupendous delusion.

THE RESULT REACHED. 149

In lands where liberty prevails, where education is universal, light will spread, the truth will become known, and the claims of Rome will be rejected, necessarily. And we would be glad to see that Church, repudiating all that is false in the past, and conforming herself to the inspired, infallible Word of God, and to the Light of the present age, become the teacher of the truth, and return to the simplicity and purity which characterized her in her primitive history, before she was corrupted and contaminated by worldly prosperity, and the seductions of temporal power.

Set free from her alliance with the world, casting aside mere human traditions; adhering to the truths taught by Peter, her assumed Founder, and by Paul, her divinely appointed Evangelist; directing her followers to Christ the only Mediator and Priest; adopting a Spiritual and Intelligent worship; she may look for the presence and gift of the Holy Spirit; she may become a blessing to mankind, and augment the glory of God in the conversion, enlightenment, and salvation of souls.

This whole question might be regarded as settled by the general consent of the most enlightened scholarship as here shown; but as other writers of Antiquity of great authority have been appealed to, who would seat Peter in Rome, these will be examined in detail, in order to learn if their testimony is of value, and can reverse the verdict which has been here rendered.

CHAPTER XVII.

Rome's Appeal to Antiquity.

In our investigation of this question we have presented all authentic documents, Inspired and human, which have come down to us from Antiquity to the year 170, which could throw light upon Peter's relation to the city of Rome.

Not one word has been discovered which asserts that this Apostle was ever in Rome, or in the West.

This ought to be sufficient to settle the matter historically; but inasmuch as the Church of Rome has presented other documents to prove her position, we will briefly examine them.

THE CLEMENTINA.

All these documents can be readily shown to be Romances, upon which all later traditions are based. Those styled the Predicatio Petri and the Clementines are the imaginative literature of the Christians of that age, who were able to read the manuscripts of that time. These works are similar to the Chronicles of the Cid; the tales of Roland; the stories of Arthur; and more recently the Scottish Chiefs; all fictitious narratives of the exploits of veritable heroes.

Cotelerius, an eminent Roman Catholic critic, classes the Predicatio Petri among "libri Pseudopigraphi Apocryphi;" and says that it was written by a person "painfully unskilled in writing, and putting together fictitious narratives." (Pat. Ap. i. 490.)

Simon, who has written the most exhaustive treatise in English on the Petrine claims, states (p. 30): "Its name seems to have been one of the main sources of the modern error about Peter's having left the East. As to its supposed testimony, however, upon this subject, the book in question is not now extant, nor is there any extract from it, in which it is pretended that there is the slightest allusion to anything of the kind."

Ellendorf, a Roman Catholic, writes: "The Church has had her time of fables. . . The Recognitions, etc, were invented. The period of these fictions belongs to the second and third centuries, and it coincides with that in which the authorities above quoted lived." (Bib. Sac., Jan., 1859, p. 99.)

Mosheim, writes (vol. i. p. 75): "The Apostolic Canons, Constitutions, the Recognitions of Clement, and the Clementina were fraudulently ascribed to this eminent father by some deceiver, for the purpose of giving them greater authority. This all now concede."

Professor Addison Alexander, on the Apostolical Constitutions, says: "They were rejected by the *Concilium Quinsextum* (692), and also by Baronius and Daillé, and are now generally given up."

Of these same writings, Riddle, in his Christian Antiquities, quotes Professor Burton of Oxford (p. 60). "They are such palpable forgeries, if they were really meant to deceive, that it would be a waste of critical labor to prove that they were not written by Clement."

Harnack, a recent critic, terms them, "a Jewish-Christian partisan romance."

"It is the work of a Judaizing Christian according to a

very peculiar form of Ebionitism. Abundantly proved by Schlieman and Neander."—Milman's Lat. Chr.

"The legend about Peter's bishopric at Rome (according to Eusebius, from the years 42–67) is derived from the heretical pseudo-Clementines and Recognitions, an authority entirely untrustworthy."—Kurtz, Church History, i. 65.

"So many Apocryphal Gospels, Epistles, Itineraries, Passions, as are counterfeited under the name of Apostles and ancient Fathers; who knoweth not to be fables and false inventions, among which this fable of Simon Magus and Peter is one."—Dr. Fulke, Wks., ii. 339.

Father Tillemont speaks of the Clementina as "full of fallacies and fables."

Father Dupin says: "All these writings are only a series of fictions and idle stories." The Dominican Father Cellier characterizes it in the same way.

"Baronius, another Romanist, calls the Recognitions attributed to Clement 'a gulf of uncleanness and filth, full of prodigious lies and forgeries.'" Nourse on Fathers. Prot. Rev., Oct., 1847, 310.

These fictions represent Clemens Romanus a noble writer (Simon's Miss. and Martyrdom of Peter, p. 54), meeting with Peter in the East, who becomes his companion in his journey.

What Peter taught, and how the father, mother, and brother of Clement are recognized and converted, are interwoven into the romance.

Peter's contests with Simon Magus are narrated, and his sending of twelve missionaries to follow Simon to Rome; but no mention is made of Peter's journey thither in the "Recognitions," though in the "Epitome" of the Recognitions there is an allusion to it. In the

Clementines, for the first time, Peter is called Bishop of Rome.

"All the Roman Catholic writers," Simon writes, p. 54, "are unanimous in declaring the 'Clementina' in unmeasured terms a mere tissue of lies and nonsense."

SAWYER, in Organic Christ., p. 49, remarks: "A Christian in the latter part of the second century undertook to resolve the principal exciting questions of his time, by a work of fiction under the title of *Ta Klementia*. Memories of Clement ; consisting of three Prologues and twenty Homilies, pretending to reveal the Apostolic traditions.

"To obviate any objections which it might encounter from its late appearance, it was prefaced by a letter from the Apostle Peter to James, in which the latter is requested to communicate the Homilies only to trustworthy brethren, under the seal of secrecy upon oath. Hom. ii. 17.

"This book makes Clement in his travels in pursuit of knowledge meet Peter in the East, from whom he receives the Gospel. In a letter of Peter to James, he gives the latter the title of Lord and Bishop of bishops, and makes him the superior of the two. It also represents, contrary to fact, Peter the true Apostle to the Gentiles, and the founder and first bishop of the Church of Rome. The work immediately gained credit at Rome, and was modified and circulated under the title of the Recognition of Clement about A. D. 230.

"These were followed by another pious forgery of the Constitution of the Apostles, written near the close of the third century. Till the latter part of the third century, the Roman Episcopacy of Peter is asserted by the Recognitions of Clement alone : a work of about

equal authority and honesty with the Book of Mormon."
—Murdock's Mosheim, i. p. 184.

As this work makes Peter Bishop of Rome, and subordinate to James, Bishop of Jerusalem, if it was of any worth as testimony, it overthrows the claim of the Pope as supreme Bishop, and that Church is welcome to it.

Dr. SALMON, in Christ. Biog., Art. Clem. Lit., an exhaustive treatise, says: "The scene of the story is all laid in the East, and the writings show no familiarity with the Roman Church. . . All through, it is James of Jerusalem, not Peter, who is represented as the supreme ruler of the Churches."

The Clementines have been here thoroughly ventilated, to show how the story of Peter's Western visit was enabled to obtain so wide a circulation, and to be so largely credited in the third century and later. IT IS THE FOUNTAIN HEAD OF THE ROMAN PETRINE CLAIMS.

DR. GEORGE P. FISHER.

Among the valuable, interesting contributions to Church history by Professor Geo. P. Fisher, is that on "Ebionitism" in the American Presbyterian Review, 1864, p. 540. He speaks of the Clementine Homilies as "a spurious production, the work of an unknown writer, and abounding in fantastic, anti-Christian ideas which could never have gained the assent of a sober-minded Christian; it represents the opinions of an individual, and not the sentiments of any important body of Christians."

How these fictions were employed in later writers to disseminate untruths, he illustrates by presenting a recent similar translation.

"Toward the close of the American Revolution there

appeared in London a history of Connecticut from the pen of Rev. Samuel Peters, who had been a missionary in Hebron in that State, but he had left in consequence of the unpopularity he had incurred by taking the side of the English Government. The work, though prefaced by protestations of fidelity and painstaking, is an odd mixture of fact and fiction. Among other fabulous stories, Peters promulgated the notion that unrecorded laws, which are styled "blue laws," of an ascetic and whimsical severity, were in force among the early Puritans of the colony. This singular, mendacious chronicle is thought worthy to be cited, though not without some expressions of distrust, by so recent an author as the worthy Dr. Hussey, in the Bampton lectures upon the history of the observance of Sunday.

"Now what would be thought of an historical critic who, at some time in the remote future, should take Peters for the governing authority in his investigation of the ancient history of Connecticut? Other documents, let it be supposed, are extant which have been universally regarded as authentic. But these, together with historians like Bancroft and Palfrey, who lived much nearer the events, and were in possession of a great amount of traditionary and documentary evidence which has since perished, he chooses to set aside. Such a course would match that taken by the critics who would convert the Clementine fiction into an authority sufficient to override the foremost historical testimonies."

And yet these fictions are the basis of the later traditions that Peter traveled to Rome, and founded there the Church of Christ.

We are justified in saying in the words of the learned

Lipsius—"At the close of the first, and up to the beginning of the second century, there was in Pauline circles, inside and outside of Rome, no knowledge of Peter's labors in that city; no knowledge of his martyrdom there under Nero." (Pres. Quar., April, 1876, p. 272.)

DIONYSIUS OF CORINTH.

The works of this bishop, A. D. 170, are lost. We have an extract in Eusebius (ii. 25), A. D. 340, which reads thus: "So also now, you by this your admonition, have again blended into one, that plantation of the Romans and Corinthians, which was first sown by Peter and Paul; for both having planted *us* here in Corinth, taught us in like manner, and then in like manner and place, having taught in Italy, they bore their testimony about the same time." This was addressed to Soter, Bishop of Rome.

On this passage Sawyer remarks: "The genuineness of this is much doubted. It certainly is false."

GLOAG, Intro. Cath. Epistles, p. 150, writes: "The earliest of the Fathers, Dionysius of Corinth, lived a hundred years after the death of Peter, and during that period there was ample time for the rise and growth of the legend concerning the death of Peter."

In a review of Dr. SCHELER on St. Peter, in N. Brit. Rev., Nov., 1848, p. 31, of Dionysius it is said: This father bears the earliest witness to the martyrdom of St. Peter at Rome, provided the epistle attributed to him by Eusebius was a genuine document. Its authenticity is, however, much doubted. At all events, the last part of the sentence of Dionysius is in direct contradiction to Eusebius (Hist. Eccl., ii. 25, iii. i.; Tertullian Contra Marc., iv. 25, and Lactantius de Mort.

Persecut., ch. ii.): the former with St. Paul's First Epistle to the Corinthians, iv. 15; compare iii. 6, 10; ix. 1, 2 ; and lastly, the remaining assertion of St. Peter having accompanied St. Paul on his journey to Rome, with the account of St. Luke, Acts xxviii."

SHEPHERD in his "History of the Church of Rome," p. 532, regards the extract from Dionysius a forgery.

" Paul is expressly contradicted. He declares, ' I have planted. Apollos watered.' Strange treatment of Peter, if he too had taught at Corinth ! Marvelous that Clement, a century previous in his Epistle to the Corinthians, when he appeals to all the holy authorities, to the Scriptures, the saints, and to Paul's Epistles, should have omitted the Apostle who ordained him at Rome, who had preached in Corinth, provided the statement of Dionysius is true."

On this statement, made a century after Peter's death, supported by no previous contemporary writer, contradicted by the words of Scripture, we can place no reliance.

Ellendorf accounts for the language of Dionysius whom he regards as "a well-informed and sensible man," thus : " In his time the oldest churches everywhere were striving to deduce their origin from the most famous of the Apostles. Had the Romans drawn Peter to Rome and associated him with Paul, Corinth did not wish to be left behind ; it does the same thing. But the story found the easier reception, as we see, from First Corinthians ; there really had been *followers of Peter* at Corinth, who had likewise formed a party there. Hence it was easily concluded that Peter himself had preached the Gospel at Corinth. The journey with Paul was thus readily added to it of itself " (p. 53).

In truth, Corinth had a stronger argument in Scripture for Peter's presence there, than Rome itself.

Dr. Chas. Hodge, Intro. Com. Epist. Romans, writes: "The tradition that Peter ever was in Rome rests on very uncertain authority. It is first mentioned by Dionysius of Corinth in the latter half of the second century, and from that time seems to have been generally received.

"The account is in itself improbable, as Peter's field of labor was in the East, about Babylon : and as the statement of Dionysius is full of inaccuracies. He makes Peter and Paul the founders of the Church of Corinth, and makes the same assertion regarding the Church at Rome, neither of which is true.

"He also says that Paul and Peter suffered martyrdom at the same time at Rome, which, from the silence of Paul respecting Peter, during his last imprisonment, is in the highest degree improbable."

Dr. John Owen, describing the untrustworthiness of the Patristic writings, says : "The truth is, the corruption and fiction of the epistolical writings in the first ages was so intolerable as that very little in that kind is preserved sincere and unquestionable.

"Hence Dionysius, the Bishop of Corinth, complained that in his own time, his own epistles were so corrupted by additions and subtractions, as that it seems he would have them no more esteemed as his." Euseb. Eccles. Hist., l. iv. c. 23.

What evidence does Eusebius present that this letter to Soter was not among the garbled correspondence which Dionysius rejected as his own ? Before receiving it as worthy of any credit, proof must be given of its authenticity ; and having none, we are plainly justified in excluding it from consideration in this pre-eminently important inquiry.

That it would not be received in any Court of justice, where even a small amount of property was concerned, requires no argument.

As this statement of Dionysius is so important in its bearing on our investigation, we give the language of Eusebius in full. He writes, book iv. c. 23 : "The same author [Dionysius] writes, respecting his own epistles, as having been corrupted. 'As the brethren desired me to write epistles, I wrote them, and these the Apostles of the Devil have filled with tares, exchanging some things and adding others, for whom there is a woe reserved. It is not, therefore, matter of wonder, if some have also attempted to adulterate the Sacred Writings of the Lord, since they have attempted the same in other works that are not to be compared with these.'"

We are compelled to rule Dionysius out of the witness box, out of respect to his protestations. It is neither just nor fair, as we have not his writings, to charge him with the invention of Peter's Western journey.

It is not remarkable, that, it having been determined to aggrandize the Church of Rome at the expense of other Christian Churches, the manuscripts of the few authors which have reached us were deliberately and systematically garbled by interested writers. We have seen how the Epistle of Clement was suppressed, because so damaging to the claims of the Roman See.

CHAPTER XVIII.

Irenæus.

This author, who lived at the close of the second century, is regarded by Roman Catholic writers as giving the most decisive testimony to the fact that Peter visited Rome, and founded there the Christian Church of that city.

His language appears so direct and positive that it has misled many Protestants. He refers to "the traditions which that greatest, most ancient, and best known of all the churches, the church founded by the glorious Apostles Peter and Paul at Rome, had received from those Apostles themselves, and has handed down through a regular succession of bishops to our day."

On these words, attributed to Irenæus, has been largely built the belief that Peter labored in Rome. An examination of them proves that, if Irenæus was an intelligent or well informed writer, he could not have penned them.

Rome was not at that time "the greatest, most ancient, and best known of all the churches." The Church of Alexandria then, and for a century afterward, largely excelled that of Rome in learning, power, and influence.

Dean STANLEY writes in his "History of the Eastern Church": "The most learned body of men assembled at Nicæa was the Church of Alexandria. The see of Alexandria was then the most important in the Old

World. . . . Its episcopate was the ' Evangelical See ' as founded by the Evangelist Mark. . . . Its occupant, as we have seen, was the only potentate of the time who bore the name of 'Pope.' . . . 'The Head of the Alexandrian Church,' says Gregory Nazianzen, ' is the head of the world.' In his own province his jurisdiction was even more extensive than that of the Roman Pontiff." Such a false statement as this discredits the remainder of the story, and seems to indicate the purpose of the writer to glorify that See at the expense of the truth, and to give it more credit by attaching the name Irenæus to it.

On the erroneous principle, so common among the Fathers, that it was right to deceive, to advance the interest of religion ; this Latin scribe would be strongly tempted to augment the grandeur of the Roman See, by inventing the bombastic statement that it was " founded by the glorious Apostles Peter and Paul," with " traditions," received from the Apostles themselves, handed down " through a regular succession of bishops to our day."

On these words, for which we have no evidence that Irenæus wrote in Greek the statement they affirm, has been built up mainly the Petrine visit to Rome, and also the so-called doctrine of Apostolic Succession, which as of a personal, tactual, uninterrupted character, connected with an assumed third Divine order of Ministers, was entirely unknown to the Primitive Church previous to Cyprian, A. D. 250 ; there being no Christian writing extant in that period which mentions it. Succession of Apostolic Doctrine the Church possesses, and a ministry from the Apostles ; but not a third Divine, ecclesiastical order. This Jerome and other Fathers assert in language as clear as possible. There is no credible testimony to a second ordination to the Episcopate, previous to Cyprian. The Pope of Rome is simply a bishop, with no Divine authority over a single Presbyter, and never possessed it.

The Papal and Sacerdotal schemes, having no support in the Holy Scriptures, rest simply for acceptance on garbled, unauthentic passages from the Fathers. Both are invariably destructive of evangelic truth, and have corrupted every body of Christians which has given them countenance.

A writer in the *Christian Observer*, November, 1853, p. 745, reviewing the mission and martyrdom of St. Peter, remarks:

"We readily admit that, till we had read Mr. Simon's work, we were accustomed to understand these passages in the popular sense; and to suppose that Peter, as well as Paul, visited that city and transacted important matters there."

As this testimony was presented (if the language is that of Irenæus) nearly a century and a half after the supposed event—an event unnoticed by any authentic writing preceding the time of this author—we are justified in declining to receive it. For with Ellendorf we may rightly believe that, "no testimony of the Fathers, made a hundred and more years afterward, can impart credibility." And with Sciarelli, in the debate in Rome on Peter in 1872, p. 24: "We must distinguish the value and force of tradition according as it is brought forward to coroborate *doctrine or fact*. When we are treating of facts, not of doctrines, tradition must be divided into two periods. In the first is to be placed the testimony of those who lived shortly after the facts to be established; in the second, the testimony of those who followed in the course of years. Testimonies of the first period have a certain value, but those of the second period, without any of the first, have no value of any sort. . . Then what avails the assent of tradition which only from Irenæus to modern times has testified in their favor?"

"The nearer we approach any true event," says SHIMEALL wisely, "the more numerous should be the vouchers of its reality and authenticity ; and that, if dependent on *tradition*, that that tradition should be proved."

In this case, unfortunately for Irenæus, it has been shown, that there is not one authentic voucher for his statements with regard to Peter.

Moreover, we have to consider that Irenæus was a *Greek*, and writes in this language ; that his works are *not extant;* and what we have of him is in a *Latin* version found some *hundreds* of years afterward.

BATES, College Lect., p. 58 : "Irenæus' extant work is a treatise in five books entitled 'A Refutation of Knowledge falsely so called,' written originally in Greek ; the greater part of the first, and fragments of the other books, are extant in that language, and there is a Latin version of the whole of ancient date, quoted by Tertullian and Augustine, but the translator was indifferently acquainted either with the language or the subject."

McClintock and Strong Encyc,. Art. Irenæus, "The text both of the Greek and Latin, as far as extant, is often most uncertain, and this has made it a difficult task for translation into English."

On Irenæus, Encyc. Britan. says : "The original Greek text, except the greater part of the first book, which has been 'preserved in quotations by Hippolytus and Epiphanius, has been lost, and the treatise has been preserved in a somewhat barbarous translation."

What evidence have we that in the Latin version there were not changes made, to manufacture evidence to establish the Petrine Claim, as already advanced in the Clementine Legends, and in forgeries so glaringly manifest in much of the Ignatian Literature, designed to aggrandize the Episcopal office?

When we read what the Roman Catholic DUPIN states with respect to the "forging ecclesiastical and profane monuments," and how "the Catholics invented false histories, false miracles, and false lives of the saints to nourish and keep up the piety of the faithful," it is manifest how little credence is to be given to this second-hand version of the earliest tradition which we possess with respect to the presence of Peter in Rome; what is there to fasten the chain to Rome and Peter, when no links are to be had for over a hundred years from the Apostle's death. Dupin Eccl. Hist., Pref. p. 8.

THE FATHERS UNRELIABLE.

MOSHEIM says of the Fathers that, in their age, this among other errors was adopted, "that to deceive and lie is a virtue, when religion can be promoted by it. . . I cannot accept Ambrose, nor Hilary, nor Augustine, nor Gregory Nazianzen, nor Jerome."

No one has been better qualified to give an opinion on this subject, and no Church historian has a better reputation for candor and accuracy than this pre-eminently learned Göttingen professor. How, earlier, in the case of Dionysius of Corinth, the works of the Fathers were designedly corrupted, we have shown in the previous chapter.

Erasmus, a most erudite Roman scholar, testifies strongly to the common Patristic corruptions. He writes (in Hilarium, Epist. lib. 28): "What is this temerity with other people's books, especially those of the Ancients, whose memory is, or ought to be sacred to us . . . that everyone, according to his fancy, should shave, expunge, and take away, change, substitute:" and again (Athan., Epist.), he says: "We have given some fragments of this sort, for what purpose? You will say, That it may hence appear with what impiety the Greek scribes have raged against the monuments of such men, in which even to change a syllable is a sacrilege.

"And what has not the same temerity dared to do among the Latins, in substituting, mutilating, increasing, and contaminating the Commentaries of the Orthodox."

The Benedictine Fathers in the Preface to Basil's Wks. (Paris, 1721), remark: "It is difficult to say how great diligence must be applied by him who wishes certainly and safely to decide respecting the spuriousness or genuineness of any work; for it is wonderful, since truth and falsehood so greatly differ, yet one frequently so much resembles the other that, in distinguishing between them, we can scarcely avoid error, unless we take great care."

Giesler, i. 82: "The later traditions respecting the Apostles and Apostolic men, which have partly been indebted for their origin to the wish of many nations to trace their Christianity up to the Apostolic age, are, to say the least, uncertain, and in part so manifestly forged that they sufficiently prove their own falseness."

"I impute," says Daillé, On the Fathers, p. 16, "a great part of the cause of the mischief to those men who, before the invention of printing, were the transcribers and copiers of manuscripts, of whose negligence and boldness in the corruption of books St. Jerome very much complained even in his time, that is: 'they write not what they find, but what they understand: and where they endeavor to correct other men's errors, they show their own,'" and elsewhere Daillé says, p. 20: "Some of the Fathers made use of these kinds of forgeries, as we have formerly said: others have favored them because they served their turn."

It seems hardly just to unfavorably criticise a writer, when we have no reliable evidence that we possess his authentic works. It will be necessary, however, to dissect this imaginary Irenæus, on whom Romanists and some Protestants greatly rely to prove that Peter ruled and labored in Rome.

It is, moreover, with respect to facts, we regret to say, that Irenæus is proved to be an inconsiderate, credulous, unreliable writer. Riddle speaks of his treatise against Heresies as "badly executed—from the pen of a writer who was not thoroughly acquainted with either Greek or Latin; it contains much sound and valuable matter mingled with much also that is weak, useless, and erroneous; disfigured by many extravagant or foolish interpretations of the Scriptures."

Among his statements is that our Saviour lived to an old age, or was fifty years old at least at the time of his crucifixion. This, he says, was "the unanimous tradition and positive testimony of all the old men who had lived with St. John and the other Apostles."

Another is "that Enoch and Elias were translated

into that very Paradise from which Adam was expelled, there to remain till the consummation of all things, and here Paul was caught up."

Canon FARRAR, in "Early Days of Christianity," speaks of "the loose translation and paraphrase of Irenæus," and further he writes, p. 398 : " we are thus obliged to discount the tales and remarks for which Irenæus refers to the authority of 'the elders,' by whom he seems chiefly to mean Papias and Polycarp.

"Now Eusebius does not hesitate to say that Papias was a source of error to Irenæus, and others who relied on his antiquity. When Irenæus says that the Pastor of Hermas is canonical ; that the head of the Nicolaitans was the Deacon Nicholas ; that the version of the LXX. was written by Inspiration—we know what estimate to put on his appeals to Apostolic tradition.

"But there is an instance of mistake or credulity even more flagrant. The whole Christian world unites in rejecting the assertion that our Lord was fifty years old when he died, although Irenæus asserts it on the authority of 'Elders who received it from the Apostles.'"

On this latter point, the Ch. Quar. Review, vol. viii. p. 29, states : "'The historical value of this testimony of S. Irenæus is much weakened by a passage in an earlier part of his great work, where he asserts that all the elders who knew St. John testify that our Lord's ministry lasted from his thirtieth year till he was between forty and fifty (ii. xxii. 5), that is for more than ten years ; whereas we have certain fixed chronological data in the Gospels to dispute this view. . . The received view of the Roman Church is that A. D. 29 is the true date, following the statements of Tertullian, S. Clemens Alex.,

Julius Africanus, and Lactantius, thereby rejecting the testimony of S. Irenæus on a point where he must certainly have had more evidence to guide him than in his Chronology of the Popes; for though he obtained the latter in his mature life, and almost certainly at Rome itself, yet it is clear that the documents there, a very little later, did not agree with his statement."

Turretin thus objects to the supposed evidence of Irenæus. Opera, iii. 149.

"To the testimony of Irenæus, who would have Peter and Paul to have evangelized and established the Roman Church, lib. 3, cap. 1, § 3, we reply (1) that he has with too great credulity adopted the opinion of Papias, and has given too much credit to the tradition of the Roman Church, already vaunting itself on account of the dominating power of the city, and boasting of its descent from other Apostles; (2) His adversaries do not trust to the opinion of Irenæus, but often contradict him; (3) The words and views of Irenæus do not agree with the Papal scheme, when they ascribe to Paul and Peter equally the founding of the Church of Rome, who governed it together, and handed down with equal authority the Episcopate to Linus, lib. 5, ch. 6."

Cunningham's Hist. Theo., p. 181, has a similar view of this matter: "Irenæus does indeed profess upon several occasions to communicate to us some information which he had received by oral tradition from the Apostles; but it so happens, providentially, that in the instances in which he does this most explicitly and confidently, he alleges in one case what contradicts Scripture, and in another what is too absurd to be believed on almost any testimony." The first has respect to the error previously considered, with respect to our Lord's life.

"In the other case he gives a very childish and ridiculous description of the abundance of luxuries and of the fertillity of the soil, especially in producing grapes and wine to be enjoyed in the days of the Millennium; a description which he alleges had been handed down from the mouth of our Lord himself."

In order to see how utterly absurd is the language referred to, we quote from Irenæus, or the writer who professes to give his words.

In L. v. ch. xxx. we read: "Forasmuch as the presbyters make mention who saw John the disciple of the Lord, that they heard from him what manner the Lord spoke of those times, and he said: 'The days shall come in which vines shall be produced, each bearing ten thousand boughs, and one bough ten thousand branches, and one branch ten thousand switches, and on every switch ten thousand bunches, on every bunch ten thousand grapes, and every grape, when pressed, shall yield twenty-five measures of wine, after the same manner also a grain of wheat shall yield ten thousand ears. . . Nor am I ignorant that every ear shall have ten thousand grains, and every grain ten pounds of fine pure flour.'"

After this statement, we may regard JORTIN as correct when he says, Eccles. Hist. i.177: "I fear it will be no easy task to clear him (Irenæus) entirely from the imputation of credulity and inaccuracy."

We have, moreover, an instance of misrepresentation of Scripture, in this writer, of which we would hardly expect the original Irenæus to be guilty.

SCRIPTURE MISQUOTED.

This is seen in his language with respect to Paul's meeting—" the *bishops and presbyters* who came from

Ephesus and *other cities* adjoining, assembled in Miletus;" when he should have said that "the bishops, who were presbyters from Miletus, alone met Paul," according to Scripture.

On this matter we quote from Dean Alford, who writes:

"This circumstance began very early to contradict the growing views of the Apostolic institution and necessity of prelatical episcopacy. Thus Irenæus, iii. 14, 2, p. 201, 'In Mileto convocatis *episcopis* et presbyteris, qui erant ab Epheso *et a reliquis proximis civitatibus.*'

"Here we see (1) the two, bishops and presbyters, distinguished, as if *both* were sent for, in order that the title might not seem to belong to the same persons.

"(2) Other neighboring churches also brought in, in order that there might not seem to be *episcopoi* in one church only. That neither of these was the case, is clearly shown by the plain words of this verse; he sent to *Ephesus* and summoned *the elders of the church* (see below on *dielthon*, v. 25). So early did interested and disingenuous interpretations begin to cloud the light which Scripture might have thrown on ecclesiastical questions.

"The E. V. has hardly dealt fairly in this case with the Sacred text, in rendering *episcopous*, v. 28, 'overseers,' whereas it ought there, as in all other places, to have been '*bishops*,' that the fact of *elders and bishops having been originally and apostolically synonymous,* might be apparent to the ordinary English readers, which now it is not."

The Italics are Alford's, and show his honesty, while they display the want of candor, and the unreliability of this writer who passes for Irenæus; when seeking to elevate the position of bishop, which he himself held, and which might naturally incline him to the tradition, that the Western Church enjoyed the peculiar honor of the presence and work of Peter.

We present another brief extract from the supposed original Irenæus, which is quoted to prove Peter's presence in Rome : " Matthew published to the Hebrews in their own dialect a writing of the Gospel, while Peter and Paul were evangelizing and founding the Church of Rome.".

But the Gospel of Matthew was written five years after our Lord's Ascension—long before either of these Apostles could have visited Rome. Baronius and Calmet place it in the year 41 ; Tillemont before 39 ; Horne in 37 A. D. As Greenwood remarks (Cathedra Petri, 1, 34) : " If this be true, it is manifest that neither Peter nor Paul could have been at Rome when they founded the church there, consequently Irenæus could not have conceived the personal presence of the Apostles as necessary to the founding of a church there, nor anywhere else."

It seems necessary, therefore, in order to make Irenæus consistent with the Scriptures, and to be worthy of credit, that we regard him as using the term "founding," as other Fathers, and Roman Catholic writers. Thus Baronius writes : " What does it mean when Peter is said to have *founded* the Church of Antioch ? They are quite wrong to think that St. Peter must have gone to Antioch for that purpose ;" and again, " As Peter's chair at Alexandria, in which it cannot be shown that Peter ever was, was founded by that Apostle, it is quite evident that his presence was not necessary to found even a patriarchal see."

TILLEMONT writes: "They hold that Peter founded the See of Alexandria, and that he did so by the instrumentality of St. Mark."

May not Peter be truly said to have been the founder of the Church of Rome through the instrumentality of those strangers of Rome who were converted by his preaching on the Day of Pentecost?

"It may well be believed," writes one, "that among this multitude, as many as one hundred returned to Rome, believers in Christ. By these, Peter's spiritual children, a Church in Rome was constituted. And a few years after St. Paul could write, 'To all who be in Rome, beloved of God, called to be saints.' And thus, as Irenæus himself says, whose testimony we are now considering. 'These are the words of the Church at Jerusalem, by which every other Church was founded.'" (B. iii. C. 12.)

Far more probable and reasonable is this supposition than that this venerable Father should be at variance with the Scriptures, and make a statement supported by no previous Christian writing.

We read also in (Book iii. Ch. 3 of) this author that "Linus I., after the martyrdom of Peter and Paul, was chosen Bishop of Rome." On the other hand Eusebius asserts that "Peter and Paul made Linus Bishop of Rome."

Thus, we see, as CHILLINGWORTH writes, "Some of the Fathers are against others, and the same Fathers are against themselves."

It has not been a gracious task thus to expose the errors, and childish and absurd statements of one who has been revered as a Saint and worthy Confessor. It has been necessary, however, as he has been used, by interested parties, as a witness to a historical error productive of vast harm.

We are compelled to believe either that we have not in the Latin translation the true sentiments of Irenæus, or that this writer is undeserving of the fair reputation he has held.

In either case, the statements with respect to Peter's Roman residence which have been offered in evidence as to this claim are utterly unworthy of confidence, and would necessarily be thrown out of any Court of justice.

Therefore, the ancient testimony most relied on to establish the visit of Peter to Rome by Papal authors must be rejected, and, as with the figurative interpretation of Babylon, be regarded as of no value whatever in the inquiry in which we are now engaged.

CHAPTER XIX.

"The Trophies" of Caius.

CAREFUL and thorough investigation of all statements by writers of the first two centuries of Christianity, with respect to the life of Peter, has shown that there are no documents extant which testify to a visit of this Apostle, in any period of his life, to the city of Rome.

The last writer quoted, and regarded as the most important witness for the claims of the Roman Church, we have seen, presents no testimony worthy of credence, that Peter was ever personally present in Rome.

Irenæus, to whom we refer, wrote at the beginning of the third century. As no evidence can be found before his time with respect to the Apostle's residence in Rome, the case might be closed here; but inasmuch as we wish to leave no point unsettled with respect to this question, which nearly 200,000,000 of nominal Christians regard as of vital, essential importance, we shall notice other ancient writers who are claimed by Roman, and some Protestant authors, as important witnesses to establish the fact of the visit of Peter to Rome.

"The conclusion which follows from the fact of St. Peter being Bishop of Rome is important, and one which every Catholic looks upon as the foundation of his faith."

So writes Rev. S. B. Smith, D. D., in his "Teachings of the Holy Catholic Church," New York, 1884, with the imprimatur of Cardinals McCloskey and Gibbons, Bishops Gilmour, Lynch, and Elder.

This statement establishes the importance of our question, and justifies the expenditure of time and labor here bestowed upon it. If we have removed that which is the Foundation of that church, according to the authorities above presented ; if our conclusions are sound and true, where is the standing of the Church of Rome, and of what value are her exclusive, arrogant, and damnatory claims ?

The existence of St. Peter's Church, and the assertion that it is built on the spot where the Apostle was crucified, by order of Nero, confirms multitudes in their belief of Peter's martyrdom in Rome. The statement upon which that claim is founded is that of Caius, or Gaius, an ecclesiastical writer of Rome under Bishop Zephyrinus, A. D. 215, who is quoted by Eusebius (ii. 25). Bishop Lightfoot suggests that Caius and Hippolytus were the same person, Caius=Hippolytus.

A Roman controversalist writes in the London *Times*, January 16, 1851 : "That Peter founded the Church at Rome is expressly asserted by Caius (apud Eus. Lib. ii. c. 24, alias 25), a priest of Rome under Pope Zephyrinus, A. D. 202 and 218, who relates that his body was then (buried) on the Vatican Hill, and that of St. Paul on the Ostian Road."

Father McCorry, another Roman author, examining this question, says : "The sixth witness is Caius—a Roman—whose words are peculiarly touching. He declares : 'I can point out to you the trophies of the Apostles Peter and Paul. For whether you direct your footsteps to the Vatican, or to the Ostian way, the trophies of those who founded the Roman Church present themselves to our view.'"

Baronius, Valesius, and Feuardent among Roman, and Pearson and Lardner among Protestant writers, appeal to the testimony of Caius. It would be astonishing, if we knew not the ways of some Roman controversalists, to learn that Caius does not insert the names of either Peter or Paul in his statement, as quoted by Eusebius.

We give the language of Caius in the version of ELLENDORF, Roman Catholic Professor: "I can show you the monuments (*Trophæa*) of the Apostles; for when you go out to the Vatican, or to the road to Ostia, you will find the same monuments of those who founded this Church" (Eusebius ii. 25).

Ellendorf further proceeds: "If we suppose this to be authentic it proves nothing at all. The monuments (or trophies) may signify graves; but who says that these 'monuments of the Apostles' were the graves of Peter and Paul? Those men are called Apostles in the Holy Scriptures and by the Fathers, not only who were the Apostles specially, but likewise their pupils and followers. Thus Luke (Acts xiv. 13) names Barnabas an Apostle; so Paul often calls Titus, Timothy, Silas, etc., his fellow Apostles; so Clemens of Rome is called by Clement of Alexandria, who was a contemporary of Caius, an Apostle. (Stromata, iv. 17.) Among the Apostles, also, to whose graves Caius points, we may properly understand those of Paul, and many of his companions who, with him, founded the Church at Rome, and who died there with him, or after him, in the faith. The addition, that they were the graves of those who founded the Church of Rome, necessarily points to the interpretation; while it is a matter of fact, according to the Holy Scriptures, that the Church of Rome was *founded* by *Paul* and his disciples, but in no wise by Peter and his followers."—Bib. Sac., January, 1859.

Thus reasons this learned and candid Roman Catholic. Moreover, the existence of monuments or trophies to any Apostle, is no evidence of the burial of that person in that particular city. Ancient writers tell us that it was customary to erect such memorials to the departed worthies in all the principal cities.

Thus, Stephen had a trophy in Ancona; Peter at Constantinople, in the days of Eusebius; St. Lawrence at Ravenna, though far from the place of his martyrdom; and Ignatius at Antioch, though he suffered in Rome. The authorities on this point may be seen in Simon's "Mission and Martyrdom of Peter," p. 88.

BARONIUS, the Roman historian, writes: "The least fragment of the relics of any saint is equivalent to the entire of that saint's body" (Index); and, again (A. D. 55, par. 15): "Each city imagined itself possessed of the Martyr's blood, on account of the trophy or tomb erected in consequence of its efficacy."

The criticism of BOUZIQUE, the French jurist, is to this effect: "Evidently, he (Eusebius) makes the (passage of Caius) say more than the words involve. Eusebius, who never saw Rome, may in good faith have made a mistake here, misled by the legend which was then accounted veritable history. . . The inscription on these monuments, without date, and which are not mentioned by either Irenæus, or Justin, or Clement of Rome, or any author of the first two centuries, proves nothing else than that at the epoch when they were raised the legend was accepted by the Romans" (vol. i. 369).

SHEPHERD, in his "History of the Church of Rome," p. 532, well remarks: "The attempts to prove that St.

Peter had been at Rome by quoting the inscription on the tombstones there, and Caius to confirm them, and Dionysius of Corinth to prove that Peter had been in Italy (all forgeries, I have no doubt), furnish a most conclusive argument against Supremacy. The writer (it cannot be Eusebius) tells us he adduces these things, 'that the history of Peter dying at Rome may be the more accredited.' Accredited? If the Roman theory be true the Supremacy which was founded had been a constant fact before the eyes of the Church for the previous 300 years. . . Objection, then, to believing that Peter had died at Rome, there could have been none. There might have been doubts A. D. 70; but A. D. 330, after an admitted authority of three centuries, there could have been none—that is, if the Roman story be true. But if the unbelievers be so numerous as to attract the notice of the historian, or, rather, if this is an insertion into the history of Eusebius, the Supremacy, founded upon St. Peter having died at Rome, must be a fable."

NEANDER on Caius, i. 380, remarks: "These graves do not furnish incontestible evidence. When the report was once set afloat, the designation of the locality where the Apostles were buried could easily be added."

"Jerome interprets this as referring to the graves of the Apostles Peter and Paul. Eusebius does the same. But this is putting on the language of Gaius more than it expresses."—SAWYER's Orig. Christ., p. 48.

"When we look at this statement, we find that it affirms merely that the Apostles were in that persecution; the town where the martyrdom took place is the Christian's trophy—even though not his tomb."—PLATTNER on Caius, Descrip. Rome, ii. 152; Baur i. 256.

"With respect to what *Eusebius* says of the testimony

of a presbyter named *Caius*, that about the beginning of the third century he saw the graves of Peter and Paul at Rome, it may easily be accounted for : it was the age of pious fraud, when the relics of saints could be found almost everywhere; and in the next century the wood and nails of the cross were discovered! Those who can believe these things, may have a credulity large enough to swallow up the testimony of Caius."— J. OWEN, Vicar of Thrussington.

WILLET writes on this subject, Synopsis, x. 13; "How shall you believe that it is St. Peter's sepulcher which is showed at Rome, seeing you have made so many mockeries already, making the world believe that Peter's body is sometimes in one place and sometimes in another? Half his body you say is at St. Peter's in Rome; half at St. Paul's; his head at St. John's Lateran; his nether jaw with the beard, at Poictiers in France; many of his bones at Tiers; at Geneva part of his brain (Fulke ad Rom. etc.). You see we may as well doubt whether Peter's body be at Rome, as in any of these places."

ANOTHER DIFFICULTY.

Another difficulty remains to be considered in the argument founded on the words of Caius.

The spot where Peter's remains are stated to be buried, was in Nero's magnificent Circus, surrounded by altars and oracles, where no corpse—much less that of a malefactor—would have been allowed to be buried. Here was the site of Pompey's theater. The site is identified by the Obelisk erected by Ptolemy Philadelphus at Alexandria, which was removed to Rome and placed in this Circus.

Nardini, in his "Roma Antica," writes somewhat ironically: "If the bodies of St. Peter and the martyrs were buried where St. Peter's Church now stands, it is strange that the Circus could still remain there. Perhaps Nero, the inhuman author of the Christian massacres, was compassionate enough to destroy his Circus in order to provide them a place of sepulture; yet the Circus was certainly standing in the time of Pliny. Perhaps Nero permitted it to serve two ends at once —a Circus for the Gentiles, and a Catacomb for the faithful."

J. C. Gray, Bib. Museum, iii. 261, remarks: "The first and best evidence of the Apostle's suffering at Rome is his 'trophy' or sepulcher, in the Vatican (Eus. ii. 25). Now it is certain that at this time this spot was included in Nero's magnificent Circus, surrounded by altars and oracles, where no corpse, much less a malefactor's, could be interred. Then, quoting Nardini, he adds: "Having myself no faith in Nero's compassion or toleration, I take this fact to be conclusive evidence that Peter was not buried in the Vatican. The conclusion is, *he was never in Rome at all.*"

Ellendorf takes the same view. He argues: "Whether these monuments signify signs of victory or graves; yet it is improbable that at the Vatican, near the tombs of the Scipios, that is, the way to Ostia or the public road, there were the tombs of the Apostles, and decorated with inscriptions, at a time when the persecutions raged, when the populace often destroyed Christian churches as soon as they discovered them, and left nothing uninjured which was holy to them; at a time when the Emperor and his officers commanded everyone to blot out the Christian name."

ANOTHER DIFFICULTY.

The question may be properly asked: If one trophy be recognized as genuine, why not all?

Take for example what they call *St. Peter's Chair*, elevated in their great Cathedral 120 feet from the ground, and placed under a tabernacle of brass, in honor of which Mass is celebrated, and before which Cardinals bow themselves. This is relied on, like 'Caius' Trophies,' as one of the convincing proofs that Peter was Bishop of Rome.

Cardinal Wiseman says: "I am certain of the mission and presence of St. Peter at Rome, from the presence of the chair of St. Peter in the Basilica of the Vatican."

When the French held Rome in the beginning of the century, they chose two noted Romanists, Champolion, and the Abbé Lanci, Professor in the Roman University, to examine the mysterious chair as to its origin.

Lanci makes the following report: "I have examined the chair of St. Peter at Rome. It is not of the age of Augustus, but belongs to the fifth century of the Christian era; its architecture was not yet discovered in the Augustan age.

"To my great astonishment, I found in this chair twelve little plates of ivory, on which were sculptured the twelve labors of Hercules; so that, in my opinion, it was the chair of one of the Emperors, or of some consular man, in the decay of the Roman Empire."

ANOTHER TROPHY.

We have room but for one more description of a "trophy" or evidence of the presence of Peter in the Imperial City. The Roman Breviary, which has the Inprimatur of the Pope, has this account of *Peter's Chains:* "During the reign of Theodosius the Younger, when Eudocia his wife had visited Jerusalem for the sake of fulfilling a vow, she was favored with many presents. Above all others she received the illustrious gift of an *iron chain*, adorned with gold and gems, which they declared was the same with which the Apostle Peter had been bound by Herod.

"Eudocia, piously venerating the chain, afterward sent it to her daughter Eudocia, who brought it to the Pontiff; and he in turn showed her another chain, with which, under the reign of Nero, the same Apostle had been bound. While, therefore, the Pontiff was comparing the Roman chain with that which had been brought from Jerusalem, it happened that they became so united together that there appeared to be not two chains, but one made by the same workman."

This event was regarded as so remarkable that, in honor of it, a Church was erected, under the name of St. Peter ad Vincula. Miracles were said to be wrought by these chains; devils were expelled by their touch, and diseases instantly cured. The 1st day of August is set apart as a festival in honor of the miracle of St. Peter's chains.

Is further proof needed of Peter's visit to Rome, than is furnished by the *Trophies, the Chair,* and *the Chains?*

In this examination we have seen how thoroughly the supposed evidence of Caius fails, in like manner with all other testimony which has been presented, to prove the improbable story that the Apostle Peter left Babylon in Chaldea, with its numerous Hebrew population, to wander to far Rome in the West, to take part with Paul and his numerous coadjutors in the Church founded and superintended by the Apostle to the Gentiles.

We close our examination of Caius with the decisive words of the *North British Review*, November, 1848, p. 33.

"In the first place it has not been considered that the words of Caius are only by Eusebius referred, evidently contrary to their sense, exclusively referred to *St. Peter and St. Paul;* and in the second place, the supposition of public monuments having been erected to the Apostle in the *second* century at Rome, and in the immediate vicinity of the Vatican, is so preposterous that it is surprising how it could at any time have gained even momentary credence.

"The Neronian persecution at its first outbreak was of a most overwhelming character, and the assumption of any Christian having been permitted to witness the sufferings of his fellow believers, much less to pay the last honors to their earthly remains, without being made to share their fate, is wholly inadmissible.

"What became of the mutilated bodies and scattered ashes of the innocent victims to a national calamity and a tyrant's recklessness, God only knows, and no Christian probably ever knew; and as the principal scene of their sufferings was the very locality named by Caius (Tacitus, *loc. cit.*), it appears to us scarcely to admit of a doubt but that all the Roman presbyter meant to say when he wrote the words quoted, and used the word ' Apostle,' in its more extended sense, was, Whether you turn to the Vatican or to the Via Ostia, the above presents but one scene of suffering; every spot reminds you of a Christian dying for his faith; every stone is a trophy of the martyrdom of those who constituted the earliest Church."

CHAPTER XX.

Tertullian and Hippolytus.

That the aggrandisement of the See of Rome was a leading motive of the ancient authors in bringing Peter from Babylon in Parthia to the Imperial city, has been here freely asserted.

Foulkes, a Roman Catholic, in his "Christendom's Divisions," i. p. 23, gives some warrant for this charge. He says: "Rome in addition to any mere Imperial privileges, had another, that had infinitely more charms for Christendom, namely, the pre-eminence of its Apostolic origin.

"As it was the only See in the West which could boast of that distinction, so it was the only See in all the world which had been founded, not by one Apostle, but by two, and these the greatest of all the Apostles. This incomparably more than the other, is the fact so glowingly dwelt upon by SS. Irenæus, Tertullian, Cyprian, Athanasius, Augustine, and others who have testified to the prerogatives of the Church of Rome."

D'Aubigné, Hist. i. 11, explains the growth of the Roman claim: "'The Bishops of the West favored this encroachment of the Roman Pastors, either from jealousy of the Eastern bishops, or because they preferred subjection to the Pope, to the dominion of the temporal power. On the other hand, the theological sects which distracted the East, strove each for itself to gain an interest at Rome, hoping to triumph over its opponent by the support of the principal of the western Churches. It was highly flattering to the Roman bishop to be styled the successor of the Chair of Peter."

DAVIDSON, Intro. N. Test., i. 412, offers another suggestion in this connection : "The more the basis of the whole tradition is examined, the lighter it will appear. The Babylon of the Epistle contributed to it, while it was the interest of the Jewish Christians to put their leader along with Paul, in preaching to the church of the Imperial city, and suffering death under the same Emperor. Early Christian writers were credulous and uncritical. They repeated the statement of predecessors, and added to them without much discernment and consistency. To judge fairly of evidence was not their talent."

DAILLÉ remarks with respect to early Christian authorship, On the Fathers, p. 45 : "The blessed Christians of these times contented themselves, for the greater part, with writing the Christian faith on the hearts of men, by the beams of their own sanctity and holy life, and by the blood shed in martyrdom, without much troubling themselves with the writing of books."

TERTULLIAN.

Among these early writers and advocates of Peter's visit to Rome, Tertullian (A. D. 245) is among those most confidently appealed to.

OWEN, Intro. Calvin's Tracts, iii. 272, says: "The many authorities adduced respecting Peter being at Rome, may be reduced almost to two, *Irenæus and Tertullian*. They were the first, as it were, to stamp a kind of authority on this report, and also on others to which no credit is given even by those who would have the Fathers to be almost infallible."

TERTULLIAN, an advocate, residing at Rome, naturally sought to increase the influence of that church. He writes, vol. i. 486, Oxford Ed. :

"If thou art near to Italy, thou hast Rome, where we also have an authority close at hand. What a happy Church is that in which the Apostles poured out their doctrines with their blood ; where Peter had a like passion with the Lord ; where Paul had for his crown the same death with John, where the Apostle John was plunged into boiling oil, and suffered nothing, and was afterward banished to an Island."

Here we have a *third* Apostle introduced, the more extensively to glorify his church—Irenæus, as we have seen, was contented with *two*.

This statement with respect to the Evangelist John, having no contemporaneous authority, discredits greatly Tertullian's testimony.

GLOAG, Intro. Cath. Epis., 150, writes : "Tertullian writes with the martyrdom of Peter and Paul at Rome the story that John was cast unhurt into a caldron of boiling oil, which is now generally regarded as a myth."

BACON, Lives, p. 317 : "Meisner, Cellarius, Dodwell, Spanheim, Heuman, and others overthrow it entirely as a baseless fiction. They argue against it, first, from the bad character of its only ancient witness. Tertullian is known as most miserably credulous, and fond of catching up these idle tales ; and even the devoutly credulous Baronius condemns him in the most unmeasured terms, for his greedy and undiscriminating love of falsehood. . .

"In this decided condemnation of the venerable Tertullian I am justified by the example of Lampe, whose reverence for the authority of the Fathers is much greater than of most theologians of late days. He refers to him in these terms, 'whose credulity in catching up idle tales is well known in other instances.'"

GREENWOOD, Cath. Petri, i. 44 : "The story of the immersion and safe exit of St. John from the caldron of burning oil, is I believe abandoned, by all judicious authors, as a baseless fiction."

KITTO, Art. St. John, Dic. Bib., states : "Tertullian relates that, in the reign of Domitian, John was forcibly conveyed to Rome, where he was thrown into a cask of oil ; that he was miraculously released, and then brought to Patmos. But since none of the ancient writers, besides the rather undiscriminating Tertullian, relate the circumstances, and since this mode of capital punishment was unheard of in Rome, we ought not to lay much stress upon it." Comp. Mosh. Diss. Eccles. Hist., i. 417.

BROWN, Com. on John, asserts : "That John was thrown into a caldron of boiling oil, and miraculously delivered, is one of those legends which, though reported by Tertullian and Jerome, are entitled to no credit."

MEYER styles it : " A manifestly false tradition."

It is not remarkable, from what we know of the temperament and habits of mind of Tertullian, that he was a manufacturer of traditions.

CHAMBERS' Encyclopedia describes him as " a man of strong and violent passions, who loved and hated with intensity. He was narrow, bigoted, and uncharitable."

FARRAR writes of him : "He often seems to care more for the immediate victory than for the discovery of the truth. He is often at variance with himself, because he improvises his convictions; and is more intent on prostrating his opponent than on examining the ground of the opinion. He often condescends to the grossest sophisms, the most irritating word-splitting, and the most violent abuse."

NEANDER thus describes him, Hist. i. 683: "His fiery and positive disposition, and his previous training as an advocate in rhetoric, early impelled him, especially in controversy, to rhetorical exaggerations. When he defends a cause, of whose truth he is convinced, we often see in him, the advocate, whose sole anxiety is to collect together all the arguments which can help his case, it matters not whether they are true arguments, or only miserable sophisms."

Tertullian accepted the statement of Justin Martyr with regard to Simon Magus, which is so largely embellished in the Clementine fictions. It was doubtless from these that he derived his view of Peter's journey to Rome.

Of this Simon Magus fiction, GREEN, Apos. Peter, p. 117, states: "The tradition gathers strength as it proceeds. Justin as we have seen, in the *second* century, brings Simon Magus to Rome, but not Peter; the writer of the Clementines, in *the third*, brings Simon Magus and Peter together in controversy, but in Cæsarea, not Rome: Eusebius and Jerome, in the *fourth* century, combine these narratives into a detailed story of Peter's bishopric in the city, in the course of which he is vanquished by argument and eloquence."

As an evidence of this conflict in Rome, between Simon and Peter, visitors are shown the marks in the stone pavement made by Peter's knees, when Simon fell through the air, by the power of Peter's prayer.

Tertullian's *credulity* in this matter is thus criticised by Neander, p. 454 : " Tertullian, who had more familiar knowledge of Roman Antiquities, might be expected, it is true, to know better ; but even he was too prejudiced in such cases, too ignorant of criticism, to institute any further examination with regard to the correctness of a statement which was in accordance with his taste, and which besides came to him on such respectable authority. The more critical Alexandrians take no notice of the matter." Among his false and antiscriptural notions were prayers for the dead, the corporeality of the human soul ; and the common absurdities and extravagances of the Fathers, in regard to angels, and demons, and kindred topics. See Cunningham's Doc. Theo., p. 160.

He held the Papal notion with regard to Peter. He writes, p. 471 : " Was anything hidden from Peter, who was called the rock whereon the Church should be built, who obtained the Keys of the Kingdom ; and the power of loosing and binding in heaven and on earth ?"

With Rome, too, his final appeal was not to *Scripture*, but to *the Church*. He says : " To the Scriptures, therefore, we must not appeal. . . What Christ did reveal must be proved in no other way than by those churches which the Apostles themselves founded. . . Let him prefer those, received by the greater numbers, and the weightier authorities, to those held by the fewer and less weighty." To give Rome the predominance, through a triple Apostolate, Tertullian transfers Peter from Parthia, and John also from the East, to be combined with Paul, and thus glorify the See of the Imperial City : and this on the strength of legends which he as a lawyer would know to be unworthy of credit. When we add that Tertullian was the father of Sacerdotalism; with his other errors, we may regard him as the advance guard of the Papal system.

But as a credible witness, this retailer of fables, this unscrupulous advocate, this unscriptural teacher, cannot be accepted in a case of such profound importance as we are considering. He adds nothing of value to the arguments of those who hold that Peter deserted Babylon in Parthia, for Rome.

HIPPOLYTUS.

This author (A. D. 222) is quoted by Dr. Samson and others, as a witness in favor of Peter's visit to Rome.

There is much uncertainty with respect to his residence.

NEANDER writes concerning him, i. 681 : "As neither Eusebius nor Jerome was able to name the city in which he was bishop, we can say nothing more definite in the matter : and neither do those later accounts which transfer his bishopric to Arabia, nor the others, which place it in the neighborhood of Rome, deserve consideration."

Dr. CAVE places him in Aden, Arabia ; BUNSEN at Ostia ; some make him a Roman presbyter : while others, endeavoring to reconcile his denunciation of the Roman bishop with the Papal view, regard him as an Anti-Pope.

GUASSEN on the Canon, p. 312, remarks: "Hippolytus, one of the most learned men of antiquity, no less celebrated in mathematics and astronomy than in sacred learning, was an intimate friend of Origen. He taught both in the East, and in the West; for having been, as supposed, Bishop of Aden in Arabia, he came to the capital of the Empire, about A. D. 325, labored there a long time, and even, as is believed, underwent martyrdom there." Guassen regards Aden as Portus Romanus, and adds: "This fact, maintained by Cave (Hist. Lite. Sacr. Nov.), is utterly rejected by Mr. Bunsen. But the argument of Cave remains, and we do not think he has been refuted."

Wherever he was, he appears to have had little respect for the Roman bishop. Farrar says of him, Lives of Fathers, i. 89: "Hippolytus occupied a position of extreme antagonism to two Popes, whom he describes as *fancying* themselves bishops. One of these, Zephyrinus (A. D. 202–217), he describes as a weak and venal dunce; and of Calixtus (A. D. 217–222), he speaks as 'a cheat and sacrilegious swindler, an infamous convict, an heresiarch.' We remain ignorant whether he was orthodox or heretical, a catholic or schismatic, a priest or a bishop, a Pope or an Anti-Pope, an excommunicated sectarian or a martyred saint. Dr. Lightfoot has suggested that Caius and Hippolytus were one and the same person, Caius=Hippolytus."

HATCH, Origin of Christ. Ch., p. 104, writes: "Two recent Jewish writers, Annelini and Grisar . . . have endeavored to show that he (Novatian) was the author of the Philosophenomena (more commonly but without certain grounds) assigned to Hippolytus." We cannot wonder that even Döllinger, with his great powers, failed in adapting Hippolytus to modern papal ideas.

This author utterly fails as a reliable witness in this present inquiry. Of his works, "Scarcely one has come to us without mutilation; concerning almost every work we ascribe to him there has been controversy whether it is really his."—Smith and Wace, Dict. Biog.

And when we read his language about Peter and other Apostles, we see at once that we may class him with the authors of the Clementina. We read, vol. ii. 130-34, of his Works: "Peter preached the Gospel in Pontus and Galatia, and Cappadocia and Betania, and Italy and Asia, and was afterward crucified by Nero in Rome, with his head downward, as he had himself desired to suffer in that manner." He also undertakes to give us the fields of labor of all the Apostles, and the manner of their deaths, as for instance, Andrew, Philip, and Bartholomew were crucified; the two latter with their heads downward; the two, James and Thomas, were likewise martyred. John, Matthew, Jude, Simon, and Matthias died natural deaths.

Not content with giving us the history of the Apostles, we are favored by this marvelously informed writer with the fields of labor of all the Seventy, whom he also enumerates. He includes among these *all the names in Paul's Epistles*, with many others.

As a specimen of his remarkable knowledge, we give this statement: "Mark the Evangelist, bishop of Alexandria, and Luke the Evangelist, belonged to the Seventy disciples who were scattered by the offense of the word which Christ spake, 'except a man eat my flesh and drink my blood, he is not worthy of me!' But the one being induced to return to the Lord, by Peter's instrumentality, and the other by Paul's, they were honored to preach that Gospel, on account of which they also suffered martyrdom, the one being burned, and the other being crucified on an olive tree."

He also makes bishops of over *fifty* of the seventy,

giving us their names, and also those of their respective churches.

Here is a man of whose residence we are ignorant. In writings attributed to him, we have a great variety of statements for which there is no contemporaneous evidence, and which carry on their face absurdity and impossibility. It is manifest he draws on his imagination for his facts. He adds nothing to our knowledge of Peter's history. No one is, therefore, warranted in making an appeal to Hippolytus, in their investigations.

CHAPTER XXI.

Origen, Clemens, Cyprian.

It is not a pleasant task to remove the halo which has surrounded the early writers of the Christian Church who have received the title of saints, and with regard to whom distance has lent enchantment to the view. But the truth must be told that with regard to their writings the authenticity of much is doubtful, and they cannot be relied on to prove events of importance, like those which have here been investigated. They are credulous, uncritical, and at times deceive, to carry their point and to promote religion. See chap. xviii.

With regard to the history of Peter, we have presented the testimonies which have been regarded as most important, and have seen that for a century and a half after the death of this Apostle, not a line of evidence which would have weight in a court of justice has ever been presented to prove his presence in Rome. Nothing later than this period could be of any value, for no facts bearing on the case could be substantiated. Still, as the Roman Church appeals to later eminent writers, we shall give them brief consideration, as this is sufficient, we think, to prove them valueless.

Origen (a. d. 253), among the most brilliant and learned of the Fathers, is quoted as placing Peter in Rome. He says: "Peter appears to have preached through Pontus, Galatia, Bithynia, Cappadocia, and

Asia, to the Jews who were scattered abroad, who also, finally, ἐπι τελει, coming to Rome, was crucified with his head downward, having requested to suffer in that way." Eus., iii. 1. Origen differs from Tertullian, who states that Peter died the *same* death as our Lord.

Of Origen, Adam Clarke tells us: "He was a thorough critic, learned and pious, but credulous in the extreme, and capable of believing and teaching the most absurd notions for grave truths."

DAILLÉ, with regard to the authenticity of his works, writes, Fathers, p. 6: "As for Origen, Cyprian's contemporary, we have very little of him left, and the greatest part of that too miserably abused and corrupted; the most learned and almost innumerable writings of this great and incomparable person not being able to withstand the ravages of time, nor the envy and malice of men who have dealt much worse with him, than so many ages and centuries of years that have passed from his time down to us."

The NORTH BRITISH REVIEW, on St. Peter, November, 1848, p. 33, remarks: "It is *possible* that Peter may have gone to Rome, ἐπι τελει, as Origen has it, *but there is not the very remotest reason for such a supposition.* The latter Father informs us that it was generally contended St. Peter had written his first Epistle not from Babylon in Persia, but from Rome in Italy under the symbolical name of Babylon. Here we have the key to the whole tradition of St. Peter's sojourn and death at Rome. It rests solely on that positive error." The reasoning of this writer appears so clear and conclusive from his examination of the Patristic controversy, that we give it in full.

"We say the symbolical interpretation of the date of

St. Peter's first Epistle is a positive error. Yet, though an anomaly in itself, it has been defended, and defended by Protestant writers, too.

"But there are *two generally acknowledged facts* which baffle all the most subtle arguments, and will irresistibly bear us out in our assertion : The symbolical allusion to Rome by the name of Babylon was not known before the Revelation was written. The first Epistle of St. Peter was written before the Apocalypse.

"On the other hand, the symbolical allusion to Rome in the Revelation having become generally known, probably *a long time* before the presence of St. Peter at Rome is ever mentioned by the tradition, which we have seen was not the case till toward *the third century*, we have the strongest possible reason to conclude that the tradition derived its origin from that allusion, and from it alone.

"Thus we can in the most satisfactory manner account for what is, otherwise, altogether unaccountable ; the contradictory reports of the tradition in regard to the time of St. Peter's arrival at Rome, and to the simple fact of his death at a period, moreover, at evident variance with his own Epistles ; the fabulous history of his combat with Simon the magician, and other absurdities ; and above all, the absence of every authentic information as to his Apostolic labors for the space of time of nearly twenty years (for of the events in *Persia* how little comes even now to our knowledge), and *the utter ignorance of the whole Christian Church, during the first one hundred years after St. Peter's death, as to his ever having set foot in Rome.*

"It appears to us, therefore, all but certain that St.

Peter, as he chiefly, since the time of the council of the Apostles, lived and taught; so, a martyr to his faith in Christ, he died in Babylon."

With respect to the manner of Peter's death, in which he differs from Tertullian, as stated, we find no contemporaneous evidence.

GREEN, Apostle Peter, 171, writes: "Clement and Irenæus knew nothing of it. Tertullian, with whose gloomy enthusiasm the story would have been peculiarly congenial, says simply that Peter had a like passion with our Lord. Origen, as quoted by Eusebius, is made to say that the Apostle was crucified with his head downward; but this seems to have arisen from a misconception of Origen's words, which simply mean that Peter was fastened to the cross by the head. From this misunderstanding the account undoubtedly sprang, and Jerome last of all gives the legend a full form. A story which required more than three hundred years to get into shape, and which is besides intrinsically improbable, can scarcely be otherwise than rejected. The manner of the great Apostle's departure has been wisely left in uncertainty, and we need not desire to raise the veil."

SIMON, Mission, etc., 124, speaks of another uncertainty in regard to Origen's statement: "Valesius frankly acknowledges that Eusebius does not tell us that Origen attested what is said about St. Peter, though Valesius assumes that Origen may have done so. 'Eusebius,' he says, 'has not clearly pointed out what is the commencement of Origen's words, which remarks Father De La Rue repeats in his edition of Origen. Both these writers, therefore, admit that we cannot infer from what Eusebius says, that Origen had ever heard of the conjecture that contradicts the Scriptural account of Peter's martyrdom at Babylon."

Nourse, On the Fathers, Prot. Rev., October, 1847, p. 310, further confirms the uncertainty which exists with regard to Origen's writings. He remarks: "These Fathers are not only made to say what they never did say, but are introduced as silent on subjects on which they did speak. Of these there are many instances which can be proved. This, too, was practiced by ecclesiastical writers toward each other. Thus, Ruffin professes to translate Origen, Eusebius, and others from the Greek into the Latin, but there is scarce a page in which he has not added or omitted something. Jerome admits this, and recommends Ruffin for it, saying, 'that he had interpreted the good and useful, and left out the bad.' The Greek text of Origen is in a good measure now lost, and we have to depend upon Ruffin's translation. Hilary did the same thing."

If such men as Ruffin, Hilary, and Jerome approve of such practices, what little confidence can be placed in the unknown translator of the lost works of Irenæus; the Father most relied on, as we have seen, to substantiate the presence of Peter in Rome; Irenæus, whose Greek has come down to us in an unauthenticated barbarous Latin version?

If we have Origen's own words, and his statements are true, then the view taken by Roman authors, Popes and others, of Peter's twenty-five-years' Roman residence, is flatly contradicted by this author, who says that Peter came to Rome, ἐπὶ τέλει. He comes in conflict, too, with Eusebius and Jerome, on this point—another case of Patristic disagreement.

CLEMENS ALEXANDRINUS.

Clemens (A. D. 192–217) and Cyprian (A. D. 250) are also appealed to in support of Peter's Roman residence.

The former, accepting the tradition of the Elders, that Babylon meant Rome, regards Mark's Gospel as written at the latter city, under the supervision of Peter, though the date is not mentioned. He has also his legend with regard to Peter's wife. He says, Clark's Ed., 11, 45 : " They say accordingly that the blessed Peter, on seeing his wife led to death, rejoiced on account of her call and conveyance home, and called very encouragingly and comfortingly, addressing her by name, ' Remember thou the Lord ! ' Such was the marriage of the blessed, and their perfect disposition toward those dearest to them."

Clemens' language is a strong condemnation of the unscriptural celibacy of the Roman Popes and priests, which is defended on the ground of a supposed superior purity in the unmarried state. This system certainly seems to place the Roman clergy in a higher spiritual condition than even the supposed inspired Founder of their communion. But this is only one of the numerous inconsistencies of that Church with Holy Scripture.

CYPRIAN.

Cyprian, Bishop of Carthage, in his letters, writes of "Peter's Chair, and the principal Church where sacerdotal unity took its rise. . . Peter, also, to whom the Lord committed his sheep to be fed and guarded; upon whom he founded and established that Church."

But as "The Chair" was commonly used to express "The Doctrine," and Peter could be said to have founded the Church of Rome by means of his converts at Pentecost, such vague language presents no evidence that he supposed Peter to have visited Rome in person, which is our present inquiry.

Cyprian spoke of Tertullian as his "Master." He appears to have adopted from him his sacerdotal sentiments, his reliance upon the Church and tradition, as the ground of belief; and upon Peter as the Rock. And adding his own self-originated scheme of Episcopal unity, based upon an uninterrupted Episcopal succession, he corrupted the simplicity of the Gospel scheme, and paved the way for Popery with all its errors.

We have thus far examined all authors referred to on the question of Peter's history, who are worthy of notice in this examination, save one, who, though later, has furnished us with much of the testimony considered.

No light of value has been thrown upon the inquiry by these writers. As to Peter's Roman visit—we may justly say with EDGAR, Var. Popery, p. 70: "The cotemporary and succeeding authors for a century and a half, such as Luke, Paul, John, Clemens, Barnabas, Hermas, Ignatius, and Polycarp say nothing of the tradition. The intervening historians between Peter and Irenæus on this topic are as silent as the grave. Cotemporary historians, indeed, say no more of the Apostle Peter's journey to Rome, than of Baron Munchausen's excursion to the moon."

LANCIANI'S DISCOVERIES.

Before proceeding to the examination of the statements of Eusebius, we will briefly notice a work by LANCIANI, a distinguished Roman archæologist and explorer. In his "Pagan and Christian Rome," a work of great interest and value, he devotes twenty-five pages to an attempt to prove the presence of Peter in Rome.

A Roman Catholic; accepting the Papal legends of the Apostle's residence, bishopric, death, and burial in the Imperial City; "trifles light as air" appear to him "confirmation strong as proofs of Holy Writ."

P. 123 he begins by asserting: "For the archæologist, the presence and execution of SS. Peter and Paul in Rome are facts established beyond the shadow of a doubt by purely monumental evidence."

"Monumental" evidence is strong evidence where there are facts to back it. But inasmuch as the great volume of scholarship outside the Roman communion rejects the Roman visit and residence of Peter, and locates him at Babylon, the Jewish center, and his divinely appointed field as the Apostle of the Circumcision; something more than assumption is required to bring him to Rome, where no reasonable motive could draw him. Lanciani appeals to Döllinger, Bishop Lightfoot, and De Rossi in support of his views. But Döllinger, a Romanist, is satisfactorily answered by Ellendorf, De Marca, and others of the same communion; Bishop Lightfoot, by an older writer of the same name and pre-eminently fitted for the investigation; and De Rossi, by laymen of judicial training, who pronounce the Peter legend as absolutely devoid of proof.

Lanciani's authorities appeal to Clement and Ignatius. DÖLLINGER says: "That Peter worked in Rome is abundantly proved; that his presence in Corinth is obviously connected with the journey to Rome; and no one will accept the one and deny the other." It has been seen that the language of Clement and Ignatius bears rather against the Papal claim, and the omission of Paul to mention, in his letter to Corinth, Peter as a fellow laborer, is conclusive against that Apostle's presence there. See p. 157.

Lanciani refers to the Ebionite "Preaching of Peter," and cannot regard it as a "groundless fable." It has been shown in the examination of the "Clementina," p. 150-6, what these Ebionite productions were worth as testimony. Lanciani appeals also to Eusebius. The value of his evidence will be seen in the next chapter.

P. 125 : "There is nothing to contradict the assumption of his journey to Rome, and his confession and execution there. . . The fact was so generally known that nobody dreamed that it could be denied." We reply that no rational motive has been assigned for the visit of Peter to Rome. He had abundant work in his proper field of labor in Babylon. He is not connected with Rome in the Scripture, nor in authentic documents which have reached us.

Greenwood, an able English barrister, rightly says: "In truth no positive or circumstantial statement of the tradition of Peter's residence and martyrdom in Rome is to be met with in any Christian writer prior to Eusebius. . . With the exception of the strange gossip collected by Eusebius, principally from Papias, about St. Peter's pursuit of Simon Magus, and the composition of St. Mark's gospel, no witness to the fact of St. Peter's presence in Rome at any period of his life has been produced, other than Eusebius himself ; and *he* only speaks to a belief founded upon the infirm statements and vague allusions to which we have already adverted."

Lanciani alludes to monumental evidences, erected by

Constantine; to Eudoxia's church ad Vincula; to the 29th of June, Peter's anniversary; to children named after him; likenesses made of Peter and Paul after the second century. What Eudoxia's testimony was worth was shown in a previous chapter. Engravers would likely produce likenesses of Peter, for the same reason that the silversmiths made silver shrines of Diana, for profit; but such manufactures no more proved, in the one case, that Peter had seen Rome, than in the other that the image of the goddess had fallen down from heaven.

Lanciani then describes the Circus of Nero and the graves near it. He states that one of the coffins he found had the name of *Linus* upon it, though it might be, he acknowledges, the termination of the name Marcellinus. On the authority of the "Liber Pontificalis," he claims that " Linus was buried side by side with the remains of the blessed Peter in the Vatican, October 24." Now what is the reputation of this "Liber Pontificalis," on which Lanciani mainly rests for proof that Peter was buried in Rome? Neander styles it "that untrustworthy collection of the lives of the Roman Bishops," vi. 8. Powell on Succession, p. 218, Am. Ed., states: "That this Pontificale is a forgery is proved by numerous authors; among others see Howell's 'Pontificale,' Dupin's 'Bibliotheca Patrum,' Jewel's 'Defense.' . . It is justly denominated a forgery by Dr. Comber." Foye's "Romish Rites," etc., says of it: " The *Pontificale*, or lives of the Popes, the *Decretal Epistles*, and the Roman Martyrology, are all notorious forgeries. The two former were gotten up for the special purpose of advancing the Papacy. (See Dean Comber in Gibson, vol. xv. p. 97, and also Bishop

Pearson's Posthumous Dissertation.)" After describing the chair and a statue of St. Peter, Lanciani again refers to the "Pontificale" for his final and conclusive proof of this question.

The story is, p. 149, that Constantine placed a cross of gold over the gold lid of the Apostle's coffin, weighing 150 pounds. It happened in 1594, while Giacomo della Porta was leveling the floor of the church, the ground gave way, and he saw through the opening the grave of St. Peter, and upon it the golden cross of Constantine. The Pope with two cardinals was called to view it. Looking through the opening the Pope beheld the cross, and was so much impressed that he caused the opening to be closed at once. A manuscript deposition as to the fact is said to exist.

Just three hundred years ago this marvelous sight was seen, and this coffin of Peter, according to this legend, there remains, a silent witness to the fact of his burial at Rome.

If Rome has this evidence that Peter came to the West, why not display it, and put to rest the doubts with respect to the subject?

The connection of the story with the "Liber Pontificalis" is enough to destroy its credit, and since Lanciani has no more, nor stronger evidence to establish the fact, we are justified in asserting that there is no *monumental* testimony to show that the Apostle Peter was ever in the city of Rome.

It has already been substantiated that there are no *documents* which assert the facts, which are worthy of credence.

Any historical assumption which can produce neither monumental nor documentary proof is rejected by intelligent men; and though there may be *ecclesiastical* reasons why Peter should be regarded as the First Roman Bishop, to sustain the Church of Rome, her Pope, and her Priests, in their domination over the consciences of their followers, the verdict of history cannot be reversed. Babylon in Parthia will be regarded and revered, as the scene of the labors of the Chief Apostle; as the spot where his heroic soul departed to Paradise, and from which his glorified body will ascend to be forever with his Lord, and with the Church of the First-born in Heaven.

CHAPTER XXII.

Eusebius.

One of the most remarkable features in the matter we are considering, is that the main reliance of the advocates of the affirmative, rests on the works of an author who wrote over two centuries and a half after the death of Peter. Eusebius, Bishop of Cæsarea, A. D. 325, is the Father of Church History. Dupin writes: "Without the history of Eusebius we should scarcely have any knowledge not only of the history of those first ages of the Church, but even of the authors who wrote at that time." Scaliger, another profound historian, states: "All we have received concerning the Church, from Trajan to Constantine, we owe to Eusebius."

Our examination of the authors who precede Eusebius, has shown that they present no reliable nor satisfactory evidence that Peter ever left the West, to visit the city of Rome, or that there he resided, and ruled the Church.

Eusebius presents in his history some vague statements from the lost writings of Dionysius, Papias, and Gaius. Our examination has shown that if these quotations are authentic, they give us no valuable light on the question. As testimony to an important historical question they are of no account. The advocates of the Roman residence of Peter are, therefore, compelled to rely on the sole opinion of Eusebius, who appears to have credited the then prevailing view that Peter had visited that city.

An important inquiry suggests itself : What value did Eusebius place on his own statements? He writes (B. i., ch. 1): "Acknowledging that it is beyond my power to present the work perfect and unexceptionable, I freely confess it will crave indulgence, especially since, as the first of those that have entered upon the subject, we are attempting a kind of trackless and unbeaten path." Again, "We are totally unable to find even the bare vestiges of those who may have traveled the way before us." This author with respect to some of his statements uses the Greek terms " Phasi," "eoiken"— equivalent to the French, "On dit"—which we may render, " It is reported."

EDGAR, Var. Popy., p. 70, thus speaks of this uncertainty : "The fiction of Peter's visit to the metropolis of the world began to obtain credit about the end of the second century, . . . the tradition seemed doubtful to Eusebius. He introduces it as something reported, but not certain. The relation, to the Father of Ecclesiastical history, was mere heresay."

GAVAZZI, in the contest at Rome, 1872, says emphatically : "Michaelis excludes the opinion that Babylon signifies Rome. Grotius, instead, finds this opinion reasonable. Eusebius does not find it reasonable at all. He speaks of the letter, 'It is pretended it was written from Babylon,' and finds that intending Babylon for Rome, 'too daring a metaphor.' And note the words : ' It is pretended it was written from Babylon.' Eusebius thus excludes this supposition. But, now, if Eusebius excluded it, what matter that afterward a

Grotius should have come to admit it? And Jerome? Jerome says, in his commentary upon the 14th of Isaiah, that to interpret for Rome is to follow *Judaical words:* and then he says: 'Who could concede that Babylon was called Rome?'"

Herzog's Encyclopedia, while giving due credit to the good qualities of Eusebius, affirms: "The fidelity of the narrative is sometimes invalidated by inaccuracy and credulity ; sometimes by being fitted to the Procrustean bed of theological prejudices. Doctrinal considerations obscure and narrow his historical horizons. Even chronological mistakes abound."

Conybeare and Howson, St. Paul, etc., p. 712, Phil. Ed., 1877, on the growth of this tradition, remark: "The tradition which makes Peter Paul's fellow worker at Rome, and the companion of his imprisonment and martyrdom, seems to have grown up gradually in the Church, till at length in the fourth century it was accredited by Eusebius and Jerome.

"If we trace it to its origin, it appears to rest on but slender foundations." Referring to the writers previously examined, it continues : " This apparent weight of testimony, moreover, is much weakened by our knowledge of the facility with which unhistoric legends originate, especially when they fall in with the wishes of those among whom they circulate ; and it was a natural wish of the Roman world to represent the Chief of the Apostles as having the seat of his government, and the site of his martyrdom, in the chief city of the world."

The Church Quar. Rev., October, 1888, p. 226, Rev. of Livius, says on this subject : " If a mistaken view of history once becomes current, it does not become more true, by the number of times it is repeated. If the tradition of Peter's Roman Episcopate can be shown to date from the third and fourth century, it may be repeated ten thousand times, and be none the more true . . . The historical proof of the Petrine claim consists of stringing together extracts without criticism, and without regard to their authority."

In view of these facts, how vain, how dangerous, how indefensible, for a body of Christian men to make the eternal salvation of our Race to depend upon a supposed event, for which the only reliable testimony they can produce is the conjecture of one historian, who has, confessedly, presented no certain evidence of the tradition we are considering!

LAYMEN ON EUSEBIUS.

We present the testimony given by candid laymen of judicial minds, men better prepared, generally, to judge of the nature and value of evidence.

BUNSEN observes of Eusebius and other writers on this question : "They were evidently men of the East whose knowledge of the Western church was notoriously defective ; who wrote centuries after the Apostle's day, and were evidently doubtful of it as of a mere rumor."

BOUZIQUE, French historian and statesman, writes with respect to Gaius, quoted by Eusebius : "Eusebius, who never saw Rome, may in good faith have made a mistake here, misled by the legend which was then accounted veritable history. . . When he testifies in his own name he employs forms more or less dubitative, such as "It is said," "They think," etc. . . Whatever his own thought, Eusebius had too much prudence to contradict the common opinion of his Church ; but, as historian, he could not deny the unlikelihood of these diverse accounts ; hence the precautions of his style in the narratives of the last years of the two Apostles." (Hist. of Christianity, i., 369.)

GREENWOOD, in his " Cathedra Petri," i., 42, remarks: "In truth, no positive or circumstantial statement of the tradition of Peter's residence and martyrdom at Rome is to be met with in any Christian writer prior to Eusebius. Though he was himself convinced of the authenticity of the tradition, yet the poverty of his proofs shows clearly enough that it had not made the impression upon the Church, or attained to that maturity, in its view which so important a fact, if only tolerably supported, would lead us to expect. . . With the exception of the strange gossip collected by Eusebius, principally from Papias, about St. Peter's pursuit of Simon Magus, and the composition of St. Mark's Gospel, no witness to the fact of Peter's presence in Rome, at any period of his life, has been produced other than Eusebius himself ; and *he* only speaks to a belief founded upon the infirm statements and vague allusions to which we have already averted." Vol. ii. p. xi, he says : " Every rational inquirer must pronounce a tradition to be spurious when he finds contemporaries, eye-witnesses, actors in the scene, know nothing of the facts on which it rests. Tertullian and Dionysius may have believed the tradition. There is no doubt that three centuries after the event Eusebius did believe it."

MCGAVIN, a Scotchman, in his " Protestant," i., 702, a work which Robert Hall describes as " the most powerful confutation of the principles of the Popish system in a popular style of any work we have seen," and of whom Edgar says: " He was a man of sense, discrimination, admirable precision and honesty," writes:

"Nothing that these fathers (Origen and Eusebius) have written tends to prove the fact of the Apostles having been in Rome, except that there was a vague tradition on the subject, which is surely a foundation extremely slender for building such a fabric as the Church of Rome professes to build upon it. . . We know how difficult it is to come at the truth with regard to persons who lived within a few years of our own time, especially if no written mention of them has been preserved. It must have been much more difficult in the first stages of the Christian era, and in the disturbed state of the Roman Empire, to ascertain any fact with regard to the life and death of men who were so generally abhorred and so cruelly persecuted as the Christians were, except what they and their cotemporaries have written.

"Though the writers who spoke of Peter's having been at Rome had lived within fifty years of his death, they would not have been able to ascertain the fact without great difficulty; surely, then, when two or three hundred years have elapsed, it must have been impossible to know anything of the matter with certainty. There were few authors and no printing in those days. Real facts, with regard to a man so politically insignificant, could only be transmitted from mouth by persons still more obscure; and by the time of Origen or Eusebius, no man could tell what was true and what was not, except what the Christian churches had preserved as the authentic testimony of eye and ear witnesses; that is, just what we have in the New Testament, and nothing more can be depended upon."

SIMON, the English barrister who spent months in the British Museum examining exhaustively this subject, says: "Eusebius . . . tells us that he gives all the facts that had come down to his times respecting the Apostle Peter. In this history he is supposed to assert that St. Peter was in Europe, and that he was not put to death (as the Scriptures indicate) at Babylon. But it will be seen that he asserts neither of these alleged facts. . . Eusebius, it must not be forgotten, wrote nearly three centuries after the events in question could have occurred, and had, as we have seen, no intervening record of them to advert to, although there were no less than 150 ecclesiastical writers who had preceded him, some of them extremely voluminous. His sole authority, therefore (for such it would have been), could under such circumstances have had no weight whatever. No historical event, no event, even merely traditional, has ever been accepted, or ever could be accepted, as authentic upon the sole testimony of a writer who lived so many generations after the supposed period. . . Eusebius asserts no one thing, important or unimportant, that Peter is even ever said to have done in person at Rome. Not one day is indicated that he passed there; not one spot on which he trod there; not one word stated that he uttered there; not one person mentioned to whom he spoke there." (Miss. and Martyrdom of Peter, p. 144, 45.)

R. W. KENNARD, Esq., another able London advocate, referring to Simon's work, in the report of his controversy with McLachlan, p. 49, says: "I boldly and advisedly assert that there is no *evidence* to show that St. Peter ever was at Rome, much less that he ever assumed the office of Bishop of Rome, or that of Universal Patriarch." He fully indorses Simon's work.

An American layman, Dr. D. F. BACON, in his exhaustive "Lives of the Apostles," pp. 235-39, writes: "In justification of the certainty with which sentence is pronounced against the whole story of Peter's having gone to Rome, it is only necessary to refer to the full statement on pp. 245-50, in which the complete array of ancient evidence on this point is given by Dr. Murdock. If the support of great names is needed, those of Scaliger, Salmasius, Spanheim, and Bower, all mighty minds in criticism, are enough to justify the seeming boldness of the opinion that Peter never went west of the Hellespont, and probably never embarked on the Mediterranean."

With respect to Eusebius Bacon remarks, p. 221: "Eusebius enlarges the stories of Justin and Irenæus by an addition of his own. . . From this beginning he goes on to say that Peter went to Rome in the second year of Claudius to war against this Simon Magus, who never went there; so that we know how much the whole tale is worth by looking into the circumstance which constitutes its essential foundation. The idea of Peter's visit to Rome at that time is nowhere given before Eusebius, except in some parts of the 'Clementina,' a long series of the most unmitigated falsehoods, forged in the name of Clemens Romanus, without any certain date, but commonly supposed to have been made up of the continued contributions of several impudent liars during different portions of the second, third, and fourth centuries."

We have seen how the authority of Eusebius is rejected by the critical minds of these competent German, English, French, Scotch, and American laymen. Ellendorf, an accomplished Roman lay professor, has been shown to be in full accord with their views.

A SUGGESTED PARALLEL CASE.

The value of the testimony of Eusebius may be estimated rightly by presenting a parallel case. Let us suppose that in the course of a century the Church of Rome becomes thoroughly evangelized, which we sincerely desire; that at that late day an American writer of history should state that, in the year 1572, the greatest soldier of France and fifty thousand other Christians were massacred by Roman Catholics with the consent of their King; that the Bishop of Rome publicly offered thanksgiving in church for the event; ordered a Jubilee; a painting of the horrible scene, on the walls of his palace, and commemorating medals to be struck; and, moreover, urged the King of France to proceed further in his exterminating scheme. Further suppose that no preceding historians had narrated this event, and that all proof presented was some ambiguous language of three writers not authenticated, whose works were no longer extant. Could men living at that time be expected to place reliance on a story of that nature, of events attributed to so distant a period? Eusebius has no greater claim for reliance on his fanciful and improbable tale about Peter.

But how came a writer of the ability of Eusebius to accept the tradition concerning the journey of Peter to Rome? He appears to have been deceived, together with Irenæus and Tertullian, by the statement of Justin Martyr, with respect to the statue at Rome to the Sabine deity, Semo Sangus or Sancus. Justin, who knew little Latin, regarded this as referring to Simon Magus, whom tradition had carried to Rome, where, by his magical arts, he had induced the Romans to rank him among the gods. Justin makes this statement in his address to the Emperor Antoninus. Neither Justin, Irenæus, nor Tertullian connects Peter with the narrative.

The Clementine fictions do; but these are known to be "unmitigated falsehoods," as we have seen. Eusebius not having been at Rome, and misled by the language of Papias, Dionysius, and Gaius, which we have shown to be untrustworthy, proceeds to commemorate the circumstance previously unrecorded, except in the Clementina: that Peter traveled from the East to the West, to vanquish the blasphemous sorcerer, Simon Magus.

By a singular providence, in the year 1574, there was excavated from the very spot, on an island on the Tiber, indicated by Justin, the image with the inscription to which he refers. It was recognized as a heathen deity. Justin, like Simon, was a Samaritan, and knowing of his arts, the more readily imagined that the Romans had deified him.

SAWYER, Organ. Christ., p. 47, writes: "The error of Eusebius is traced through Clemens Alexandrinus, A. D. 220, to a misunderstanding of Justin Martyr, A. D. 168; interpreting the inscription of a statue of the Roman Deity Semo, of Simon the Magician, Acts 8: 4, 10, 18. This mistake led to a fabulous history of the supposed combat of Peter with Simon, and the supposition of his residence at Rome."

GIFFORD, Intro. Rom. Speaker's Com. on Eusebius, remarks: "This arbitrary and erroneous combination of traditions which had no original connection, may possibly have been suggested to Eusebius by the historical connection between Simon Magus and Simon Peter, in Acts. viii., or more probably he may have borrowed it from the strange fictions of the 'Clementina,' 'Recognitions,' and 'Homilies,' and 'Apostolic Constitutions.' It is most important to observe that these traditions, preserved by Papias and Clement, have not the slightest connection of persons, time, or place with Justin Martyr's story of Simon Magus."

Dr. Murdock, in his Manuscript Lectures, quoted in Bacon's "Lives," p. 231, after presenting all the Patristic authorities claimed with respect to Peter's visit to Rome, thus concludes:

"So far as the later Fathers contradict those of the first three centuries, they ought to be rejected, because they could not have so good means of information. Oral tradition must in three centuries have become worthless compared with what it was in the second and third centuries; and of written testimony which could be relied on, they had none except of the early Fathers.

"Besides, we have seen how these later Fathers were led astray. They believed the fable of Simon Magus' legerdemain at Rome, and his deification there. They read the Clementine fictions and supposed them to be novels founded on facts. In their eulogies of Peter, they were fond of relating marvelous and affecting stories about him, and therefore too readily admitted fabulous additions. And, lastly, the Bishops of Rome and their numerous adherents had a direct and an immense interest depending on this traditional history— for by it alone they made out their succession to the chair of Peter, and the legitimacy of their ghostly power."

The want of information with respect to the Apostle, is clearly proved by his glaring mistake with regard to the time he ascribes to his Roman visit. It will be observed that he fixes this time in the second year of

Claudius, A. D. 42. But the Scriptures plainly contradict this statement, as do also the Roman authors Cellier, Baluze, Pagi, Dupin, Hug, Feilmoser, Klee, Herbst, Ellendorf, Maier, and Stengel.

The value of the testimony of Eusebius with respect to the presence of Peter in Rome may be gathered from the opinions of the learned writers, lay and clerical, here presented. They agree in pronouncing it as unworthy of acceptance as evidence, on the subject discussed in these pages.

We respect Eusebius for much that he has written. We owe to him the first formal list of the Books of the New Testament. He has handed down to us the names of many Christian heroes who suffered martyrdom, with notices and historical events deeply interesting to the Christian Church. But he little imagined that, in presenting as history, the traditions of his time concerning Peter, he was aiding in building up the most formidable foe to the progress of Christian truth and righteousness which the Church has ever encountered; and whose work of evil is still in operation.

It has been seen that we possess no authentic statement before Eusebius, that the Apostle Peter ever was in Rome, deserving of respect; and that Eusebius had no sure evidence on which to base his belief in this matter.

And thus the chief pillar on which the Pope bases his claim to the universal Headship of the Church, and the right to curse all who reject his Supremacy, has no better foundation than quicksand. The truth of history pronounces this Peter-Roman legend a baseless Fiction.

CHAPTER XXIII.

Professor Ramsey's Theory.

A WORK of great interest and value has recently appeared, entitled, "The Church in the Roman Empire before A. D. 170," by W. M. Ramsey, M. A., Professor in Aberdeen, and formerly Professor in Oxford, pp. 494.

The author has personally investigated the country of Asia Minor, and has written ably about it. A portion of his work is devoted to the various persecutions of Christians there, and the condition of the churches.

Chapter xiii. is closely related to the present inquiry, inasmuch as it discusses Peter's First Epistle, and the letters of Clement and Ignatius.

The theory that Professor Ramsey explains and defends is : that the language of Peter's Epistle cannot be made consistent with the nature of the persecution in the time of Nero, but must refer to the Flavian period ; consequently the Epistle of Peter must have been written as late as A. D. 80. He also advocates a twenty-five years' residence for Peter in Rome.

His words are these, p. 281 : " They (the Christians) suffer for the Name (iv. 14–16) pure and simple ; the trial takes the form of an inquiry into their religion giving them the opportunity of 'glorifying God in this Name.'

"The picture is here complete. We have the fully developed kind of trial which we suppose to have been instituted about 75-80, and which was carried out by Pliny as part of a fixed policy of the Empire toward the Christians. These circumstances are essentially different from those of the Neronian period." P. 242, "Under Nero . . . The trial is held and the condemnation is pronounced, in respect not of the Name, but of serious offenses naturally connected with the Name," etc.

The decision of this question is naturally dependent upon the locality of Peter. Was he in Parthia in a place of safety when he wrote, or in a situation where punishment was imminent?

Our author concedes that we have no accurate information concerning the events of the Church in this period. He says, p. 253: "In the dearth of contemporary trustworthy authorities we are compelled, unless we leave this period a blank, to have recourse to hypothesis," and p. 189: "In a subject of such difficulty as the history of the early Church, a subject about which the only point that is universally agreed upon is its obscurity," etc.

We have maintained in this inquiry that the question was one of probabilities, and that the position that Peter labored and wrote in Parthian Babylon, had a vastly greater preponderance of probability—and hence the 330 authors quoted, or enumerated, had embraced and defended this view.

Professor Ramsey has evidently not appreciated the argument for Peter's Parthian residence, else he would not have used these words, p. 287: "That Babylon should be understood as the Chaldean City, appears to conflict so entirely with all record and early tradition, as to hardly need discussion."

Before this extreme statement can be received,

we must ask our author to answer the arguments of Lightfoot, Michaelis, Turretin, Edersheim, and Bishop Wordsworth ; of the historians, Neander, Niebuhr, Guerike, and Kurtz ; Milman, Robertson, Stanley, and Murdock ; of Roman scholars, De Marca, Dupin, Hug, and Ellendorf ; men who represent the predominating opinion of the learned outside the Church of Rome ; authors who assert that there is no reliable evidence that Peter visited Rome, but that he lived, and died, in the East, and that his letters were written prior to A. D. 70.

We assert that Peter must be established at Rome, before we can admit our author's hypothesis. The language of Peter has been shown by competent writers to be reconcilable with that of a person in a place of safety, and if this view is sound he could not have addressed his letter from Rome, after the persecution of Nero.

We will briefly examine Professor Ramsey's objections to the opinion that Peter lived and wrote in the Parthian Babylon.

P. 282 : "While the tradition that St. Peter perished in Rome is strong and early, the tradition about the date of his death is not so clear. . . The tradition that he lived for a long time in Rome is also strong, and as Dr. Harnack justly says, 'It is difficult to suppose that so large a body of tradition had no foundation in fact.'" Harnack on "Peter" in the Encyc. Brit., 9th ed.

We observe here that the earliest tradition that places Peter in Rome is contained in the Clementina, and this is the fountain head of the legend. Harnack himself styles this work "A Jewish-Christian partisan romance." The Encyc. Brit. here referred to, Art. Popedom, says :

"It is maintained by a great majority of Protestant scholars that there is no proof that Peter was ever in Rome at all."

With regard to Peter's death, Origen and Tertullian, contrary to our author's view, place it in the time of Nero. Authors quoted in this volume make it clear that we know nothing concerning Peter's death; that it is not even certain that he died a martyr's death.

P. 283. Tertullian is mentioned as stating that Clement was ordained by St. Peter, and we read: "The latter passage is the strongest evidence we possess on the point, and it clearly proves that the Roman tradition during the latter part of the second century placed the martyrdom much later than the time of Nero."

In chapter xx. we have shown that this author was unworthy of credit, and his statement has no force. As to Clement's ordination by Peter, authors like Dick, Ellendorf, Edgar, and Turretin (see pp. 44–47), argue that it is morally impossible that Clement in his Epistle would have omitted all reference to the fact if it had occurred.

P. 286. Another objection is thus stated: "That this epistle was written from Rome I cannot doubt. It is impregnated with Roman thought to a degree beyond any other book in the Bible. . . That a Jew whose life had been spent in Palestine and Chaldea should write so *Romanized* a letter is even more improbable."

If Mark was with Peter at Babylon acting as his secretary, as the ancients all declare, and his intimate associate, the difficulty may be only apparent.

DA COSTA, a brilliant Hebrew layman of Holland, suggests that Mark was the "devout soldier" sent by Cornelius to Peter—one of the first Gentile converts, and hence endeared to him. Mark's Roman name and the Roman phrases in his Gospel are thus explained. There is no evidence that Mark and Peter were in Rome together.

BLEEK, Intro. Mark, vol. ii., says : " When 1st Peter was written Mark must have been with Peter in Babylon." MEYER writes, Intro. Com. Mark : " At 1 Peter, v. 13, we find Mark again with his spiritual father Peter at Babylon. His special relation to Peter is specified by the unanimous testimony of the ancient Church as having been that of interpreter. . . This view is plainly confirmed by Jerome, ad Hedib. ii." Archbishop THOMSON, Speaker's Com. Intro. Mark : " Somewhat later Mark is with Peter in Babylon. Some have considered Babylon to be a name given here to Rome in a mystical sense, surely without reason."

SAWYER, Organic Christ., p. 47 : " Mark's supposed residence at Rome depends upon the supposition that Peter resided there, and has no other foundation. Mark was Peter's companion at Babylon." FAUSSETT, Bib. Encyc. : " After Paul's death Mark joined his old father in the faith at Babylon. . . The tradition (Clem. Alex. in Euseb.) that Mark was Peter's companion *at Rome* arose from misunderstanding Babylon to be *Rome*."

It has been remarked that the Gospel of Mark contains more Latin expressions than the other Gospels. It would be reasonable, therefore, that Peter's Epistle, written likewise in conjunction with Mark, would be somewhat *Romanized* in its tone ! See pp. 82–86.

Moreover, Silvanus, a Roman citizen, was at the same time with Mark, a companion of Peter. Silvanus, who had visited the churches addressed by Peter, in Paul's company, had, it is fair to believe, brought news to Babylon of their condition. McClintock and Strong on Peter, write: "It is highly probable that Silvanus, considering his rank, character, and special connection with those churches with their great Apostle and founder, would be consulted by Peter throughout, and that they would together read the Epistles of Paul, especially those addressed to the churches in those districts. . .

"It has been observed above that there is good reason to suppose that Peter was in the habit of employing an interpreter; nor is there anything inconsistent with his position or character in the supposition that Silvanus, perhaps also Mark, may have assisted him in giving expression to the thoughts suggested to him by the Holy Spirit." These authors place Peter in Babylon.

JEROME, Epist. cxx. c. x. ad Hed., writes: "Paul, therefore employed Titus as an interpreter, just as the blessed Peter employed Mark, whose Gospel was composed by the latter out of the narrations of the former. And the Epistles also which are ascribed to Peter differ from one another in style and character and verbal structure, from which fact it is evident that he had been constrained to make use of different interpreters."

Valesius, Dupin, and De Marca, eminent Romanists, hold that Peter's Epistles were written from Parthian Babylon. The objection to *Romanized* expressions does not seem valid. See p. 86.

A FURTHER OBJECTION.

Professor RAMSEY holds that Christianity had not extended so widely as to warrant an epistle earlier than A. D. 75-80, to be addressed to the provinces mentioned in 1 Peter i. He says: "It is inconceivable that before A. D. 64, it had spread away from that line (the main line of intercourse across the empire) through the northern provinces," and again : " The congregations of Asia Minor were composed of persons who had been Pagans (iv. 2, 3). It is contrary to all reasonable probability that they contained any appreciably large Jewish elements."

We do not think the facts justify these statements. If Peter's Epistle had been written as early as 64, the Gospel must have been preached for thirty years in " Pontus, Asia, Cappadocia, Phrygia, and Pamphylia," which included the greater portion of the region mentioned in the Epistle. Hebrews, converted in Jerusalem on the day of Pentecost, had returned to their homes to preach Jesus, who was their acknowledged Messiah. Annually, subsequently, they had visited Jerusalem, and had heard the Gospel preached. Must we believe that the Gospel was without effect in these regions for thirty years ? Were those converts silent about Jesus ?

BACON, in his exhaustive life of Peter, writes, p. 137 : " The foreign Jews, then at Jerusalem, being witnesses of these wonderful things, would not fail, on their return home, to give the above affair a prominent place in their account of their pilgrimage, when they recounted their various adventures and observations to their inquiring friends. Among these visitors too, were probably some who were themselves converted to the new faith, and each one of these would be a sort of missionary, preaching Christ crucified to his countrymen in his distant home, and telling them of a way to God which their fathers had not known."

Bacon further says, pp. 238–241 : " The First Epistle of Peter contains at the close a general salutation from the Church in Babylon to the Christians of Asia Minor to whom it is addressed. . . . High associations of historical and religious interest gave all around him a holy character. . . . Inspired by such associations and remembrances, and by the spirit of simple truth and sincerity, Peter wrote his First Epistle, which he directed to his Jewish brethren in several sections of Asia Minor, who had probably been brought under his ministry only in Jerusalem, on their visit there in attendance on the great annual feast, which, in all years, as in that of Pentecost, on which the Spirit was outpoured, came up to the Holy City to worship ; for there is no *proof* whatever that Peter ever visited those countries to which he sent this letter. . .

"The main purport seems to be to inspire them with courage and consolation under some weight of general suffering then endured by them, or impending over them. Indeed, the whole scope of the Epistle bears most manifestly on this one particular point—the preparation of its readers, the Christian communities of Asia Minor, for heavy sufferings."

The natural supposition is, therefore, that there were congregations of Jewish Christians in these provinces at an early period, to whom a comforting and encouraging letter might be addressed. Such is the view taken by Eusebius, Jerome, and Theophylact ; by Erasmus, Calvin, Grotius, Bengel, Hug, and Pott. Michaelis, Credner, Neudecker, Mynster, Davidson, Storr, and Jowett, hold that the letter was to Proselytes. On the other hand, many eminent writers think it was written to Gentiles, such as Augustine, Luther, Wettstein, Steiger, Bruckner, Mayerhoff, Weisinger, Neander, Reuss, Schaff, Huther, Schneckenburger, Baur, and Hilgenfield.

When there is such great diversity of opinion among scholars of equal merit, it is plain that there is no decisive force in the objection offered by Professor Ramsey, that there were not converted Hebrews in the provinces mentioned in First Peter, at the period at which the Epistle has been generally regarded as written.

The true meaning of the term "Dispersion" used by the Apostle we regard as indicated by Canon Farrar: "The Dispersion of which St. Peter is mainly thinking is a spiritual one. He is writing to all Christians in the countries which he mentions." Eadie, in his Commentary on Galatians, agrees with Farrar in this view.

We have given in previous pages testimony from Wm. Smith, Wordsworth, Faussett, Milman, and others, as to Hebrew converts being addressed in the Epistle.

De Marca, an eminent Romanist, writes: "Although the ancients supposed Peter to have here meant Rome, Scaliger can be shown to be right when he says that this letter was writen from Babylon itself, to those dispersed Jews whose provincial synagogue depended upon the Patriarch of Babylon."

Professor Shedd, Com., wisely suggests: "That this is the literal Babylon is favored by the fact that the First Epistle of Peter was addressed to the Jewish Church in Asia Minor (1 Peter ii.), whose condition and needs must more naturally come under the eye of an Apostle on the banks of the Euphrates, than on the banks of the Tiber."

Lange, Com. 1 Peter, confirms this view: "Peter appears for some time to have had his sphere of labor in the Parthian empire, since he sends salutations from his co-elected in Babylon (1 Peter v. 13), which is probably not to be understood of Rome, but of Babylon in Chaldea. Many Jews were dispersed there and Christianity was early diffused in those regions. . . The First Epistle of Peter has no record of churches already organized, but makes mention of "elect strangers of the Dispersion."

THE MAIN OBJECTION.

The greatest difficulty, as has already been shown, which Professor Ramsey has with regard to giving an early date for Peter's Epistle, is that its tone and expressions do not harmonize with the character of the Neronian persecution. He writes, p. 279 : "The view that First Peter was written between 64 and 67 would involve a modification of our theory, and an admission of the view which we have deliberately rejected, that the development from the condemnation of Christians for definite crimes, to the absolute proscription of the name, took place before the conclusion of Nero's reign."

We remark here that our author's view of the date of Peter's First Epistle differs essentially from that of the great body of scholars, who have examined the subject.

Among authors of note, Hug and Dupin, Romanists; Bloomfield, Lardner, Faussett, Davidson, Wiesler, Guerike, Steiger, Dewette, Thiersch, and Michaelis, regard it as written between 60 and 65. This is the common opinion. Alford dates it 63-67.

When an author undertakes to reverse the accepted view of the world's scholarship generally, and to advocate a theory which is vastly opposed to the probabilities of the case (for we have no accredited documents here), a theory which removes the Apostle Peter from Babylon, where the Scripture locates him, and places him in Rome, where he had no call, and where he was not wanted; we properly demand reasons which are self-evident, or facts which have not been previously known. We do not find these in this volume, with respect to Peter. Others who have carefully analyzed the Epistle, and have investigated the facts of history, as far as known with respect to the various Christian persecutions, find no difficulty in reconciling the expressions of the Apostle with circumstances of Nero's reign.

In reply to the position taken by Professor Ramsey, we prefer to present the argument of others who have thoroughly examined the subject.

Bacon, an erudite American layman, before quoted, Lives, p. 243, writes: "The conclusion is inevitable that there was in the condition of the Christians to whom Peter wrote a most remarkable crisis just occurring— one too of no limited or local character; and that throughout Asia Minor, and the whole Empire, a trying time of universal trouble was immediately beginning with all who owned the faith of Jesus. The widely extended character of the evil necessarily implies its emanation from the supreme power of the Empire, which, bounded by no provincial limits, would sweep through the world in desolating fury on the righteous sufferers; nor is there any event recorded in the history of those ages, which could thus have affected the Christian communities, except the first Christian persecution, in which Nero, with wanton malice, set the example of cruel, unfounded accusation, that soon spread throughout his whole Empire, bringing suffering and death to thousands of faithful believers."

Bacon holds, in opposition to Professor Ramsey, that the persecution was for *the Name*. "Nero charged the Christians, as a sect, with his own atrocious crime, the dreadful devastation by fire of his own capital ; and on this ground everywhere instituted a cruel persecution against them. In connection with this procedure the Christians are first mentioned in Roman history as a new and peculiar class of people, called *Christians*, from their founder, *Christus;* and in reference to this matter, abusive charges are brought against them. . . Not even a conjecture can be made, much less any historical proof be brought, that beyond Palestine any person had ever yet been made to suffer death on the score of religion, or of any stigma attached to that sect, before the time when Nero involved them in the cruel charge just mentioned. . .

"It is evident that the Epistle was not written in the same year in which the burning occurred ; but in the subsequent one, the twelfth of Nero's reign, and the sixty-fifth of the Christian era. By that time the condition and prospects of the Christians throughout the Empire were such as to excite the deepest solicitude, and the great Apostle, also, though himself residing in the great Parthian Empire, removed from all danger of injury from the Roman Emperor, was by no means disposed to forget the high claims the sufferers had on him for counsel and consolation. This dreadful event was the most important which has ever yet befallen the Christians, and there would certainly be just occasion for surprise, if it had called forth no consolatory testimony from the founders of the faith, and if no trace of it could be found in the Apostolic records. . .

"From the uniform tone in which the Apostle alludes to the danger as threatening only his readers, without the slightest attention to the circumstance of his being involved in the difficulty, is drawn another important confirmation of the locality of the Epistle. He uniformly uses the second person when referring to trials; but if he himself had then been so situated as to share in the calamity for which he strove to prepare them, he would have been very apt to have expressed his own feelings in view of the common evil. Paul, in those Epistles which were written under circumstances of personal distress, is very full of warm expressions of the state of mind in which he met his trials; nor was there in Peter any lack of the fervid energy that would burst forth in similarly eloquent sympathy on the like occasion. But from Babylon, beyond the bounds of Roman sway, he looked on their sufferings only with that pure sympathy which his regard for his brethren would excite; and it is not to be wondered, then, that he uses the second person merely in speaking of their distresses."

Bacon, moreover, states: "That this Neronian persecution was as extensive as it is here made to appear, is proved by Lardner and Hug. The former in particular gives several very interesting evidences in his 'Heathen Testimonies,' especially the remarkable inscription referring to this persecution found in Portugal." (Test. of Anc. Heath. c. iii.)

Farrar's "Early Ages of Christianity," with respect to the date of the Epistle, says, "He is writing to those who, although their faith was undergoing a severe test, like gold tried in the fire, were yet mainly liable to danger rather than to death. They were exposed to false accusation as malefactors, to revilings, threats, and a general system of terrorism and sufferings.

"Now this is exactly the state of things which must have existed in the provinces after the Neronian persecution. The crisis marked out the Christians for a special hatred above and beyond what they experienced as being in the eyes of the world a debased Jewish sect. It even brought into view that name of 'Christians,' which, though invented by the jeering populace of Antioch as early as A. D. 44, had not until this time come into general vogue. . .

"Some have attempted to prove that the state of things referred to could only have existed during the persecution of Trajan (A. D. 101, Swegler, Köstlin, Baur), which is, of course, equivalent to saying that the Epistle is spurious. But, considering that we find traces of trials at least as severe as those to which St. Peter alludes some time *before* the Neronian persecution had broken out, and in the Apocalyptic letters to the seven churches of Asia *after* it had broken out, the whole argument is groundless."

PRESENSÉ, it will be seen by referring to p. 113, regards the Epistle as having been written from Babylon at a period preceding that of Nero.

In reply to Swegler, who dates the Epistle in the time of Trajan, McClintock and Strong remark: "The tranquillity of tone in this Epistle would be remarkable under any persecution, in that it is of calm, heroic endurance which trusts in an unseen arm and has hopes undimmed by death; that the persecution of Christians, simply for the Name which they love, was not an irrational ferocity peculiar to Trajan's time; that in the provinces Christians were always exposed to popular fury and irregular magisterial condemnation; that there is no allusion to judicial trial in the Epistle, for the word $\dot{\alpha}\pi o \lambda o \gamma \iota \alpha$ does not imply it; and that the sufferings of Christians in Asia Minor, as referred to or predicted, do not agree with the recorded facts in Pliny's letter, for according to it they were by a formal investigation and sentence doomed to death. (Huther, *Einleit*, p. 28.)

"The persecutions referred to in this Epistle are rather such as Christians have always to encounter in heathen countries from an ignorant mob easily stirred to violence, and where the civil power, though inclined to toleration in theory, is yet swayed by strong prejudices, and prone from position and policy to favor and protect the dominant superstition."

The main difficulty of Professor Ramsey with regard to Peter, his residence, and Epistle, seems to have been considered and effectually removed by these competent and thorough critics.

THE PAPAL COMMENDATION.

A greater interest has been aroused in Professor Ramsey's volume in the fact, that his view has been publicly commended by Leo XIII., and a gold medal bestowed upon the author for his scholarly and valuable work. His personal exploration of Asia Minor has thrown much needed light upon that region, where Christianity made early and rapid progress. St. Paul's connection with the work is most ably investigated, and treated in an unusually interesting and vivid manner. It is not, however, with the experience of Paul that the Pope is especially concerned, but that the book brings Peter to Rome, and thus serves to prop up the ecclesiastical fabric which depends for its support and its existence on that supposition, but for which there is no proof, as has been shown in the present examination.

It has been seen that the writer does not regard our

author as having established his theory with respect to Peter, nor that he has met successfully the arguments of the competent scholars who have been quoted.

The predominant view of the world's scholarship outside the Roman communion, has settled the question, that there is no reasonable or satisfactory evidence that Peter ever deserted the East for the West, or that anyone ever supposed it for a century after his death.

The Roman edifice is weakening with time, and with the progress of modern thought and investigation. May that Church look to Paul, its founder, for light and direction. Peter in no wise can benefit it by a supposed personal presence as the first Pope, or by the possession of his remains. His *words*, if studied and heeded, may prevent the downfall which surely attends every work which is built on wood, hay, and stubble, and not on the everlasting foundations of "*the Truth as it is in Jesus.*"

CHAPTER XXIV.

Recapitulation.

"The office of the Head of the Church is claimed by the Pope as the successor of St. Peter. The adversary of the Papacy who devotes his energies to the undermining of the position is so far logical; and he manifests his appreciation of the value of time. Could the Papacy be dislodged from it, there would be left him no vantage ground, the occupation of which would enable him to retrieve his loss. . . . Now the simplest way of proving that the Bishop of Rome is not the successor of St. Peter is . . . by establishing, as a stubborn fact, that St. Peter himself, the presumed source of the Papal claims, never was Bishop of Rome, in fact, that he never was in the Eternal City."

Thus writes Rev. Reuben Parsons, D. D., in "Studies in Church History," A. D. 1886, with the imprimatur of Archbishop Corrigan of New York.

We need no better evidence of the importance of the topic here discussed. We repeat the words of Cardinal Perrone presented in chapter first:

"None but an apostate Catholic could make the assertion that 'St. Peter was never at Rome.' The reason of this fact (namely, that no Catholic could make this assertion) is that the coming of St. Peter in Rome and the seat there established by him is connected, as the indispensable condition, with an article of our faith;

that is, the Primacy of Order and Jurisdiction belonging of Divine right to the Roman Pontiff. Hence it follows, that he cannot be a Catholic, who does not admit the Coming, the Episcopate, the Death of St. Peter in Rome." (Cardinal Perrone's "St. Peter in Rome," 1861, p. 32.)

This language is taken from Professor Clement M. Butler, Butler's work " St. Paul in Rome," p. 267, written in Rome, in reply to statements made in an address in that city by Cardinal Manning. Dr. Butler writes: "To the Romanist it is essential that he should prove that St. Peter presided over the Church of Rome. On that assumed fact is erected the most important doctrine—next to that of salvation by the death of Christ—ever proclaimed to man. If true, it is a truth on which the salvation of myriads rests. If false, it is a portentous falsehood, the evil results of which no imagination can conceive. It rests on the fact that St. Peter was in Rome. If he was not there, it falls to the ground a convicted and dead lie. Now it will be admitted that such a fact should have proof that is unimpeachable, abundant, and undoubted."

We shall recapitulate the evidence on which we rest our case, that there is no proof that is unimpeachable, abundant, or even undoubted. Nay, more, in the homely words of McGavin: "There is no sensible man who would venture the value of a new hat that Peter was Bishop of Rome. . . That he was Bishop of Rome, or that he ever saw Rome, yet remains to be proved."

In further proof of the vital bearing of this subject on the Papal position, we repeat the words of Dr. S. B. Smith in his "Teachings of the Holy Catholic Church," indorsed by Cardinals McCloskey and Gibbons, Bishops Gilmour, Lynch, and Elder. "The conclusion which follows from the fact of St. Peter being Bishop of Rome is important, and one which every Catholic looks upon as the foundation of his faith."

ANTECEDENT PROBABILITIES.

Before reviewing the argument let us glance at the antecedent probabilities in the case. And here the *a priori* argument is immensely in favor of those on the negative side of this question, acknowledged to be fundamental by the Romanists.

First: From the position of Peter as Divinely appointed missionary to the Hebrew people; coupled with the fact, as shown, that the great mass of the Jewish nation were in the East, in and around Babylon in Chaldea, from which region his first Epistle is directed.

Intercourse was constant between Palestine and Babylon. The latter was reckoned a part of the former. The distance to Rome by sea was three times greater, and still more so by land. All the circumstances combine to detain Peter in his peculiar work in the East, for which he was fitted; the field to which he was called by the Spirit.

Second: From the fact that St. Paul was in Rome, aided by a band of competent co-workers; and therefore, that Peter's co-operation was not needed. The circumstances do not appear to have warranted the expense and risk of a long, laborious, and exhaustive journey. Besides, we have reason to believe that Peter's appearance in Rome would not have been welcomed by the great Apostle already there. Already had these two foremost of that band been in collision. The dissimulation of Peter had aroused the indignation of the fiery-tempered Paul; who had previously been engaged in a sharp contention (*paroxysm* in the Greek), with the devout Barnabas on a matter of Missions.

Doubtless, as in Corinth, where parties had arisen between the followers of the two Apostles, such rivalry would have been intensified by the presence of Peter in Rome. The Apostle to the Gentiles would have again come into antagonism with the Apostle to the Circumcision; and from the history and character of the two men, peaceful co-operation among them and harmony in the Church under the circumstances would have been a moral impossibility. If Paul went into a *paroxysm* of strife with the mild Barnabas, he would have allowed no interference from the impetuous Peter, whom "he rebuked to his face." Of all the Apostles, Peter would have been the last to have intruded upon the special field of Paul. If we credit him with but little prudence, he never would have traveled to Rome while Paul was in charge.

Third: The principles laid down by both men in their letters indicate this opinion. Paul says expressly that he built on "no other man's foundation" (Rom. xv. 20; 2 Cor. x. 16), and certainly he would have allowed no man as a rival in his field of labor, except he was expressly needed. The abundance of laborers in Rome made Peter's presence wholly unnecessary. Peter, moreover, expressly condemns an intrusion of this kind. He discountenances in his first Epistle (v. 20) all— *allotrio-episcopizing*—overseeing the affairs of others; intruding as a "bishop in another's field," as the Greek has it. The Apostle in going to Rome would have acted contrary to his own inspired directions to the Church.

Fourth: A very serious objection arises to the presence of Peter in Rome, from the disputes concerning the authenticity and genuineness of the second Epistle of Peter. Eusebius, who is the main reliance for the claim of Peter's presence in Rome, writes of the Apostle's second Epistle, I. III, c. III: "I have understood only one Epistle to be genuine and admitted by the ancient fathers." The Epistle was not received into the Canon until the Council of Hippo, A. D. 393. The Church of Rome accepts this Epistle as genuine, but can that Church explain the early doubts concerning it if the Apostle had been Bishop of Rome? Would Peter have kept secret from the Church that he had written two Epistles? We may regard it as absolutely certain that if written at Rome by Peter, the intelligence would have reached the Universal Church, and there would have been no doubts on the subject.

Kennion in his "St. Peter and Rome," p. 7, well writes: "If the second as well as the first Epistle was written on the banks of the Euphrates or Tigris, the martyrdom which he then looked forward to as soon to take place might most readily account for it; for I do not think we have any very clear account of the Parthian Church in those days. If when Peter was put to death, most of his fellow-Christians in the same place, or on the same journey, suffered with him; if in the Parthian war, which was then raging or soon afterward broke out, the remains of that Church were swept away, and few copies of this Epistle left, the doubts which have existed are fully explained.

"And, if so, another difficulty may perhaps be got

rid of ; for St. Jude's Epistle, with which that of Peter is obviously connected, is also one of the doubtful ones. And though we know little of St. Jude's later history, various traditions speak of him as in Edessa, Assyria, and Persia ; that is, in the near neighborhood of St. Peter ; and nothing is more likely than that the latter should embody those burning words of his fellow Apostle, in the letter which he was then about to send to the Churches of Asia Minor."

Dr. LITTLEDALE, in his "Petrine Claims," p. 73, writes : "The fact that the Second Epistle of Peter is amongst the disputed books of the New Testament, and that St. Jerome, whose warm attachment to the Church of Rome makes certain the opinion of that Church would weigh much with him, is one of those who doubt its genuineness (de Vir. Illust. i.), is strong presumptive evidence against St. Peter having been at Rome when it was written. For if he had been there, the local Church must needs have been in a position to say whether he had or had not addressed such an epistle to the whole Catholic Church ; and his single attestation would have ended the controversy. Clearly nothing more was known at Rome than elsewhere on the point."

Dr. WELLS in Sacred Geography, p. 261, on this matter of St. Jude, presents interesting thoughts which will be seen on p. 104.

The removal of the doubts which have affected so many minds with respect to this portion of the Sacred Canon, is one of the good effects of making clear the truth, that the *a priori* argument, and the verdict of history are positively and, we may say, decisively, against Peter's journey to the West.

Fifth : Lightfoot, as we have seen, p. 89, suggests : " The consideration that Peter ended his days at Babylon, is very useful, if my judgment fail not, at the setting out of ecclesiastical story." Among the points cleared up by establishing Peter in his true locality at Babylon is the field of labor of his fellow Apostle among the Circumcision, John the Evangelist. In chapter xiv., we have shown the strong probability that John labored in Parthia with Peter until his later years, when the Church's needs required his presence in Ephesus.

Sixth : It seems highly reasonable that, as on account of the ancient tendency to idolatry, Jehovah concealed the body of Moses from the Israelites ; for the same reason Providence has kept from the certain knowledge of man, the later residence and the burial place of the most highly honored, and foremost of the Apostles of our Lord.

The fearful idolatry which has so sadly characterized the Church of Rome with respect to the human Mother of our Lord, and to the remains of martyred saints, would have been greatly intensified if the bones of Peter could have been discovered and identified. They have never been found. No man knoweth of his sepulcher unto this day. So has the Lord ordered it. Peter was buried in Babylon, and from that spot shall he rise on the Resurrection morn. He will be surrounded by his fellow martyrs, and not by that long, dark catalogue of men who have been falsely claimed to be his infallible successors.

The justice of the charge of idolatry may be gathered from Father Hardouin's words on p. 6, where he affirms that Rome had Peter's head, and " that it ought to be duly worshiped."

Bishop Wordsworth, Com. on 1 Peter, uses impressive language on this topic. He says:

"The obscurity in which the history of St. Peter is involved after his delivery from his imprisonment, A. D. 44 (Acts xii. 17), is very remarkable. It seems providential.

"It may be ascribable to the same causes as the silence of Holy Scripture with reference to the Blessed Virgin Mary. It is like a prophetic protest against the errors which grew up afterward within the Church, and fastened themselves with a semblance of reverence on his venerable name; like ivy which injures the tree it dresses up with its foliage. There is, therefore, it is probable, an eloquent significance in this silence."

Dr. William Hague, "Christianity and Statesmanship," p. 134, eloquently writes:

"The learned and diligent Michaelis has shown good reason to believe that Peter wrote his Epistles from the Chaldean Babylon, and that there, amid the scenes around which clustered hallowed memories of Ezekiel and Daniel, he spent the last days of his Apostleship. The renowned temple in Rome which bears his name is said by some to be built on his tomb.

"There is no proof, however, that his mortal remains were ever laid in a Roman sepulcher, but we are rather led to the conclusion that He who caused the body of Moses to be hidden from the Israelites permitted also the body of the Apostle to rest in some quiet seclusion, that none might be tempted to offer his saintly relics the incense of an idolatrous worship.

"From his home in the far East he sent his last Epistle to the great Christian family, declaring to them that his Lord had shown him that 'he must shortly put

17

off this tabernacle.' That tabernacle has long since mingled with its kindred dust, but his works survive it. His name is still fragrant. His recorded words are living oracles, and as an inspired Apostle, having authority, he still sits on his throne judging the tribes of Israel."

It is an act of reverence thus to ascribe to Divine Providence the hiding of the remains of the chief Apostle, and we justly claim that the Heavenly blessing has descended upon those who have magnified and followed the inspired words of Peter, rather than upon those who have boasted of his personal presence, and have unduly honored his pretended remains.

No intelligent Pope would have selected one like Peter for a mission to Rome, while Paul was its guide and leader. It is a false interpretation of our Lord's words to him, with a desire to secure his name for Rome's aggrandizement and supreme power, which can account for the historical fiction we have examined. That Rome should prefer to Paul's doctrines of grace and a pure Gospel, the Jewish exclusiveness and devotion to tradition characteristic of Peter before his conversion, is not surprising when we contemplate her history, her influence, and her works! The doctrines of Rome are as wide as the poles from the plain teaching of Peter's Epistles.

And if Rome is ever to return to the doctrine of Holy Scripture, to the Inspired Gospel, it must be by accepting the Truth as taught so clearly and copiously by her true Founder, the Apostle Paul. In the letters of Peter the same is contained, and the doctrine of Paul indorsed. From both Rome has departed, and has succeeded to the views and temper of both Apostles, as they were in their days of Jewish exclusiveness, prejudice, and religious bigotry and uncharitableness, before enlightened by the Holy Spirit.

May the spirit of the converted Paul and Peter descend upon the teachers and rulers of that Church and the vast millions under their rule and instruction; that souls may be enlightened and saved; the Divine Head of the Church be glorified; stumbling blocks in the way of the world's advance in light, knowledge, purity, and happiness be effectually removed!

FORM AND ORDER OF EVIDENCE.

It remains now briefly to recapitulate the form and order of Evidence previously produced.

It has been shown that in the first century, in the writings of the only two authors whose works have reached us, Clement and Ignatius, nothing whatever is said concerning Peter's presence in Rome. Evidence is presented that in the five authentic documents of the century following Peter's death, which exist—the works of Polycarp, Barnabas, Hermas, Justin, and the Didache—there is no statement to be found that Peter visited Rome, or died there.

An examination of the Scriptures makes it clear that they contain no allusion whatever to the presence of Peter in Rome. Such omission presents a strong and apparently conclusive negative argument against his presence there.

It, moreover, establishes the fact that the knowledge of the locality where Peter labored and died is of no essential importance to the Church, and that no doctrine dependent on the Apostle's residence affects the welfare of Christians.

If it were otherwise, the Word of God would have

given light on the subject. The Apostle himself does not seem to be aware that the locality of his life or death was of any importance to the Church of Christ.

The question with respect to Babylon mentioned by the Apostle was carefully examined; and it was made evident that the overwhelming weight of testimony was in favor of the opinion that Babylon in Chaldea was meant. The names of 330 leading Continental, English, and American writers, besides Roman authors, who hold that Babylon was the Chaldean city, and not Rome, have been given.

The fictions, such as the Clementina, from whence the story of Peter's visit to Rome was derived, were shown to be utterly unworthy of credit by the admission of eminent Romanists and others. The statements of Caius and of Dionysius quoted by Eusebius; then of Irenæus, Tertullian, and Hippolytus; of Origen, Clemens, and Cyprian; and lastly of Eusebius, were critically examined, and, it is claimed, were clearly seen to present no evidence on the subject deserving of respect or confidence. Writers later than Eusebius are of no weight as evidence.

Stress has been laid in the examination on the opinion of *legal* minds, of jurists, Protestant and Roman; who, investigating the subject critically, have given their unanimous verdict: the case not proven with respect to Peter's visit to Rome; no reliable evidence whatever on the part of the affirmative.

Marsillius and Dumoulin, Roman Catholic lawyers; Simon, Greenwood, and Kennard, English barristers; Bouzique, an eminent French jurist; after a judicial investigation concur in this verdict. Ellendorf, a Roman Catholic lay professor in Berlin; Bacon, an accomplished American scholar ; McGavin and Kitto, Scotch savants of extensive research ; all laymen ; consequently more free from theological bias and ecclesiastical prejudice than clergymen, and better prepared to sift testimony impartially, are compelled to affirm that, according to all the evidence obtainable, the Apostle Peter never entered the city of Rome.

If the conclusions here presented are just, the claims of the Church of Rome do not rest on solid foundations ; certainly not sufficient to lead us to trust in a religion which depends for its authority over mankind on the presumption that Peter was in Rome, was Bishop of Rome, and has handed down to the occupants of that See supreme power over all bishops, ministers, and members of the Church of the Lord Jesus Christ. There is here presented complete vindication for the action of all who have protested against and seceded from the Papal power ; and in view of its almost universally deleterious and corrupting influence where it is not checked and modified by a predominating Protestantism (witness Italy, Spain, Mexico, and South America), is it not the duty of all intelligent and devout Christian people to resist the Papal Church, to endeavor to enlighten its members, and thus bring them into the full liberty and light of the children of God ?

If this main pillar of the Roman Catholic Church is thus seen to rest on quicksand, why may not other supports of that Institution be equally insecure ?

They may be equally destitute of authority from the Word of God, or authenticated history. Transubstantiation, Purgatory, the Adoration and Immaculate Conception of the Virgin Mary, Papal Infallibility, Sacramental Grace, a Sacerdotal Caste endowed with absolving authority—all these may be sustained neither by Scripture, history, nor sound reason. Would it not be well for Roman Catholics to thoroughly investigate these matters, and not run the risk of entering eternity ignorant of revealed Truth, and with minds full of fables and delusions—the life-long victims of superstition.

When this whole system of Papal doctrine is rejected by the great mass of intelligent and educated Christians, as in England, Germany, and the United States, where the mind and conscience are free, and where education is universal; rejected as opposed to Divine Revelation, and the belief of the primitive Apostolic Church; is there not a serious responsibility laid upon the cultivated members of this Communion; and do not the words of our Lord Jesus Christ to the people, convey a serious admonition: "Why do ye not of yourselves judge that which is right?" Luke's Gospel, xii. 57; and again: "In vain do ye worship me, teaching for doctrines the commandments of men," Matthew xv. 9.

THE END.

ADDENDA.

"St. Peter, dating his epistle from Babylon, was not then at Rome."—John Fox, "Book of Martyrs," p. 16.

M. Hobart Seymour, in his edition of Fox's work, p. 16, Worthington Company, New York, writes: "It was during the life of our author, John Fox, that the Rhemish Testament was published, and though he little thought that the Papists would identify Babylon with Rome, yet his 'Acts and Monuments' were scarcely before the world when the Rhemish annotators—finding no evidence in the Scriptures to prove that Peter was ever at Rome—did actually fasten upon the dating of his first epistle from Babylon and explain it as a mystic name for Rome."

Cartwright, who was a contemporary of Fox, and wrote his "Compilation of the Rhemish," etc., during the lifetime of our martyrologist, thus writes: "That Peter sat not in Rome, is confirmed in that Peter writes from Babylon in Chaldea, and not in Italy. This is an evident reason, for that this Babylon was a place of principal abode of the Jews, towards whom Peter's charge principally lay. Gal. ii, 7. Whereas at this time the Jews were not suffered to make their abode in Rome. Acts xviii, 2. Whereunto may be added that, writing to the dispersed Jews, and making rehearsal of divers countries wherein they were, he leaveth out Chaldea, which, considering the great numbers that remained there still after the return into Judea out of captivity, he would not have done, unless Chaldea were the place from whence he wrote his Epistles."

The force of this argument is clear. Three fourths of the Jewish nation at that time were in the Chaldean or Mesopotamian country. As these Hebrews are not addressed by the one divinely appointed as their evangelist, the argument seems irresistible that the apostle must have been in their midst, and hence could not have been writing from Rome or any other place besides Babylon, from which he plainly dates his letters. 1 Pet. v, 13.

PRINCIPAL AUTHORITIES QUOTED.

Simon's "Mission and Martyrdom of St. Peter." This volume contains all patristic authorities in the original.
Greenwood's "Cathedra Petri," Vols. I, II.
Bacon's "Lives of the Apostles."
Ellendorf, "Bib. Sacra." July, 1858; January, 1859.
Lipius, "Pres. Quar. Rev.," November, 1848, Trans. by S. M. Jackson.
North Brit. Rev., November, 1848. Rev. of Scheler.
New Brunswick Rev., May and August, 1854.
Christ. Observer, London, Nov. 1853. Rev. of Simon.
Church Rev., July, 1848. Dr. S. M. Jarvis.
Meth. Quar. Rev., South. January, 1856, Dr. T. V. Moore.
New Englander, January, 1871, Dr. E. Harwood.
Shepherd's "History of the Church of Rome."
Trevor's "Rome from the Fall of the Western Empire."
Robin's "Claims of the Church of Rome."
Seabury's Answer to Dr. Harwood. New York, 1871.
Edgar's "Variations of Popery."
Bower's "Lives of the Popes."
Brown's "Peter the Apostle never in Rome."
Bouzique's "History of Christianity," 3 vols.
Report of Discussion in Rome. February, 1872.
Dr. Littledale's "Petrine Claims."
Sawyer's "Organic Christianity."
Wiesler, Kitto's Journal of Sacred Literature.
Dr. Hatch, Encyclopædia Brit., article, "Peter."
Edersheim's "Life and Times of Jesus the Messiah."
Michaelis, in Adam Clarke's Com. on 1 Peter.
Farrar's "Early Days of Christianity."
Dr. E. W. Samson, Bap. Quar. Rev., July, 1873.
Turretini Opera, Vol. III, (p. 144–50). Ed. New York.
Lightfoot's Sermon, 1 Peter, v. 13. Vol. VII, p. 1.
Canon F. C. Cook, "Speaker's Commentary."
Wordsworth "on the Canon;" "Com. on Revelation."
Ramsay's "Church in the Roman Empire."
Lanciani's "Rome, Pagan and Christian."
McDonald's Com. on St. John.
S. R. Green's "Life of Peter."
Kennion's, "St. Peter and Rome."
McGavin's "Protestant."
Elliot on Romanism.
Butler's "St. Paul in Rome."

INDEX.

Alexander, J. Addison, 63, 151
Alford, Dean, 90, 170, 227
Artaud, 25
Arrowsmith, 11
Auberlin, 78

Bacon, 15, 39, 48, 120, 124, 127, 129, 186, 221, 224, 228, 230
Bagby's Travels, 12
Barnes, Albert, 94
Barnabas, 53
Barrow, Dr., 80
Baronius, 28, 59, 76, 95, 176, 177
Barras, 3
Baratier, 26
Bates, 163
Baumgarten, 63
Bellarmine, Cardinal, 4, 25, 59, 61, 77, 117, 152
Benson, Dr., 41
Bethune, 13
Bishop, Alex., 11
Bleek, 84, 222
Blaikie, 13
Bloomfield, 75, 100
Bower, 10, 19
Bonzique, 38, 66, 77, 209
Bradford, 8
Browne, J. H., 9
Brown, 79, 86, 187
Bryennios, 47, 56
Bull, Bishop, 9, 74
Bunsen, 26, 32, 209
Butler, Prof. C. M., 16, 235

Calmet, 69
Calvin, 62, 100
Canon Law, Church of Rome, 2
Caron, Father, 6
Cains, 174, 175, 179, 182
Cave, Dr., 190
Catechismus Romanus, 3
Ceillier, 25

Chambers, 187
Chevalier, 32, 34
Chillingworth, 172
Clarke, Dr. Adam, 10, 87, 109, 195
Clemens, Alexandrinus, 133, 199
Clement, 9, 32, 35, 39, 40, 43–49
Clementina, 152
Coleman, 32
Cotelerius, 150
Conybeare, 208
Copleston, Bishop, 10
Cook, F. C., 93
Coxe, 19
Cranmer, 8
Creed of Pope Pius IV., 2
Cumming, J., 99
Cunningham, 168
Cuyler, Dr. T. L., 73
Cyprian, 199, 200

Da Costa, 86, 221
Daille, 166, 185, 195
Daubigne, 184
Davidson, 12, 109, 131, 185
De Cormenin, 6, 70
De Marca, 226
Depradt, 21
Deutsch, Dr. Emanuel, 115
Dick's Theology, 10, 44
Dionysius, 158, 159
Doddridge, 89
Dollinger, 132, 201
Dowling, 15
Duff, 60
Dupin, 69, 152, 164
Du Moulin, 5

Echard, Lawrence, 103
Edersheim, 116
Edgar, 11, 46, 60, 200, 207, 210
Ellendorf, 6, 44, 64, 65, 68, 143, 151, 157, 176, 180
Elliot, Charles, 13, 74

247

INDEX.

Ellicott, Bishop, 84
Emerton, 14
Encyc. Britan. 13
Eusebius, 76, 77, 158, 159, 167, 178, 183, 206, 207, 212, 213, 214, 217, 238
Erasmus, 70, 165

Faber, Geo. S., 6
Fairbairn, 103
Family Ex. Cat., 3
Farrar, 67, 81, 141, 143, 167, 187, 191, 230
Faussett, 40, 82
Fenardent, 24
Fisher, Dr. Geo., 154
Foulkes, 184
Fulke, 97, 152
Froschammer, 44

Gaussen, 190
Gavazzi, 117, 119, 120, 207
Giesler, 40, 165
Gifford, 215
Gloag, 156, 186
Guerike, 113
Gray, J. C., 180
Green, S. R., 130, 188, 197
Greenwood, 10, 28, 36, 125, 171, 187, 202, 210
Grotius, 126

Hague, 241
Hall, Robert, 10, 210
Hardouin, 6, 240
Harman, 84
Harnack, 151, 202
Hatch, 191
Herzog, 208
Hermas, 54, 55
Hertzog, 72, 73
Hilary, 198
Hill, 10
Hippolytus, 190, 191, 193
Hodge, C., 13, 97, 158
Howson, Dean, 90, 208
Hooper, 8
Hopkins, J. H., 91
Horne, T. H., 87, 171
Hovey, 99
Howe, John, 9
Hug, 70
Hurst, 14
Hussey, 155
Huther, 232

Ignatius, 25, 30, 31, 44, 51, 141, 243
Irenæus, 160, 163, 167, 170, 174

Jacobus, 13
Jarvis, Dr., 78
Jerome, 60, 76, 78, 84, 134, 198, 208, 223
Jewel, 18
Jortin, 169
Josephus, 71, 79, 101, 102, 115, 123
Justin, 55, 65, 214, 215

Kennard, R. W., 12, 212
Kennion, 45, 238
Kenrick, 34
Kuinoel, 120
Kirwan, 75
Kitto, 10, 79, 109, 115, 187
Kurtz, 8

Lampe, 139
Lange, 226
Lansing, 14
Lanci, 181
Lanciani, 200, 201, 202, 203, 204
Lardner, Dr., 33, 34, 35, 36, 41, 109, 128, 141
Leland, Father, 6
Le Moyne, 52
Lightfoot, Bishop, 32, 54, 132
Lightfoot, Dr. John, 8, 87-89, 122
Lillie, 99
Lipsius, 57, 58, 156
Littledale, Dr., 12, 91, 239
Livius, 208
London Times, 175

Marsilius, 6, 66
Merivale, 102
Massey, 12
McCorry, 26, 33, 38, 175
McClintock, 106, 163, 231
McDonald, 20, 123, 124
McGavin, 11, 210, 235
McGiffert, 76
McKnight, 70
Meyer, 60, 72, 84, 187
Michælis, 79, 107, 108, 109, 123
Milman, 101, 152
Milton, 135
Moore, 15
Mosheim, 151, 164
Murdock, 39, 213, 216
Murray, Dr. N., 14, 72, 75

INDEX. 249

Nardini, 180
Neander, 8, 72, 112, 178, 188, 189, 190, 203
Newton, 95
New Englander, 15
New Brunswick Review, 48
Nicephorus, 83
Niebuhr, 91
North British Review, 13, 43, 183, 195
Nourse, 16, 198

Origen, 195, 197, 198, 221
Owen, J., Vicar, 27, 110, 179, 185
Owen, John, Dr., 8, 158

Papias, 74, 77, 78
Parsons, Rev. R., 1, 234
Pearson, 26
Peck, Dr. Geo., 18
Perrone, 4, 235
Plattner, 178
Polycarp, 52
Poole, 98
Powell, 11
Prelim. Diss., 70
Presensé, 113, 231
Princeton Review, 15

Quarterly Review, 167, 208

Ramsay, 218, 219, 220, 223, 227
Ranke, 7
Rhenish New Testament, 97
Rennel, 104
Reuss, 114
Rice, N. L., 16
Riddle, 32, 151, 166
Robertson, 102
Robinson, Edw., 105
Ruffinus, 198

Salmon, Dr., 154
Salmond, 104
Salmasius, 7
Samson, Dr., 92, 141, 142, 190
Sawyer, 16, 27, 82, 153, 156, 178, 215, 222
Scaliger, 7

Scheler, 43, 156
Schottgen, 78
Schurer, 114
Seeley, 11
Shedd, 106, 226
Shepherd, 157, 177
Shimeall, 14, 163
Simon, 34, 37, 77, 151, 197, 211
Smith, Rev. S. B., 1, 174
Smith, Dr. Wm., 125
Smyth, 13
Snodgrass, 16
Southern Review, 8
Spanheim, 7
Stanley, Dean, 105, 160
Steiger, 85, 112
Stowe, 106
Strong, 14, 106, 163, 231

Taylor, W. C., 125
Taylor, W. M., 14, 98
Tertullian, 185, 186, 188, 189, 221
Thomson, Archbishop, 85
Thomson, W. M., 140
Thompson, R. E., 14
Tillemont, 152, 172
Timpson, 11
Townsend, 138, 139
Trevor, Canon, 72
Turrentin, 6, 7, 46, 59, 61, 75, 110, 168

Uhlorn, 47

Valesius, 77, 86, 223
Van Oosterzee, 7
Vatican Council, 2
Vedder, H. C., 14

Wake, Archbishop, 54
Wells, 104, 239
Wesley, John, 91
Whedon, 91
Whittaker, 74
Willet, 8, 179
Wiseman, 181
Wordsworth, Bishop, 96, 104, 132, 138, 241
Wright, W. A., 102
Wylie, J. A., 11, 29, 62